TELLING LIES
IN MODERN AMERICAN
AUTOBIOGRAPHY

Timothy Dow Adams

Telling **LIES**

in Modern American

Autobiography

The University of North Carolina Press

Chapel Hill and London

© 1990 The University of North Carolina Press

All rights reserved

Library of Congress Cataloging-in-Publication Data

Adams, Timothy Dow.
  Telling lies in modern American autobiography / Timothy Dow Adams.
    p. cm.
  Bibliography: p.
  Includes index.
  ISBN 0-8078-1888-7 (alk. paper)
  1. American prose literature—20th century—History and criticism.
2. Autobiography.   3. Authors, American—20th century—Biography—
History and criticism.   I. Title.
PS366.A88A34   1990
818'.540809492—dc20   89-35380
                                                    CIP

Portions of this book have appeared in somewhat different form in the following: Chapter 2, "Gertrude Stein: 'She Will Be Me When This You See,'"
appeared in a shorter version in *Publications of the Arkansas Philological Association* 6 (1980). Chapter 4, "Richard Wright: 'Wearing the Mask,'" was
published in *Modern Selves: Essays on Modern British and American Autobiography*, edited by Philip Dodd (London: Frank Cass, 1986). Chapter 6, "Lillian Hellman: 'Are You Now or Were You Ever?,'" was published in a different form in *Critical Essays on Lillian Hellman*, edited by Mark Estrin (Boston: G. K. Hall and Co., 1989).

A section from an unpublished manuscript in the Sherwood Anderson Collection has been reprinted with permission of the Newberry Library in Chicago, Illinois.

The paper in this book meets the guidelines for permanence and durability
of the Committee on Production Guidelines for Book Longevity of the
Council on Library Resources.

Design by April Leidig-Higgins

Manufactured in the United States of America

94 93 92 91 90   5 4 3 2 1

FOR GAIL AND PAUL

CONTENTS

PREFACE

Art lies in concealing art.—Ovid

All autobiographers are unreliable narrators, all humans are liars, and yet, as I will be arguing throughout this book, to be a successful liar in one's own life story is especially difficult. Because what we choose to misrepresent is as telling as what really happened, because the shape of our lives often distorts who we really are, and because, as Roy Pascal reminds us, "consistent misrepresentation of oneself is not easy," even those autobiographers with the most problematic approach to lying should be valued for telling the truth of their lives.[1] As Leslie Stephen wrote, "It may be reckoned, too, as a special felicity that an autobiography, alone of all books, may be more valuable in proportion to the amount of misrepresentation it contains."[2] I believe autobiography is the story of an attempt to reconcile one's life with one's self and is not, therefore, meant to be taken as historically accurate but as metaphorically authentic. My judgments throughout are based on Marcel Eck's standard, as expressed in his *Lies and Truth*: "We will be judged not on whether we possess or do not possess the truth but on whether or not we sought and loved it."[3]

Much autobiographical theory has focused on the boundaries of the genre. Rather than declaring what is or is not autobiography or suggesting that autobiography with an extensive degree of fictionality is less than true to life, I am interested in the reasons behind deliberate lying, the uses and significance of lying in autobiographies that fall on the borderline in the geography of genre. Throughout *Telling Lies in Modern American Autobiography* I will be concerned with genre, not because I think that we can ever agree on exact lines of demarcation, but because the ambiguity of genre is a major reason these writers have been thought of as liars. Autobiographers seldom make a distinction between autobiography, autobiographical novel, memoir, memories, or reminiscence, genres with different ideas of truthfulness. Rather than deploring the lack of a completely satisfying definition of autobiography, I am attracted to the genre because of its generic ambiguities that allow the writers I have chosen to get at the truth of their lives by using the truth standards of not only fiction and nonfiction but also biography, diary, and memoir.

I have selected the life stories of Gertrude Stein, Sherwood Anderson, Richard Wright, Mary McCarthy, and Lillian Hellman mainly because their books are complex. The autobiographies of these five modern Americans are especially difficult cases because of the apparent lies that permeate the form and content of each work. For each of these writers, charges of lying, and even fraud, have centered on lies, omissions, inaccuracies, and suppressions and on misleading forms: Gertrude Stein's biography of herself, Sherwood Anderson's three contradictory autobiographies, Richard Wright's "record of childhood and youth," Mary McCarthy's "memories," and Lillian Hellman's underdeveloped "portraits."

Lying in autobiography is not just something that happens inevitably; rather, it is a highly strategic decision, especially on the part of literary autobiographers. In Stein's *The Autobiography of Alice B. Toklas*, lies take the form of the traditional American tall tale or hoax with the author simultaneously exaggerating her importance to the literary world of the time and presenting through the book's form Toklas's most characteristic personal quality—a predilection for disguising herself as another person. Sherwood Anderson's three autobiographies—*A Story Teller's Story, Tar*, and *Sherwood Anderson's Memoirs*—are often contradictory; yet, their casual use of the facts of the author's life results in an accurate portrait of the real Anderson.

Richard Wright's *Black Boy* often does not feel truthful because the inability to tell the truth is his central metaphor for both his youth and the childhood of all black children growing up in the pre-Depression American South. Wright's persona is confessing to his difficulty with hypocrisy that makes lying—signifying or wearing the mask—at once a constant necessity and a nearly impossible performance, especially for a poor liar whose tone frequently gives him away. Mary McCarthy's *Memories of a Catholic Girlhood* uses a bad confession in the Catholic sense, coupled with less than precise distinctions between truth and what she calls half-truths, to undercut both the sacrament of confession and the confessional mode historically central to autobiography. Lillian Hellman's four personal narratives—*An Unfinished Woman, Pentimento, Scoundrel Time*, and *Maybe*—present an autobiographical character with an ever-increasing sense of memory's mendacity. For Hellman, a concern with the surface of life, with the unfinished in the sense of unvarnished life, gives way to a palimpsestic autobiographical act that both repents and reports the satisfaction inherent in its own inconclusive rhetorical stance—a stance of yes, no, maybe so.

Throughout *Telling Lies in Modern American Autobiography*, my standard is not literal accuracy but personal authenticity. For me, narrative truth and personal myth are more telling than literal fidelity;

the autobiographer's reasons for telling lies are more important than absolute accuracy. In this work, I hope simultaneously to resolve some of the paradoxes of recent autobiographical theory and to reconcile those paradoxes by looking at the classic question of design and truth in autobiography from the underside—that is, with a focus on lying rather than on truth.

ACKNOWLEDGMENTS

My work in autobiography began in Benjamin DeMott's National Endowment for the Humanities seminar at Amherst College in 1974. Since that time, I have been supported by too many teachers, colleagues, friends, and administrators to name each individually. However, I want particularly to thank the following people. At Emory University, I was helped by Liliane Arensberg, Robert Detweiler, William Dillingham, Trudy Kretchman, Elizabeth Stevenson, and Virginia Trombley. At West Virginia University, I am especially grateful to Marcia Aldrich, Dennis Allen, Rudolph Almasy, Patrick Conner, Winston Fuller, Richard Isomaki, Thomas Miles, Kevin Oderman, Frank Scafella, Cheryl Torsney, and Hayden Ward. I thank Deans Thomas Knight and Gerald Lang for financial support for research. Penny Pugh and Judi McCracken of West Virginia University's library have been invaluable.

I appreciate the institutional support for research and writing from the National Endowment for the Humanities, which provided me with a summer stipend to work on the Lillian Hellman chapter, and West Virginia University, which awarded me a Senate Research Grant. I am particularly grateful to Richard Brown and Paul Gehl at the Newberry Library for a Short-Term Fellowship that enabled me to work on the Sherwood Anderson chapter and especially to Diana Haskell, Frances Kao, Florence Sadler, Diana Robin, Michael Palencia-Roth, and Cristanne Miller whose presence made my stay valuable.

Others who have helped me in various ways include James R. Bennett, Temma Berg, Henry Louis Gates, Jr., Gerald McDaniel, Ira Bruce Nadel, Shirley Neuman, James Olney, Anna Shannon Elfenbein, and Doris Falk Stillman.

I am thankful for the encouragement of Iris Tillman Hill, Sandra Eisdorfer, and Mary Repaske at the University of North Carolina Press.

Finally, I would like to thank the two people who have been the most helpful in my work, Albert E. Stone, Jr., and Paul John Eakin.

TELLING LIES
IN MODERN AMERICAN
AUTOBIOGRAPHY

INTRODUCTION

Design and Lie in
Modern American Autobiography

Autobiography is stranger than fiction which as everybody knows must be stranger than life.—Jane Lazarre, *A Slight Distortion of the Truth*

The modern era in autobiographical theory began in 1960 with the publication of Roy Pascal's now classic *Design and Truth in Autobiography*. Since then, virtually all autobiographical theorists have arranged their arguments within a complex, interconnected spectrum based on the terms in Pascal's title. *Design* has been treated under such headings as genre, form, mode, and style; *truth* has been handled in a bewildering variety of ways, including its relation to fiction, nonfiction, fact, fraud, figure, memory, identity, error, and myth. The word *autobiography* has frequently been analyzed in terms of its three separate components: *autos* or self, *bios* or life, and *graphe* or writing.

The consistent attempt to write about autobiography by working with these terms has produced, in the thirty years since Pascal's benchmark, a multitude of scholarly activity—books and articles, including bibliographies, collections of essays, special issues of journals, and journals devoted to the topic (*Biography*, *Prose Studies*, and *A/B: Auto/Biography Studies*); the formulation of both the Modern Language Association Nonfictional Prose Division and the Modern Language Association Autobiography and Biography Discussion Group; and countless papers delivered at conferences, followed by entire conferences and symposia devoted to particular aspects of the subject. The latter include Black Autobiography (College Language Association—hosted by Fisk University and Tennessee State University), the Self and Other (University of Louisville), Women's Autobiography and Biography (Stanford University), Symposium on Canadian Autobiography (University of Ottawa), the First International Symposium on Autobiography and Autobiography Study (Louisiana State University), the Autobiography Conference (University of Southern Maine), and Autobiography and Avant-garde (Johannes Gutenberg University).

What this critical outpouring of over a quarter century has produced is a paradox—an astonishing ability to generate lively and valuable commentary on and ingenious and helpful readings of an enormous variety of autobiographical texts, despite a general agreement that autobiography cannot really be defined. As early as 1965, William Spengemann and L. R. Lundquist defined autobiography by its indefinable quality: "The modern autobiographer needs an especially flexible form, one that can always outrun attempts to define it."[1] And by 1979, autobiographical criticism had reached such an impasse that Paul de Man described it as nearly pointless.

> The theory of autobiography is plagued by a recurrent series of questions and approaches that are not simply false, in the sense that they take for granted assumptions about autobiographical discourse that are in fact highly problematic. They keep therefore being stymied, with predictable monotony, by sets of problems that are inherent in their own use. One of these problems is the attempt to define and to treat autobiography as if it were a literary genre among others.[2]

No matter how complicated or complete our attempt, creating an airtight definition of autobiography is virtually impossible. The word under which all of this critical work has been done, however defined, has produced a variety of positions, ranging from those critics, such as Mutlu Konuk Blasing, who would collapse the boundaries and expand the canon to include anything with an autobiographical feel to those, such as Barrett John Mandel, who argue that autobiography and fiction are completely separate genres and that a line of demarcation between them should be drawn.[3] For Paul de Man, the solution is to think of autobiography, not as a genre, but as "a figure of reading or of understanding that occurs, to some degree, in all texts."[4] According to Avrom Fleishman, we should begin, not by asking "what is autobiography?," but by questioning "how the age-old activity of writing life stories has organized itself at various periods of literary history."[5] Despite his exhaustive scholarship and sophisticated arrangement, Fleishman's emphasis on the life-writing process rather than on the outcome, the autobiographical act over the autobiographical corpus, results in his analyzing *David Copperfield*, *The Mill on the Floss*, and *Sons and Lovers* as though no distinctions exist between "The Autobiographical Novel and the Autobiography," which is the title of Roy Pascal's initial foray into autobiographical theory in 1959.

In an essay focusing on James Olney's *Autobiography: Essays Theoretical and Critical*, Jonathan Loesberg nicely summarizes the impasse of the 1980s in autobiographical theory: "Critics seem to wind up either playing fast and loose with genre in order to protect the most

fundamental aspects of autobiography or insisting on maintaining generic distinctions in fairly rigid ways in order to call into question the
bases of that genre."[6]

In a 1980 essay "Autobiography and the Cultural Moment," Olney
points out the immediate paradox of dealing with autobiography
critically: the danger, on the one hand, that we will define autobiography out of existence is counterbalanced with the tendency, on the
other, to see every text as a form of autobiography.[7] This paradox is
complicated by the assumptions that all readers instinctively know the
difference between autobiography and other genres and that all of our
critical energy has been wasted on an issue that would not matter
much if it could finally be resolved. What Olney saw as particular to
the cultural moment in which he wrote his essay is actually a recurring
pattern; we are still at work trying to resolve the particular paradoxes
of autobiography, wrestling with the same questions asked by such
classic autobiographers as Rousseau and Augustine.

What power exists within or behind the complex arguments formed
by repeatedly examining autobiography in terms of design and truth?
How can we proceed when our best theorists argue that autobiography is not really a genre, not finally distinct from fiction, not even
definable—a narrative that pretends to be written by a self-conscious
self who is actually only a linguistic construct? Like the profound novels and valuable criticism produced since the celebrated "death of the
novel" or the exhaustive list of new fiction written in the twenty years
since John Barth published his well-known essay "The Literature of
Exhaustion," autobiography, as well as its theory, thrives precisely because of its paradoxical position.

Whether the key terms around which this chapter is organized are
taken individually or together, the inescapable conclusion is that each
word is complicated, ambiguous, inseparable from other terms, and
finally paradoxical. Design, truth, and autobiography collectively name
the autobiographical paradox. This form of writing, which may or
may not be a genre, possesses a peculiar kind of truth through a narrative composed of the author's metaphors of self that attempt to reconcile the individual events of a lifetime by using a combination of
memory and imagination—all performed in a unique act that partakes
of a therapeutic fiction making, rooted in what really happened, and
judged both by the standards of truth and falsity and by the standards
of success as an artistic creation.

Although I believe that these paradoxes are essential to autobiography and that any attempt to resolve them completely would destroy
the compelling charm of the form, I also believe that behind the con-

fusions they represent lies one unstressed problem, a problem that calls for the addition of one more key term to the original three—*lying*. Virtually all of the discussion about autobiography I have been summarizing focuses on truth. Throughout all of the critical efforts to sort out these paradoxes, few theorists have dealt with lying itself, despite the fact that autobiography is synonymous with lying for many readers.

For the remainder of this chapter, I will attempt, on the one hand, to resolve some of autobiography's paradoxes by the introduction of lying as a key term and, on the other, to argue that the paradoxical ambiguity of autobiography—the impossibility of ever completely separating or refining either the word itself or the terms used in discussing it—is in a sense both its strength and its most defining characteristic.

Design

If consciousness were not a liar, it would have no problems. . . . It could not lie to itself, since it would not be aware of what it had to lie about.—William Earle, *The Autobiographical Consciousness*

Most theoretical arguments about design are really about genre. Our difficulties with defining autobiography have caused more than just a bemused embarrassment for literary historians; questions about autobiography as a genre have implications wider than mere academic classification. For example, Mary McCarthy and Lillian Hellman were embroiled in a lawsuit involving charges and countercharges of lying, based—as I show in chapter 6—in part on misunderstandings on both sides of questions of genre. Although the protagonist of Richard Wright's *Black Boy* is named Richard, some of the events Wright attributed to this character's life actually happened to other people, a fact he justified by calling his book *Black Boy* rather than "The Autobiography of Richard Wright." And yet Janet Cooke, a reporter for the *Washington Post*, lost her Pulitzer Prize, her job, and her reputation when she invented a young black boy called "Jimmy" to stand for thousands of black children whose lives have been blighted by poverty, racism, and drugs. Sherwood Anderson was notorious for creating false backgrounds for his own family members and for inventing myths about himself, all of which he recorded in his autobiographies despite the fact that they often contradicted each other. In contrast, Michael Daly, a writer for the *New York Daily News*, was fined for

having invented "Christopher Spell," a typical British army soldier in
Belfast.

Recently, Alastair Reid was castigated for creating composite characters and locations in his *New Yorker* pieces about Spain. Joanne Lipman, a *New Yorker* staff writer, says Reid "took disparate elements from different places—a bar here, a bartender or television speech there—and moved them around and put them in a whole different place and made a poetic whole." According to Lipman, Reid used real people but also "'disembodied voices' asking 'the questions that a lot of people in Spain were asking at the time' [1982], as did Hemingway in numerous stories that served both for journalism and for fiction."[8] However, the *New Yorker*, which prides itself on meticulous research and absolute separation of fact from fiction, has in the past allowed the use of composite, semifictional autobiographical pieces by Frank Conroy and others, including Mary McCarthy, that blend fact and fiction.[9]

Clearly, freelancer Christopher Jones was being dishonest to plagiarize portions of André Malraux's novel *The Royal Way* (1930) in a documentary that appeared in the *New York Times Magazine* about Jones's supposed journey inside Cambodia, and most commentators seemed to agree that Clifford Irving deserved a prison sentence for having made money from Howard Hughes's autobiography, which Irving himself wrote. And yet Gertrude Stein adopted a similar tactic in *The Autobiography of Alice B. Toklas*, as did Margaret Foster who wrote *Memoirs of a Victorian Gentleman by William Thackeray*, or William Styron in his *The Confessions of Nat Turner*, or Danny Santiago, the putative author of *Famous All Over Town*, who turned out to be a seventy-three-year-old Anglo named Dan James.

All of these instances involve some controversy and a charge of fraud, as is the case with all of the books I treat in detail in subsequent chapters. Although it is tempting to treat these cases as problems of New Journalism or anomalies of autobiography, eventually it becomes apparent that virtually all autobiographies are anomalous and that the world of autobiography is replete with similarly problematic cases.

D. H. Lawrence might have been thinking of American autobiography when he wrote that "Americans refuse everything explicit and always put up a sort of double meaning. They revel in subterfuge. They prefer their truth swaddled in an ark of bullrushes, and deposited among the reeds until some friendly Egyptian princess comes to rescue the babe."[10] The history of American autobiography is filled with generic confusions bordering on fabrication. Such originally nonfictional autobiographical forms as the Indian-captivity narrative and the slave narrative quickly gave way to fictional versions, and early American literature is characterized by works that combine travel writing, almanacs, journals, diaries, and fiction in ambiguous proportions. The early blend of journalism and the tall tale, whose importance for Gertrude Stein will be discussed in chapter 2, can be exemplified by the case of Davy Crockett, celebrated hero of 200 books—including three autobiographies, none of which he wrote himself—and of a recent exhibit at the Smithsonian Institution. American autobiographical writing from Hawthorne, Melville, Thoreau, Whitman, and James to the present is constantly ambiguous in terms of genre, with both historical authenticity and deliberate confusion between fiction and nonfiction, between literal and fictional prefaces, as constants.

Research has revealed more and more the problematic, generic confusions of many classics of American nonfictional prose. Mary Chesnutt's *A Diary from Dixie*, which was assumed for years to be an authentic Civil War diary, has lately been revealed to be a fictionalized version, which was written after the war was over, of a real diary, whereas James Weldon Johnson's *The Autobiography of an Ex-Coloured Man*, a novel, was so often taken for a real autobiography that the author was forced in compensation to write a nonfictional account of his life.

By the late 1960s, the acceptance of New Journalism and the nonfictional novel, the relaxing of libel laws, and the spirit of social revolution had combined to produce autobiographies that deliberately flaunted whatever conventions of the genre remained. From their titles and subtitles alone, we can see basic problems inherent in such books as Herbert Gold's *Fathers*, subtitled *A Novel in the Form of a Memoir*; Gore Vidal's *Two Sisters*, subtitled *A Memoir in the Form of a Novel*; Frederick Exley's *A Fan's Notes*, subtitled *A Fictional Memoir*; Rosellen Brown's *The Autobiography of My Mother*; Toby Olson's *The Life of Jesus*, an autobiographical novel; and Michael Anania's *The Red Menace*, advertised as "a memoir in the form of a novel." In addition, the authors of numerous autobiographical books have deliberately taken a stand on the border between traditional autobiography, autobiographical novel, and fictional autobiographies—stories in autobiographical form of fictional people—such as Ernest Gaines's *The Autobiography of Miss Jane Pittman*.

What are we to make of such "factual fictions," to use Albert E. Stone's term, as Norman Mailer's *The Armies of the Night*, Frank Conroy's *Stop-Time*, Jonathan Baumbach's *Reruns*, Ronald Sukenick's *UP*, Raymond Federman's *Double or Nothing*, subtitled *A Real Fictitious Discourse*, Thomas Rogers's *The Confessions of a Child of the Century by Samuel Heather*, or Philip Roth's *My Life as a Man*? Roth's work, which he calls mock autobiography, is divided into two parts: the fictional Peter Tarnopol's autobiographical narrative, "My True Story," and this hero's "fictional fiction," called "Useful Fictions."[11] Adding to the confusion, in Roth's recent work *The Counterlife* we discover that Nathan Zuckerman, protagonist of the three novels by Roth collected as *Zuckerman Bound*, is a literary character invented by Tarnopol and that Zuckerman's fictional fiction includes thinly disguised parodies of Roth's *Portnoy's Complaint*.

James McConkey, author of *Crossroads, Court of Memory*, and *To a Distant Island*, was praised by Noel Perrin for having invented a genre with no name, but McConkey's books are actually borderline autobiographies very much like Nicholas Delbanco's *In the Middle Distance*, which the author calls a novel though it features a character named Nicholas Delbanco, and George Cain's *Blueschild Baby*, whose protagonist likewise shares a name with the book's author. Many of these books have adopted the stance of the narrator of John Barth's "Anonymiad": "I found by pretending that things had happened which in fact had not, and that people existed who didn't, I could achieve a lovely truth which actuality obscures—especially when I learned to abandon myth and pattern my fabrications on actual people and events."[12] Deliberate generic confusions have even entered the world of biography in such books as John Updike's *Bech: A Book*, Steven Millhauser's *Edwin Mullhouse: The Life and Death of an American Writer, 1943–1954 by Jeffrey Cartwright*, and Susan Cheever's *Home before Dark*, a biography of her father, John Cheever, that is called "a biographical memoir."

All of these examples, which stand for many others, clearly indicate that no definition can outwit the modern author, no solid distinction can or ought to be made between confession, autobiographical novel, mock autobiography, or autobiography, even though we can sometimes isolate nearly pure specimens of each. Sometimes it is tempting to join with Barrett John Mandel and declare that all of the taxonomic questions I have been referring to are "academic sleight of hand" because "autobiographies and novels are finally totally distinct—and this simple fact *every reader knows*."[13] But behind that declaration lies a problem that cannot be made to go away simply by commanding our word processors to replace autobiography with autobiographical. The question of design in autobiography persists as a problem, persists because it is always connected, in the most basic and in the most sophisticated analysis, with complicated terms such as reality and truth.

Not only do authors sometimes have difficulty in determining precisely what genre they are working in, but they also deliberately blur the genres for rhetorical effect. John Fowles, for instance, interrupts his novel *The French Lieutenant's Woman* to comment on his character's reality:

> But this is preposterous? A character is either "real" or "Imaginary"? If you think that, *hypocrite lecteur*, I can only smile. You do not even think of your own past as quite real; you dress it up, you gild it or blacken it, censor it, tinker with it . . . fictionalize it, in a word, and put it away on a shelf—your book, your romanced autobiography. We are all in flight from real reality.[14]

As if this confusion of genre were not problem enough, critics of autobiography must also distinguish between historical truth, propositional truth, personal truth, psychological truth, narrative truth, and conditional truth. Sissela Bok begins her classic book on lying by distinguishing between "the *moral* domain of intended truthfulness and deception, and the much vaster domain of truth and falsity in general." For Bok: "the moral question of whether you are lying or not is not *settled* by establishing the truth or falsity of what you say. In order to settle this question, we must know whether you *intend your statement to mislead*."[15] But for the autobiographer, part of the game includes trying to keep the reader off balance, trying to disturb what Philippe Lejeune calls "The Autobiographical Pact."[16] Where Lejeune sees the combination of names, title page, preface, and library classification as working together to signal a generic pact, many autobiographers, not entirely certain themselves, try to remain deliberately ambiguous about genre. Modern autobiographers, seeking to regain the ambiguity that naturally surrounded the novel at its beginnings, want to keep the reader guessing about the precise degree of fictionality within their text. No matter how we look at design in autobiography, we would be wise to remember Paul John Eakin's words: "Fictions and the fiction-making process are a central constituent of the truth of any life as it is lived and of any art devoted to the presentation of that life."[17]

Like magicians, poker players, or baseball managers, autobiographers must continually claim that they have nothing up their sleeves, nothing in the cards, nothing planned for the next pitch, all the while deliberately sending a steady stream of false and true signals, hints and feints designed to keep the game going. Although Bok is certainly right to judge lying in a frame outside of the general world of true versus false, her claim that lying is determined by the intention to mislead must be modified when applied to autobiography. Bok stresses that in situations where the rules permit mutual deception, lying is acceptable and should no longer be considered lying. Within the complicated, shifting rules for autobiography, however, the exact degree of deception intended or allowed is open to debate, a fact that makes Pascal's key terms so difficult to handle.

Truth

Truth is stranger than Fiction, but it is because Fiction is obliged to stick to possibilities; Truth isn't.—Mark Twain, *Pudd'nhead Wilson's New Calendar*

A promise to tell the truth is one of autobiography's earliest premises. "The assumption that, from his privileged position vis-à-vis himself, the autobiographer will tell the truth," according to Shirley Neuman, is "the most fundamental article of good faith between autobiographer and his readers."[18] As fundamental as truth is to autobiography, modern readers have increasingly come to realize that telling the truth about oneself on paper is virtually impossible. Even if writers could isolate "the truth" of their past, how could they know it would remain true as they wrote, much less in the future? How would readers know if they were reading the truth, and how could writers separate poetic truth from factual truth, psychological truth from family truth? Is it more important to be true or to ring true? How could any autobiographer, particularly a fiction writer, resist inventing telling episodes that present a life story more truthfully than what actually happened? Neuman asks, "If the autobiographer does scrupulously recount what he *believes* to be true about his self (or to have been true at the time about which he is writing), how do we know that the so-called truth is not what he *wishes* were the case (and therefore may have come to believe *is* the case) rather than a verifiable presentation of himself?"[19]

The impossibility of answering questions such as these has resulted in the virtual abandonment of "extra textual demands of truthfulness," according to Loesberg, who comments that "if autobiographers claim to be telling the truth about their past lives, they are not doing very well at it."[20] Autobiographical theorists have qualified their call for truth so much that it is virtually impossible to test, and autobiographers now are said to pretend to believe their audiences think they are trying to tell the truth. Eakin summarizes the most widely accepted position: "Autobiographical truth is not a fixed but an evolving content in an intricate process of self-discovery and self-creation." Rather than trying "to expel truth from the house of autobiography and to install fiction in its stead," Eakin argues persuasively that fiction is essential to life and has its own kind of truth.[21] Eakin's position on autobiographical truth is remarkably similar to Clayton Koelb's position on literary truth, which is expressed in *The Incredulous Reader*: "We may not call a speaker/author a liar unless we have reason to suppose both conditions: first, that he or she did not believe the statement, and second, that he or she expected and solicited the audience's belief. These belong to the 'felicity conditions' for the illocutionary act of lying."[22]

Eakin's analysis, relying as it does on the dedicated work of our best theorists, is not only the most current viewpoint about the problematic position of truth in autobiography, but it is also in some ways a restatement of the problems readers have had in sorting out fiction from nonfiction from the times of such novelists as Defoe, Fielding, and Richardson to the present. Hayden White summarizes the eighteenth-century view that historiography was a literary art, a form of fiction made trustworthy through the use of rhetorical tropes. "The imagination no less than the reason had to be engaged in any adequate representation of the truth; and this meant that the techniques of fiction-making were as necessary to the composition of a historical discourse as erudition might be."[23]

Any discussion of autobiographical truth is soon caught up in questions about fact and fiction, distinctions that are nicely summarized by the following textbook discussion:

> Fact comes from *facere*—to make or do. Fiction comes from *fingere*—to make or shape. . . . Fact still means for us quite literally "a thing done" and fiction has never lost its meaning of "a thing made." Fact, in order to survive, must become fiction. Seen in this way, fiction is not the opposite of fact, but its complement. It gives a more lasting shape to the vanishing deeds of men.[24]

By this standard, autobiography might be best thought of as a thing made out of a thing done. The old arguments, which stacked fiction against nonfiction, became even more tendentious once the nonfictional novel, the New Journalism, and the postmodern era brought us such terms as factoid, pseudofactual, and docudrama. Fiction became fictitious, while critics invented new terms, such as Philip Stevick's "mock-facts" and E. L. Doctorow's "false documents."[25]

One of the most useful discussions of the important distinctions between these words is Merle Brown's. "The effort to distinguish fiction that matters from 'mere' fiction is at least as old as Augustine, who felt that a fiction referring only to itself is a lie, whereas a fiction referring to some truth is a figura." Brown's definition is clear and direct: "A fiction, or something made or made up, is fictive if it necessarily implies as part of itself the art of its making; it is fictitious, even if signifying a truth other than itself, if it does not, as part of itself, implicate the act of its making."[26]

Under Brown's rule, all autobiographies are fictive rather than fictitious because the autobiographical act always includes—and can even be defined by—a discussion of itself. All autobiographers are in a sense self-conscious, characteristically asking as they start why they are writing about themselves and why they have chosen autobiography over another form, and often questioning their own veracity. As Eakin notes, "Autobiographers themselves constitute a principal source of doubt about the validity of the art they practice."[27]

Even deciding precisely what we mean by fact will not solve the complicated problem of defining autobiographical truth, for the truth of one's self can be very different from the truth of one's life. In addition, autobiographical truth may bear only tangentially on literal accuracy. As Stephen Shapiro asserts, "Truth in autobiography is not merely fidelity to fact or conformity to 'likeness,' to the way one appears to others, but rather the projection of a story of successive self-images and recognitions of distortions of those self-images by the world; . . . autobiography may be regarded psychologically as a final attempt to persuade the world to view one's self through one's own eyes, to finally recognize what may be invisible."[28]

Because we can never know how truthful an author is being to what we can never see, we are always caught in what Shirley Neuman calls "the paradox of alterity": "The autobiographer must create a text of what he knows from the *inside* in terms of what we recognize from the *outside*."[29] Stephen Spender describes the inside-outside paradox in this way: "This inside self has a history that may have no significance in any objective 'history of the time.' It is the history of himself observing the observer, not the history of himself observed by others."[30] The implications of Spender's statement for the subject of lying are made clear by the Australian autobiographer Hal Porter, who wrote that "no one but I will know if a lie be told; therefore I must try for the truth which is the blood and breath and nerves of the elaborate and unimportant facts."[31]

The truth in autobiography—difficult to name, impossible to verify—can be better understood if we think of it as narrative rather than historical truth. Whatever else the books discussed in detail in subsequent chapters may be, they all can safely be called stories, and therefore they all partake of narrative truth. As psychoanalyst Donald Spence explains: "Narrative truth has a special significance in its own right. . . . making contact with the actual past may be of far less significance than creating a coherent and consistent account of a particular set of events."[32] Although Spence is working in the context of psychoanalysis, his displacement of historical with narrative truth is particularly apt for autobiography, which could be thought of as a written form of self-therapy. According to Spence:

> Narrative truth can be defined as the criterion we use to decide when a certain experience has been captured to our satisfaction; it depends on continuity and closure and the extent to which the fit of the pieces takes on an aesthetic finality. Narrative truth is what we have in mind when we say that such and such is a good story, that a given explanation carries conviction, that one solution to a mystery must be true. Once a given construction has acquired narrative truth, it becomes just as real as any other kind of truth.[33]

What Spence calls narrative truth is similar to the traditional storyteller's sense of propriety, of how far to go in weaving a tale out of memory and imagination. As Janet Varner Gunn explains, in discussing the Sacred Pipe story in *Black Elk Speaks*: "Truth lies in the story's *sufficiency*: in its capacity to make sense of experience told, shared, and even made newly possible for both the teller and the hearer of the story. Just as the authorship of autobiography is tacitly plural, so the truth of autobiography is to be found, not in the 'facts' of the story itself, but in the relational space *between* the story and its reader."[34]

Although current autobiographical theorists have worked through the whole issue of autobiographical truth and arrived at the conclusion that the proper question to ask about autobiography is not how much does it reproduce the life that a biographer might write of its subject, nor what is its researchable fidelity quotient, an uneasy feeling remains that some way to talk about the issue of autobiographical truth without appearing hopelessly naive must exist. In the preface to their composition textbook, William Coles and James Vopat ask the question, "If the writer of a biography or autobiography is not Telling the Truth, then even when the writer is good, what is such a writer doing? . . . What value might there be to seeing *all* written discourse as a kind of artfully (or artlessly) made work, and in this sense all writing as a kind of creative writing, all telling as a form of story-telling (rather than lying)?"[35]

Although this is a seductive theory, an easy resolution that lets us progress to writing about autobiographies themselves, there is a one-word disquieting answer—fraud. For many readers, what distinguishes Janet Cooke from Richard Wright, or Clifford Irving from Lillian Hellman, are questions of intention and remuneration that are best characterized under the heading of fraud. If Clifford Irving had labeled his autobiography of Howard Hughes a fictional reconstruction, or an autobiography in the form of a novel, he might have been seen by many as a clever inventor. What made the spurious Hitler diaries fraudulent was not their content but their claim to authenticity. As L. B. Cebik writes: "Challenges to the authenticity of the recently (1983) 'discovered' Hitler diaries do not seek to prove them to be fiction, in the sense of being a novel written in autobiographical form. Rather, disputants are seeking to prove them to be . . . a forgery."[36]

Of course, historically, the cry of fraud has been attached to those literary works, such as *Robinson Crusoe*, that cunningly blur the boundaries between genres. What Defoe did in answering charges that *Robinson Crusoe* was a fraud—that is, not a genuine travel book at all—is similar to what Vladimir Nabokov did in *Lolita* or, as I will show in chapter 2, what Gertrude Stein was doing in *The Autobiography of Alice B. Toklas*. Distinctions between fiction, nonfiction, and fraud—concepts that Thomas J. Roberts calls "the radical terms"—frequently have more to do with the generic contract, what Albert E. Stone, Jr., calls "the autobiographical occasion," and the reader's expectations than with the actual contents of the narrative.

Roberts demonstrates this phenomenon with four nonliterary events:

a. A teacher shows his pupils the three states of matter by changing ice into water and the water into steam.
b. A sleight of hand artist breaks an egg into a borrowed hat and then changes it into a baby chicken.
c. A fake spiritualist changes the handkerchief of a grieving widow into one her husband had carried.
d. A priest changes bread and wine into the body and blood of Jesus Christ.[37]

Roberts explains that the degree of fraud in each of these acts of transformation depends on a combination of situation, attitude, and intention. The sleight-of-hand artist is not fraudulent because by a smile and by calling the audience is warned that they are supposed to be tricked. The spiritualist is not fraudulent to a skeptic, who might see a spiritualist as merely a magician, a show-business performer; but to the innocent widow, the spiritualist might be as free of deception as the teacher. To an agnostic, the priest's act of transubstantiation would also be a sleight-of-hand performance but not a fraud. As Roberts says, to the nonbeliever, "The priest is honest—wrong but honest." Although he does not mention it, even the teacher could be considered fraudulent by the students if they thought his performance was designed to send a misleading signal about the next test. "Nothing is fiction or fraud or nonfiction in itself," asserts Roberts; "it becomes one or another in the human theater when an observer guesses what the performer thinks of his own behavior and guesses what he wants the observer to think of it."[38] By Roberts's standard, then, lying in autobiography is impossible because the audience begins with the assumption that the complete truth is not possible.

Lie

Men achieve their authentic reality in their most vital fictive acts, in acts that encompass and redeem within them all those fictitious elements of themselves that appear as myths, masks, personae, games, and roles, all those thick crusts that weigh us down and would bury us alive in our lies.—Merle Brown

Any discussion of autobiographical truth is incomplete without a consideration of its opposite—autobiographical lies. That lie is the closest approximate opposite to truth is part of the problem. We are accustomed to opposing truth with consequences or falsity or untruth, none of which is precisely the opposite. As Montaigne wrote: "If, like truth, the lie had but one face, we would be on better terms. For we would accept as certain the opposite of what the liar would say. But the reverse of truth has a hundred thousand faces and an infinite field."[39] That lie can be multiple is demonstrated by the ease with which a list of related terms can be generated: equivocation, duplicity, deception, manipulation, falsehood, false, distortion, perjury, feign, fakery, sham, evasion, suppression, cover-up, exaggeration, euphemism, fib, and prevarication. In addition to plain lying, we find quibbling, misleading, disinforming, duping, withholding, dissembling, disguising, glossing over, simulating, counterfeiting, embroidering, inventing, fudging, doctoring, and being mendacious. Truth is not the opposite of lie because we speak of truth in the singular and lies in the plural, with the implication being that to tell just one lie is not possible. Thus we commonly say "lying" but not "truthing" and refer to someone as "living a lie" but not as "lying a life." As L. B. Cebik remarks: "That we can successfully lie at all depends on the fact that most people tell the truth most of the time. A world of pure truth-telling is imaginable . . . but a world of pure lying would be impossible."[40]

So important is the concept of lying to autobiography that it is not surprising that Augustine is often cited as an authority on both. That Augustine is the father of Western autobiography is a commonplace; however, that his definition of lying is widely accepted within autobiography is unexpected. According to Augustine, lying consists of "having one thing in one's heart and uttering another with the intention to deceive."[41] Although this definition seems straightforward enough, for the reader of autobiographies it is unsatisfactory. First of all, how can we ever know what was in the writer's heart? How can we apply Augustine's definition to writers who are unaware of their hearts' deceptions or who are heartless? And even for the autobiographer intent on telling the whole truth, the most heartfelt images may have been mediated by memory. Sometimes authors are not aware that they are lying; at other times, writers think that they are lying but turn out to have told the truth. Augustine's definition would not be effective with the kind of lying characterized by George Orwell in *1984* as doublethink: "To use conscious deception while retaining the firmness of purpose that goes with complete honesty. To tell deliberate lies while genuinely believing in them."[42] That the classic heart-head dichotomy confuses Augustine's definition is inherent in William Maxwell's discussion of autobiographical truth in his novel *So Long, See You Tomorrow*: "Too many conflicting emotional interests are involved for life ever to be wholly acceptable, and possibly it is the work of the storyteller to rearrange things so that they conform to this end. In any case, in talking about the past, we lie with every breath we draw."[43]

Modern autobiographers have another problem with Augustine's definition; it is too close to classic definitions of irony—"a statement in which the implicit meaning intended by the speaker differs from what he ostensibly asserts."[44] That the word *irony* is derived from the Greek *eironein*, or dissembling, reinforces the parallel. Although the intention to deceive is absent from the definition of irony, many ironists do intend to deceive, their dupes being both the target of their satiric irony and those readers unable to recognize the intended effect. Aware of the difficulties of ever knowing the whole truth of anything, many modern writers are always slightly ironic, sometimes unintentionally. As Anthony Brandt reminds us, in an essay called "Lies, Lies, Lies," "When we must speak to others we speak ironically, holding truth and falsehood in balance, knowing that nothing we say is strictly true, that the best we can hope for is a vague approximation, and that no matter what we say, seeming true or seeming false, the ones inevitably most deceived by it will be ourselves."[45]

Perhaps the definitive statement about the relation of truth and lie to autobiography comes from Georges Gusdorf who declares the whole question beside the point.

> The significance of autobiography should therefore be sought beyond truth and falsity, as those are conceived by simple common sense. . . . It is therefore of little consequence that the *Mémoires d'outre-tombe* should be full of errors, omissions, and lies, and of little consequence also that Chateaubriand made up most of his *Voyage en Amérique*. . . . We may call it fiction or fraud, but its artistic value is real: there is a truth affirmed beyond the fraudulent itinerary and chronology, a truth of the man . . . who, for his own enchantment and that of his readers, realizes himself in the unreal.[46]

Initially, Gusdorf's argument is as compelling as Bok's, but in the end I believe that the inaccuracies he speaks of are not beside the point, though they are not in themselves the point. In one sense, everything that happens is to the point. Although the literal accuracy of an autobiography's words is not important, it is important that the writer chose to stray from what really happened. The complicated series of strategies behind an author's conscious and unconscious misrepresentations is not beside the point. We often discover that whether or not an autobiography rings true is as important as whether or not it is true. And although it is certainly impossible ever to ascertain the whole truth of a life and pointless to attempt to identify every minute factual error in a personal narrative, in between is a fertile field for analysis on which the following chapters of this book are based.

"She Will Be Me When This You See"

The whole of the truth lies in the presentation.—Conrad

For many readers in 1933, *The Autobiography of Alice B. Toklas* was seen, not as a clever literary device, but as a hoax, a deliberate manipulation that produced confusion, anger, and charges that the author, whoever she was, was a liar. The most famous attack came from six painters who published their "Testimony against Gertrude Stein" in a supplement to the journal *transition*. Taking the book as nonfiction, they were angry over minute factual details. They did not understand that the narrator is Toklas not Stein and that Toklas's vision of the artistic world of Paris was necessarily different from Stein's. Henri Matisse's objections, which are typical of the group's, include such petty facts as a lunch that "Alice B. Toklas" mistakenly says took place at Clamart. With a tone of indignation, Matisse corrects her by saying, "This incident took place at boulevard des Invalides, not in Clamart."[1] When Stein wrote in *Everybody's Autobiography* that "an autobiography is not a novel no indeed it is not a novel,"[2] she was hinting that the authenticity of *The Autobiography of Alice B. Toklas* is not found in terms of deeds per se but in what lies behind them.

Stein's extensive mythmaking in the autobiography, coupled with the book's deceptive form, caused contemporary readers difficulty in deciding whether *The Autobiography of Alice B. Toklas* was fiction or nonfiction, biography, autobiography or memoir, truth or lie. The *transition* attacks on Stein are marked by a curious tone of malice and anger out of proportion to the inconsequential nature of the errors to which Matisse and his colleagues objected. Similarly, Leo Stein attacked the autobiography in a letter to Mabel Weeks in which he said of his sister, "My God, what a liar she is!" Leo continued his letter with reference to Gertrude's "radical complexes," calling her "a case of Adler's deficiency and compensation."[3] Her brother's anger is hard to justify in light of his comment that "the historian investigates the facts, the autobiographer just remembers them."[4] In his own autobiography, Leo Stein admits to "a wretched topographical memory and an equally bad temperagraphical memory," which he claims are augmented by the habit of writing down dates of important happenings.[5]

Leo Stein's tone is similar to that of the six writers of "Testimony against Gertrude Stein." The fact that they respond to her book with testimony, as if she were a criminal on trial, and the fact that their responses became known as a manifesto suggest more than the usual anger at being misquoted or misrepresented. Maria Jolas calls the autobiography Stein's "final capitulation to a Barnumesque publicity." Tristan Tzara begins an anti-Stein diatribe by calling the device of speaking through Toklas a "childish subterfuge" of "two maiden ladies greedy for fame and publicity," and he ends with such phrases as "'baby' style," "simpering at the interstices of envy," "lowest literary prostitution," "clinical case of megalomania," and "the realm where lie and pretension meet the depraved morals of bourgeois society." Such expressions indicate in Tzara, the father of dada, a feeling of "strong loathing." Georges Braque makes fun of Stein's physical appearance, and André Salmon calls the book "scandalous" and mocks Toklas and Stein's relationship by calling them collectively "The Steins."[6] However, as Michael Hoffman rightfully points out, "Stein was not testifying before a jury; she was telling a story and creating a consciousness."[7]

The narrative device of writing through Alice Toklas's persona, which has been called writing "a book with her left hand," reflects not only the whole Stein-Toklas relationship but also the spirit of the time and place about which the book is written.[8] The time that the autobiography renders—Paris in the 1920s and 1930s—was characterized by a tendency toward personal myth and legend. When the "fantastic past, filled with exploits in Mexico," that Guillaume Apollinaire created for the painter Henri Rousseau began to be taken as truth, no one complained because "the denial of a history and the fabrication of myths to replace it were intrinsic to the spirit of the time and place."[9] Stein's autobiography appeared to Janet Flanner to be surrounded by "considerable mystery and some secrecy," principally because of its confusion between author and subject; however, Flanner continued, "Bernard Fay is busy making the admirable French translation and giving the hoax away."[10] That Flanner saw the book as a hoax is typical of the era, "a period marked by grand and vainglorious designs . . . a boom time of masters, of pretenders and vulgarizers of mastery," in which "no one was certain who really commanded and who shammed the possession of prodigious powers and energies, who was phony and what was genuine."[11] It was a time in which both painters and writers enjoyed the ideas of collaboration and of duping the public.

Stein's basic plan of pretending to be Alice Toklas in order to confuse her readers may have originated with Picasso. As James Mellow reports:

The collaboration between Picasso and Braque . . . was particularly close. It was even rumored that they had maliciously signed each other's paintings in order to confound the enemy. Braque maintained that they had been "engaged in what we felt was a search for the anonymous personality. We were inclined to efface our personalities in order to find originality." If "amateurs" mistook their paintings, it was "a matter of indifference" to them both.[12]

This "anonymous personality" is embodied in Alice Toklas, who said of her own autobiography, *What Is Remembered*, that "the reminiscences should be centered on Baby [Gertrude Stein] and her work. . . . I am nothing but the memory of her."[13] Just as Gertrude Stein in time came to resemble Picasso's famous portrait of her, so Alice Toklas's writing eventually seemed to an anonymous reviewer of *What Is Remembered* to "read like Gertrude Stein."[14] And like Stein, Toklas tried to write her autobiography, on which she worked in partial collaboration with Max White, as a novel instead of as the serious biography that White wanted.

Other writers of the era wrote fictionalized, collaborative autobiographies and passed them off as straightforward autobiography. David Edstrom, for example, wrote his life story with the aid of Hutchins Hapgood, the author of *The Autobiography of a Thief*. Because Edstrom was nearly mad, he began to invent episodes to "vent ruthless anger at his wife."[15] Soon Hapgood's collaboration began to affect the project so much that Edstrom's autobiography became Hapgood's biography.

The working sessions . . . consisted in Edstrom's narrating his adventures and Hapgood's recording the dictated work. The finished manuscript, however, would show Hapgood's own view. While the book was still in progress, Hapgood showed his notes to Gertrude.

"In a few days," David Edstrom recalled, "I was told by Gertrude that [Hapgood] had written a book about me."[16]

Other literary works of the period that may have influenced the writing of *The Autobiography of Alice B. Toklas* include Carl Van Vechten's *Peter Whiffle*, an autobiographical novel published in 1922 in which Whiffle, a fictionalized version of Van Vechten, purports to be the editor of his own personal narrative, a story that includes Leo Stein and Paul Cézanne as real people while fictionalizing Mabel Dodge Luhan and others. Another personal narrative told through an unusual narrator is Virginia Woolf's *Flush*, which was serialized in several of the same issues of the *Atlantic Monthly* as *The Autobiography of Alice B. Toklas*. One wonders at the confusion of the reader of the July 1933 edition of the magazine who tried to comprehend that "Alice B. Toklas" was really Gertrude Stein and that Virginia Woolf was literally demonstrating to the Brownings the truth of Stein's famous dictum that "I am me because my little dog knows me."[17]

How Many Autobiographical Acts Are There in It?

The autobiography of Rose . . . is the autobiography of Rose even if her name is not Rose.—Gertrude Stein

Many of the charges of lying that greeted *The Autobiography of Alice B. Toklas* stem from a failure to understand Stein's reasons for narrating the book through Toklas. The book is the autobiography of Gertrude Stein in the shape of a biography and memoir of the era. Stein's trick of writing her life story by pretending to write Toklas's autobiography is made more complex by the fact that the book is actually more in the form of a biography of Stein by Toklas than in the form of an autobiography of Toklas. By acting as if she were someone else writing her own biography, Stein dramatizes the double consciousness inherent in writing about one's life that Roy Pascal discusses: "The autobiographer has in fact a double character. He exists to some degree as an object, a man recognisable from outside, and he needs to give to some extent the genetical story of this person. But he is also a subject, a temperament whose inner and outer world owes its appearance to the manner in which he sees it."[18]

Realizing that *The Autobiography of Alice B. Toklas* is Stein's life story in the form of Toklas's biography of her, the reader is burdened by the dual character of the autobiographer as both observer and subject and must constantly juggle the fact that "I" in the book is Toklas with the fact that everything that "I" says was actually written by Stein. The reader must constantly keep in mind that the narrator is both Stein and not Stein at the same time.

This unique literary situation allows Stein to gain a detached perspective. If she were to name herself a genius directly, she would be an egomaniac; however, for "Gertrude Stein," a literary character, to call herself a genius through the persona of "Alice B. Toklas," another literary character, is apparently egomania twice removed. As Jean Starobinski notes, "Though seemingly a modest form, autobiographical narrative in the third person accumulates and makes compatible events glorifying the hero who refuses to speak in his own name."[19] The result is somewhat tongue-in-cheek, similar in effect to the traditional American speech idiom in which we bolster our courage by talking to ourselves. An athlete named Smith, for example, will try to cheer himself up by addressing himself in the third person: "Come on, Smith, you can do better than that." Blues singers traditionally sing songs in which they use their own names, and soldiers often speak of themselves by a nickname, as in the expression "the kid's going to pass inspection with no trouble."

Philippe Lejeune calls this device "fictive fiction":

> One can also refer to oneself using initials or even one of those nicknames you give yourself privately, or a name that already situates you as a character in a novel, as Gide does when, in his journal, he refers to himself as "Fabrice" or "X." We are here at the frontier of fiction, or rather at a "fictive fiction," if I can put it that way, since it is merely mimed within a text that is still presented as autobiographical.[20]

Lejeune emphasizes the exact form the proper name assumes in third person autobiography, stressing the rhetorical importance of the name in establishing a "figure of enunciation . . . a *mime* of social confrontation which the autobiographer is trying to trap and turn to his own advantage."[21]

Although Alice Toklas, in actual life, referred to Gertrude Stein by her first name or by the pet names "lovey" and "baby," throughout the autobiography Toklas calls her companion "Gertrude Stein," never just "Gertrude" or "Stein," except in chapter 2, "My Arrival in Paris," where she uses "Miss Stein" in telling of their initial meeting. The constant repetition of Stein's full name by her lover suggests the ironic, self-spoofing style of the American idiom that I have described. The use of Stein's full name is clearly intended for humorous effect, as shown by the following pointed observation in *The Autobiography of Alice B. Toklas*: "Everybody called Gertrude Stein Gertrude, or at most Mademoiselle Gertrude, everybody called Picasso Pablo and Fernande Fernande and everybody called Guillaume Apollinaire Guillaume and Max Jacob Max but everybody called Marie Laurencin Marie Laurencin."[22] Only Marie Laurencin, a relative outsider, is given her full name. Lynn Bloom sees this use of Stein's full name as having an "honorific" rhetorical function that gives Stein "dignity and authority that the plain, familiar 'Gertrude' or the flippant 'Gerty' would not sustain. Stein, through Toklas, thereby flouts the convention that has persisted in women's biographies throughout the centuries of addressing women subjects by their first names, regardless of their age, rank, or social status."[23]

Stein's use of Toklas as the narrator in this "autobiography-by-Doppelganger," as Bloom calls it, also has the effect of mocking the conventions that separate autobiography from biography and of challenging the requirement that the subject, narrator, and author of an autobiography be the same person. This narrative device is unique to Stein's book, though autobiographies have been written by couples, such as Will and Ariel Durant. Other writers have written about themselves in the third person in such works as Caesar's memoirs, *The Education of Henry Adams*, Norman Mailer's *The Armies of the Night*, Roland Barthes's *Roland Barthes par Roland Barthes*, and "in such publisher's material as literary prefaces, blurbs, and self-composed biographical notices."[24] Jean-Jacques Rousseau's autobiographical *Rousseau juge de Jean-Jacques* is a dialogue between two fictional characters. "One, called 'Rousseau,' admires Jean-Jacques Rousseau's books, does not know the man, but finds it hard to believe all the scandal he hears about him. The second character, 'The Frenchman,' unlike the first, has not read the author's works."[25] In another variation, Rosellen Brown published a novel, *The Autobiography of My Mother*, that uses a form of Gertrude Stein's fictive witness to tell the life story of a woman whose name, Gerda Stein, reflects its literary antecedent. Still another recent attempt to use a modified form of Stein's narrative trick is Jean-Jacques Gautier's *Cher Untel* in which "Aline Moussart, secretary to the writer X, is keeping a diary. Gradually, she gives us a description of the writer while also telling us her own story and that of her relationship with X (Untel). At the end of her journal she suggests to her employer that he 'publish the present manuscript in his own name and present the journal as fiction.'"[26]

Stein's autobiography, however, differs from all of these related cases in that its third person narrator, Alice B. Toklas, is not a fictional invention, although she appears as a partially fictionalized character in the book. Stein's attempt at copying her companion's style of speaking—Toklas's precise turns of phrase and deceptively understated wit —was a deliberate act designed for more than the egotistical, interpretive, and objective functions that Bloom isolates. Stein invented her complex technique to keep the reader off balance about her homosexuality, while she simultaneously produced an autobiography that would directly reflect both the specific atmosphere of bohemian Paris and the closeness of her loving relationship with Alice Toklas.

That readers have wondered from the beginning exactly whose

voice they were reading is a reflection of Stein's consummate skill in
mimicking Toklas's voice. When a portion of the autobiography was
printed in the *Atlantic Monthly* without any comment from the edi-
tors about the actual author, some readers assumed that Alice Toklas
was a totally fictional person, including a *New York Times* reporter
who, visiting the rue de Fleurus, was happy to find Alice Toklas " 'a
very real and efficient personality' despite the doubts that were expressed as to her existence when the autobiography appeared."[27] In
contrast, one reader took the opposite stance, addressing his article of
rebuttal directly to Toklas.[28] Richard Bridgman argues, partly from
textual evidence, for the existence of collaboration or even "one possibility . . . sufficiently heretical that no one has dared advance it directly. . . . There have been hints that Alice Toklas composed her own
autobiography."[29] But Bridgman does not offer sufficient evidence to
support his assertion. His idea, that Toklas's participation in her autobiography was more active than supposed, had been directed at Toklas
earlier, according to her biographer Linda Simon, who adds that Toklas took the suggestion as an accusation that she denied.[30]

In all of their years together, Stein and Toklas naturally assumed
aspects of each other's personality. As Donald Sutherland notes:

> It has been said that the writing takes on very much Miss Toklas's
> conversational style, and while this is true the style is still a vari-
> ant of Miss Stein's conversational style, for she had about the
> same way with an anecdote or a sly observation in talking as Miss
> Toklas has. She usually insisted that writing is an entirely differ-
> ent thing from talking, and it is part of the miracle of this little
> scheme of objectification that she could by way of imitating Miss
> Toklas put in writing something of her own beautiful conversa-
> tion. So that, aside from making a real present of her past, she re-
> created herself, or rather she created a figure of her self, estab-
> lished an identity, a twin, a Doppelganger who burst into
> publicity at once.[31]

Like F. Scott Fitzgerald, who often used his wife Zelda's actual
words and personality in his writing, Gertrude Stein had begun to
echo Toklas's voice as early as 1915 in such pieces as "Farragut or a
Husband's Recompense" in *Useful Knowledge* and "I Have No Title to
Be Successful" from *Painted Lace*. A portion of the autobiographical
Paris, France "seems to have been gotten up from the material Alice
had so far collected."[32] As James Mellow observes:

Snatches of conversation, the ruminations of the author, bits of dialogue between herself and Alice thread their way through the still-elliptical situation of her writing. It is not always clear who the speaker is—their two personalities, on occasion, become merged in a kind of marital union. Nor is it always clear whether Alice's remarks are actual or invented, in a form of interior dialogue in which Alice became Gertrude's literary alter ego.[33]

Others have expressed the nature of the Stein-Toklas relationship in similar terms. W. G. Rogers, for instance, describes their method of driving an automobile in this way: "It was as if Miss Stein's practical sense had been removed from her person and deposited in the person of Miss Toklas. The ego was in the front seat, and the alter ego in the back."[34]

Although Stein's decision to write Toklas's autobiography for her might at first seem presumptuous, another example of Stein's mammoth egotism, which turned the autobiography into a misrepresentation, she actually was deliberately expressing both the social and sexual nature of the Stein-Toklas relationship. The narrative device of blending the two women's natural conversational voices suggests how profoundly their lives were interwoven. When Toklas tells us that she often greeted visitors to their salon with the formula "de la part de qui venez-vous, who is your introducer" (13), or "by whose invitation do you come" (13), she parallels *The Autobiography of Alice B. Toklas* in which we repeatedly are forced to ask, who is introducing the world within?

This formulaic question is paralleled by questions of authorship of the autobiography; on whose part does the book come? Hemingway's famous revelation, in his autobiography, *A Moveable Feast*, of an overheard conversation between Gertrude and Alice, which broke an unwritten taboo against mentioning in print that Stein and Toklas were lesbians, also revealed that Toklas was in many ways the more powerful of the two[35]—facts that had already been revealed between the lines of *The Autobiography of Alice B. Toklas*. Because the book deliberately seems to be confusing in its identity, blending narrator and subject, confounding autobiography and biography, it is a sort of autobiography "in the closet," signaling that it is one thing on the surface, another beneath. Stein writes in the autobiography section of *The Geographical History of America* that "be is for bio. And for autobiography."[36] With this, she prefigures *The Autobiography of Alice B. Toklas* in which "to be" is for her a combination of her identity as seen from within and from without, from herself and from letting Alice "be" Toklas.

That Stein and Toklas were lovers, although an obvious and accepted fact by most of those living the bohemian life of Paris, was kept as an open secret from other expatriates, so that Toklas's standard question—"by whose invitation do you come?"—was also coded to determine whether lesbianism was to be an open or closed assumption. As Adrienne Rich writes in *On Lies, Secrets, and Silence*: "Women's love for women has been represented almost entirely through silence and lies. The institution of heterosexuality has forced the lesbian to dissemble, or be labeled a pervert, a criminal, a sick or dangerous woman." Although she sees society as forcing the lesbian into lying, Rich also wonders if "a life 'in the closet'—lying, perhaps of necessity, about ourselves to bosses, landlords, clients, colleagues, family, because the law and public opinion are founded on a lie"—can easily lead to an unconscious habit of lying in private life, "so that lying (described as *discretion*) becomes an easy way to avoid conflict or complication . . . a strategy so ingrained that it is used even with close friends and lovers."[37]

Stein's deliberate merging of her autobiographical persona with that of Toklas, designed to echo her actual merging with Toklas and to provide an eccentric cover for their homosexuality, also suggests Alice Toklas's own identity. Toklas's biographer, Linda Simon, recounts two episodes that show her delight, well before she even met Gertrude Stein, in hiding herself within a disguised identity.

> She also contrived two pranks, jesting in a role she would someday enact seriously. When she learned that a well-known lecturer was to visit San Francisco she invited her to tea and persuaded Annette [Rosenshine] to take over as hostess. A few friends would come as guests, but Alice would spend the afternoon pretending to be the maid.
>
> With Harriet [Levy], she once proposed a similar plan. Harriet belonged to a small literary group which called themselves "The Spinners" and met for meals and talks. For one of their gatherings, Alice offered to prepare the meal—provided she could again surprise her friends by appearing as the maid.[38]

So often did Toklas disguise herself—assuming the successive roles of maid, cook, wife, secretary, press agent, and publisher, making small talk with the wives of the famous, acting as a screen to keep unwanted visitors from boring Stein—that self-effacement and deliberately subverted identity can be considered Toklas's basic metaphor of self. As one visitor to the salon said, "Alice seemed always to speak of herself in the plural, automatically including Gertrude in whatever she had to say."[39] Toklas's natural predilection for submerged identity is illustrated in the story from *The Autobiography of Alice B. Toklas* that describes the French major in charge of gasoline:

> All this time of course he called me Mademoiselle Stein because Gertrude Stein's name was on all the papers that I presented to him, she being the driver. And so now, he said, Mademoiselle Stein, my wife is very anxious to make your acquaintance and she has asked me to ask you to dine with us. I was very confused. I hesitated. But I am not Mademoiselle Stein, I said. He almost jumped out of his chair. What, he shouted, not Mademoiselle Stein. Then who are you. . . . Well, said I, you see Mademoiselle Stein. Where is Mademoiselle Stein, he said. She is downstairs, I said feebly, in the automobile. Well what does all this mean, he said. Well, I said, you see Mademoiselle Stein is the driver and I am the delegate. . . . But what, said he sternly, would you have done if I had asked you to sign something. I would have told you, I said, as I am telling you now. [177–78]

Although Stein has Toklas claim she would have revealed her real identity if she had had "to sign something," this episode is representative of Toklas's most figurative self. To a military man, the driver of a vehicle in less important than those being driven, and Alice is obviously delighting in false naiveté, in pretending to be confused in order to further the confusion, in giving such ambiguous answers as "you see Mademoiselle Stein" and "I would have told you as I am telling you now"—since she is, in effect, telling us now through Stein. Not only did she delight in pretending to be Stein in a story (told by Stein pretending to be her), but she also allowed Stein to "sign something" in real life that she had actually written. Robert A. Wilson demonstrates in his bibliography of Stein's writings that "although published as Gertrude Stein's work, the English translation of *Picasso* was actually done by Miss Toklas, with some slight revision by Miss Stein."[40]

For all the innovative aspects of Gertrude Stein's speaking in her autobiography as Alice Toklas, this rhetorical device is also a modification of a classic situation that David Minter demonstrates is common to both American fiction and to autobiography. Minter sees as a familiar pattern prose works that feature two related characters, one a man with a grand design, the other a man "through whose interpret-

ing mind and voice the story of the man of design comes to us."[41]
Puzzled because her writing was largely unpublished and often misunderstood, Gertrude Stein decided to write *The Autobiography of Alice B. Toklas* partially as a way of gaining publicity for herself. The
grand design of her mammoth *The Making of Americans* and of her
enormous body of work needed someone besides herself for interpretation. But feeling that she was the only one capable of fully understanding her work, Stein decided on the narrative voice of Toklas to
explain her writing. Minter's description of the prototypical inter-
preter echoes Toklas's role, both in real life and in the autobiography:

> Moved by the baffling fate of a man of design, by failure of con-
> siderable magnitude and uncertain causes and significance, the
> man of interpretation dedicates his rational and imaginative fac-
> ulties and his linguistic resources to recounting a story so domi-
> nated by failure that it requires an act of interpretation to define
> and perhaps reclaim it. . . . The pursuits of the man of design and
> the man of interpretation are more than interlaced and interre-
> lated.[42]

Minter's scheme—which in one sense defines the most basic autobiographical stance that the autobiographer must be both the person
of design and interpretation—also parallels the Stein-Toklas persona.
Toklas, acting as "the man of interpretation," is at first baffled by the
artists and paintings she encounters in Paris, but by the book's end she
has become the one person who can best tell the story of the cubist era
and best explain the overarching plan of Gertrude Stein, "the man of
design."

Two Lives

The genius (I now slowly perceive), like the intellectual, is a product of mass cul-
ture.—Mary McCarthy, *How I Grew*

It is hard enough to make any definitive statement about the nature of
truth in fiction as opposed to nonfiction, much less to construct a
definition of the kind of truth intended for *The Autobiography of Alice
B. Toklas*. But a productive way to begin to understand Stein's kind of
truthfulness is well summarized in Shirley Neuman's phrase "the paradox of veracity" that she defines as follows: "In order to make his
readers believe in the truth of an experience so subjective that the
autobiographer alone can attest to its veracity, he will in some sense

treat that experience as if he were examining it from outside himself, as if he were a biographer."[43] Stein's treating her experiences as if they were biographical, but writing them herself, results in a clear warning that she has no intention to deceive, thereby making even the most outrageous statements and the most palpable lies into part of the autobiographical construct.

For example, in describing "Gertrude Stein's" attempts at making excuses not to see Ezra Pound, "Alice Toklas" writes:

> Gertrude Stein did not want to see Ezra again. Ezra did not quite see why. He met Gertrude Stein one day near the Luxembourg gardens and said, but I do want to come to see you. I am so sorry, answered Gertrude Stein, but Miss Toklas has a bad tooth and beside we are busy picking wild flowers. All of which was literally true, like all of Gertrude Stein's literature, but it upset Ezra, and we never saw him again. [202]

Clearly, these lame social excuses are not "literally true," and readers are being warned that this is the kind of literary truth to be found in "all of Gertrude Stein's literature." In so warning her readers that literal and figurative will not always be used literally and figuratively, Stein has set up the system that will apply throughout the book.

An example of the standard of reliability that governs the truth-value of *The Autobiography of Alice B. Toklas* is the fact that Toklas, the biographer, is willing to consider altering the truth for her own reasons, though she discusses her casual way with factual truth rather than actually misleading the reader. Beginning with the standard opening of most biographies, she writes that although "Gertrude Stein" was born in Pennsylvania, as "I am an ardent californian and as she spent her youth there I have often begged her to be born in California but she has always remained firmly born in Allegheny, Pennsylvania" (69). Toklas's desire to change Stein's place of birth in order to reflect more accurately the truth of her childhood—a desire reflected in the fact that the physical place once called Allegheny is now called Pittsburgh—is typical of what Stanley Weintraub calls the biographer's "perennial paradox": "The facts do not always add up to truth, and invention, which frequently furnishes tantalizing material for the biographer, often has its own kind of truth."[44]

For some readers, *The Autobiography of Alice B. Toklas* is a work of fiction that should be read in a special way. Michael Hoffman, for instance, believes that, because Stein was "continuously turning the events she lived through into occasions for narrative presentation," the book is a roman à clef and, consequently, that "our demands for accuracy and fairness must take second place to our demands for the writing to be interesting, the structure coherent, the observations memorable."[45] Although Hoffman's remarks accurately describe the levels of truthfulness inherent in the autobiography, there is no reason why they should apply only to fiction—"turning the events she lived through into occasions for narrative presentation" being a good working definition of autobiography as a genre.

Although many of the misstatements of time and place in the book can be attributed to Stein's faulty memory, especially considering that she cites thousands of names, dates, and places and that she was writing twenty-five years after the events had occurred, there are, nevertheless, indications that she was aware that her statements are untrue to the narrow truth of "unprofitable fact" but true to the larger impression of "telling invention."[46] Richard Bridgman has pointed out that the manuscript of *The Autobiography of Alice B. Toklas* in the Yale University library includes numerous editorial comments that question the accuracy of the book. "Sometimes Alice Toklas took emphatic exception," notes Bridgman. "When Gertrude Stein said that she had completed the job of reading proof for *The Making of Americans* by herself, Alice objected—'never.' Regarding Picasso's move to Montrouge, she commented 'no,' and supplied the correct date, '1915.' In neither instance did Gertrude Stein change her version."[47]

Stein often leaves errors in the text in order to give her narrative a spontaneous flavor and a conversational tone; for example, she has Toklas say, "It was at that time Ezra Pound came, no that was brought about in another way" (196). In another place, she stresses the remembered quality of the book by leaving in the following anecdote, even though she appears to recall little about it: "Some one once even offered us a piece of a Zeppelin or an aeroplane, I forget which, but we declined. . . . If I remember rightly it was at this time that some one, I imagine it was Apollinaire on leave, gave a concert and a reading of Blaise Cedrars' poems. . . . I remember this took place in some one's atelier" (159). This deliberately vague retelling becomes more specific when we remember Stein's E. E. Cummingsesque use of personal pronouns such as anyone, someone, and everyone in both general and specific senses.

When Matisse complained about Stein's misquoting him, "Not having seen Miss Stein since the war I could not have made the statement she attributes to me," he was only pointing out one of many times when characters in the book speak about or describe a scene at which they were not physically present.[48] Carolyn Copeland lists the anachronistic sequence of the autobiography's scenes; "the book is organized in the following sequence: 1877–1906; 1907; 1903–1907; 1874–1903; 1907–1914; 1914–1918; 1919–1932," corresponding to the seven chapters. Noting that chapters 3 and 4—"Gertrude Stein in Paris" and "Gertrude Stein before She Came to Paris"—are out of order, Copeland suggests something that bothered many members of the artistic community: since Toklas did not get to Paris until 1907, "she could not possibly have been the eye-witness first person narrator of sections three and four, since they antedate sections one and two."[49] Copeland considers the following scene in detail:

> That evening Gertrude Stein's brother took out portfolio after portfolio of japanese prints to show Picasso, Gertrude Stein's brother was fond of japanese prints. Picasso solemnly and obediently looked at print after print and listened to the descriptions. He said under his breath to Gertrude Stein, he is very nice, your brother, but like all americans . . . he shows you japanese prints. . . . I don't care for it. As I say Gertrude Stein and Pablo Picasso immediately understood each other. [46]

This scene, which took place two years before Toklas met Stein, gives the impression that Toklas was actually there in the room. "There is every indication that the picture of Leo Stein as an original bore, very much out of step with the two geniuses in the room that night, is not the conclusion of the objective narrator, but rather the result of an Alice Toklas mask which Gertrude Stein was wearing when she wrote it."[50]

This anecdote demonstrates all three of the rhetorical stances common to memoir, according to Marcus Bilson, who argues that *The Autobiography of Alice B. Toklas* is more memoir than autobiography. The author of a memoir writes as an eyewitness, a participant, or a *histor*, "to evoke the historicity of his past and to argue for the truth of his vision of history."[51] By *histor*, Bilson means the theoretical mode defined by Robert Scholes and Robert Kellogg in which the writer describes "events he has not seen with his own eyes . . . what he has overheard, read about, or accumulated by research through historical records."[52] Stein's autobiography through Toklas allows her to be simultaneously the eyewitness-participant and the *histor*. And as Georg Misch observes about memoir, "The person regarded and the person regarding are separated, while for us the identity of the two is the essential mark of the autobiography."[53] In a sense, then, *The Autobiography of Alice B. Toklas* is a mock memoir in which Toklas reports on Gertrude Stein as if she were herself a historical era witnessed by Toklas.

As a *histor*, Stein describes the now famous testimonial banquet for Rousseau. Stein's version, although different from numerous others, all of which differ from each other, has, according to Hoffman, come to stand "as an event whose absurd gaiety symbolizes the meaning of those early days of modernism." Hoffman writes that "the banquet did occur, and some of the events during it are not in question. What *exactly* did happen we shall never know."[54] Although Stein's version of the banquet may be partially inaccurate, that fact does not invalidate the historicity of the story, for the essence of history resides in a comparison of various stories about the past, a combination of what happened and what people thought happened. However, as Peter Munz observes in *The Shapes of Time*, a completely solid distinction between history and fiction is not finally possible because both are stories, narratives whose authenticity depends on comparison with other narrative.[55]

The tone of moral outrage produced in readers by Stein's autobiography is similar to the reaction of the crowd in the Petit Palais to Matisse's painting *La Femme au Chapeau*: "People were roaring with laughter at the picture and scratching at it. Gertrude Stein could not understand why, the picture seemed to her perfectly natural. . . . And she could not understand why it infuriated everybody. . . . And it upset her to see them all mocking at it. It bothered her and angered her because she did not understand why . . . just as later she did not understand why since the writing was all so clear and natural they mocked at and were enraged by her work" (35). Stein is falsely naive here; she knows the effect of her obscure style and that it will not strike every reader as perfectly clear. As she acknowledges in *Everybody's Autobiography*, "My writing is clear as mud, but mud settles and clear streams run on and disappear."[56]

The audience's reaction to Matisse's painting, their desire to attack the picture physically by scratching at it or to render it powerless as art by laughing at it, stems from the belief that they are being mocked. The crowd feels that the painting is a hoax and that by showing it in a gallery Matisse is lying to them. For artistic or literary performances, an audience does not mind being lied to, as long as it knows the artist is lying and believes it is in on the joke. But the artist must announce in some way that he or she is lying so that the audience will feel at ease in the situation. The ways that Stein announces her intention to lie to the readers of the autobiography directly influence the book's effect. If the title *The Autobiography of Alice B. Toklas*, printed without a byline, is too misleading, readers can hardly miss the implications of the frontispiece, captioned "Alice B. Toklas at the door," that depicts Ger-

trude Stein writing at a table in the background, a pictorial representation of the hint in Stein's *Tender Buttons* that "the author of all that is
in there behind the door,"[57] another suggestion of the homosexuality
partially in the closet. Furthermore, she hints in *Stanzas in Meditation*,
written just before the autobiography although not published until
later, about the nature of *The Autobiography of Alice B. Toklas*: "This is
her autobiography one of two / But which it is no one which it is can
know."[58] In still another clue, Toklas says, less than halfway through
the autobiography, of both Stein's *Ada* and *The Autobiography of Alice
B. Toklas*, "I began it [*Ada*] and I thought she was making fun of me
and I protested, she says I protest now about my autobiography"
(114). From all of these clues, Stein has made it difficult for the atten-
tive reader to miss the information, which Bridgman claims is withheld until the last sentence, "that Gertrude Stein has written Alice
Toklas's autobiography for her."[59]

In not only misleading the reader about the nature of her book but
also warning of the deception, Stein establishes that she is writing
what Thomas J. Roberts calls "fiction by intention": "A book is fiction by intention if its writer has knowingly made it factually untrue
but has also warned his reader he has done this." The kind of an-
nouncement or warning that signals a book is fiction by intention may
include an actual label such as the word *novel*, *romance*, or *tale*, or it
may consist of "certain kinds of materials—a report of a conversation
between secluded people just before they die (a conversation no living human could have heard)."[60] As Carolyn Copeland has demonstrated, many of the conversations in *The Autobiography of Alice B.
Toklas* are reported by Alice Toklas when she could not actually have
heard of or participated in them, and therefore, they act as additional
warnings to the reader that the book is not to be taken straightfor-
wardly.

Stein's use of specific concrete details adds to the verisimilitude of
the book and causes us to forget the warnings that she gives us. As
Roberts writes, "A writer may do everything in his power to deceive
us into accepting his book as wholly true, but if he gives us fair warning that it is not factually true, then we say he is writing fiction by
intention and not lies."[61] Although Roberts's category is useful in
demonstrating that factual discrepancies are not necessarily lies, *The
Autobiography of Alice B. Toklas*, for me, is not fiction by intention but
autobiography, a genre that always includes a warning that to be totally accurate about all of the factual details of a life is not possible.

From one perspective, Gertrude Stein seems to be lying directly,
whatever genre she is writing in, and for the usual reason of self-ag-

grandizement. The famous story of her final examination in William

James's psychology seminar, for instance, is, from the perspective of a
true-to-life factuality, not true. "She sat down with the examination
paper before her and she just could not. Dear Professor James, she
wrote at the top of her paper, I am so sorry but really I do not feel a bit
like an examination paper in philosophy today, and left" (79). According to the autobiography, James was so charmed by her candor
that "he gave her work the highest mark in the course" (79). However, Bridgman has shown, by examining transcripts of her college
courses, that this statement is false. "She also joined Philosophy 20b,
the 'Psychological Seminary' taught by William James in her junior
year. In the first half of that course, which was devoted to the feelings,
she received an A. But in the spring semester, when the class studied
consciousness, knowledge, and the relation of the mind to the body,
she did less well, earning only a C."[62]

Certainly, Stein might have been referring to the first half of the
course, and we do not know what grades the remainder of the class
received, but Stein appears to have misrepresented her past in the
story. However, in so doing, she is only adhering to the principle she
announces in *The Autobiography of Alice B. Toklas*. "Gertrude Stein
never corrects any detail of anybody's writing, she sticks strictly to
general principles, the way of seeing what the writer chooses to see"
(214). Stein's way of seeing, as she emphasizes again in *Everybody's
Autobiography*, was a new way of writing about the inner self that was
based on the personality seen in the publicity people create about
themselves.

> In the old days when they wrote novels they made up the person-
> ality of the things they had seen in people and the things that
> were the people as if they were a dream. But now well now how
> can you dream about a personality when it is always being cre-
> ated for you by a publicity, how can you believe what you make
> up when publicity makes them up to be so much realer than you
> can dream. And so autobiography is written which is in a way
> a way to say that publicity is right, they are as the public sees
> them.[63]

This statement is an elaboration on her well-known claim that "I am
me because my little dog knows me"—that is, we know ourselves because of inherent qualities that we can never know ourselves, but that
can only be understood from the perspective of the other.

Although the legend about her final examination for James is
probably not literally true, it is true to her conception of herself as an

eccentric genius who was recognized early by a fatherly and famous professor. The truth expressed in this story, and throughout *The Autobiography of Alice B. Toklas*, is more philosophical than historical. René Wellek and Austin Warren explain that "fiction is less strange and more representative than truth," using as an example Wilson Follet's comment about Defoe's narrative of Mrs. Veal and Mrs. Bargrave: "Everything in the story is true except the whole of it. And mark how difficult Defoe makes it to question even that whole."[64]

The Autobiography of Alice B. Toklas is, in effect, exactly the opposite of Defoe's story; nearly everything in the autobiography is slightly false, but the whole becomes true. Although autobiographers know that fiction can be more representative than truth, many readers fail to understand that autobiography is also a form of imaginative literature. Thus the usual assumption is that philosophical truth belongs to fiction, historical truth to nonfiction, when in fact autobiography, which partakes of both fiction and nonfiction, gets at truth through a combination of historical and philosophical angles.

That Wellek and Warren cite Daniel Defoe as an example of a writer who makes fine distinctions between factual and propositional truth is particularly interesting, for Gertrude Stein concludes *The Autobiography of Alice B. Toklas* with this description of what she has done: "I am going to write it as simply as Defoe did the autobiography of Robinson Crusoe" (252). Her comparison of the autobiography to *Robinson Crusoe* is one of the most significant clues offered to the nature of her autobiography. In calling *Robinson Crusoe* simple, Stein assumes a faux-naïf mask, for Defoe's book is one of the most complex in English literature in its use of disguised narration. Though modern readers and critics see *Robinson Crusoe* as a novel, Defoe's contemporaries were incensed when the book was first published because they thought Defoe "was a liar passing off invention for truth."[65]

Because the novel as a genre was not established until around 1740, Defoe's novelistic *Robinson Crusoe*, published in 1719, was judged as nonfiction. The fact that Defoe did everything he could to create the illusion of nonfiction added to his contemporaries' confusion. The original title page, for example, gave no warning that the book was not an account of actual adventures written by an actual person named Robinson Crusoe; the phrase "written by himself" and Defoe's pretense that he was merely an editor did not constitute ample warning of the book's fictive nature. Defoe prefaced his novel with the statement that "the editor believes the thing to be a just history of fact; neither is there any appearance of fiction in it."[66] Actually, Defoe based his novel on an account of a shipwrecked Scottish sailor, Alexander Selkirk. Because the novel *Robinson Crusoe* was judged as non-fiction, it received the same kind of violent attack as *The Autobiography of Alice B. Toklas*. In 1720, Charles Gildon published a parody of Defoe's novel that was characterized by a tone of "jealous outrage."[67] According to Lennard Davis, Gildon's charge was unique because it "is one of the few . . . which specifically attacks a work on the grounds that it is fictional—that is not a lie, a libel, or a distortion, but simply a fiction."[68]

To complicate the situation further, Defoe replied to Gildon's attack by writing and publishing *Serious Reflections of Robinson Crusoe* in which he pretends to be an angry Robinson Crusoe replying indignantly to the charges that his account of the shipwreck was untrue. In *Serious Reflections*: "Crusoe, who in this volume is merely a thin disguise for Defoe, then picks up an idea from Charles Gildon's attack on the first two parts of *Robinson Crusoe* and maintains that his work is actually an allegory of Defoe's life. Although he refuses to enter 'into a nearer explication of the matter,' Crusoe assures the reader that his life is an 'emblem' of the life of the author and that 'there is not a circumstance in the imaginary story but has its just allusion to a real story.'"[69] Thus we have an imagined literary character, based on an actual person, who claims that his life is a metaphor for the author who created him in the first place—which is exactly what not only Gertrude Stein but all autobiographers are doing. J. M. Coetzee's recent novel *Foe* plays with Defoe's manipulations by imagining another companion on the island, a woman who actually writes both Crusoe's and Friday's stories for them, giving the results to Defoe, who figures as a literary character in the novel.

In one of her later essays, Gertrude Stein amplifies her statement that she was trying to reproduce the simplicity of Defoe's narration: "Think of Defoe, he tried to write Robinson Crusoe as if it were exactly what did happen and yet after all he is Robinson Crusoe and Robinson Crusoe is Defoe and therefore after all it is not what is happening to him Robinson Crusoe that makes what is exciting every one." Earlier in the same essay, she says, "Narrative is what anybody has to say in any way."[70] By these two statements, Stein meant that she tried to write her autobiography so that its narrative gave a sense of time that related, in the past tense, what had happened to her and her circle in Paris, while simultaneously trying to re-create those events in the present as though they were happening as she wrote. She remarks of *The Autobiography of Alice B. Toklas* in *Everybody's Autobiography* that "the first autobiography was . . . a description and a creation of something that having happened was in a way happening not again but as it had been which is history which is newspaper which is illustration."[71]

Stein frequently combines the present tense with the past in the autobiography. For example, "The home at 27 rue de Fleurus consisted then as it does now of a tiny pavillon . . . and a very large atelier adjoining" (7), a figurative description of the physical relationship between her and Alice Toklas. Toklas begins chapter 4 with "once more I have come to Paris and now I am one of the habitués of the rue de Fleurus" (69). Describing Stein, Toklas says, "She loves objects that are breakable, cheap objects and valuable objects . . . one just broke this morning" (88), to show the continuation of the past into the very day Stein is writing the autobiography. Other representative passages include "She always was, she always is, tormented by the problem of the external and the internal" (119), "I had as was and is my habit gone to bed very early" (157), "Mary Borden-Turner had been and was going to be a writer" (170), and "I will tell the whole story as I afterward learnt it but now I must find Fernande and propose to her to take french lessons from her" (19).

In addition to trying to copy his narrative style, Stein was attracted to Defoe's habit of making outrageous statements about himself that he delivered in a perfectly serious manner. "His most original statements concern himself. What are we to think of his comparison of himself to Shakespeare and to contemporary women novelists as writers of 'little learning, but of prodigious Natural Parts?'"[72] Defoe's sense of publicity caused him, like Stein—with Toklas as her Friday— to take enormous pleasure from playfully creating false identities and legends about himself. "Even in his non-fiction he successfully hides himself behind hundreds of masks," including "Captain Charles Johnson, who briefly appeared in 1724 and 1728 as the knowledgeable economic historian of the pirates, and earned himself a place in the *Dictionary of National Biography*."[73] Defoe's predilection for disguises and outrageous claims of ability are reminiscent of Gertrude Stein's habit of making exaggerated statements about herself as a genius. In *The Autobiography of Alice B. Toklas*, she claims that she is a genius, that "in english literature in her time she is the only one" (77); elsewhere she asserts, "Yes, the Jews have produced only three originative geniuses: Christ, Spinoza and myself."[74] She also claims that her lecture at Oxford University seemed to one of her listeners, who had originally been a heckler, to be "his greatest experience since he had read Kant's Critique of Pure Reason" (235). Earlier, she claims that *The Making of Americans* was to be "a history of all human beings, all who ever were or are or could be living" (56). Obviously, such an outrageous argument is not meant to be taken literally.

Statements that make such obviously exaggerated claims as these are an integral part of another American literary tradition—the tall tale—that is characterized as "a kind of humorous tale common on the American frontier, which uses realistic detail, a literal manner, and common speech to recount extravagantly impossible happenings, usually resulting from the superhuman abilities of a character."[75] *The Autobiography of Alice B. Toklas* can be read as an elaborate tall tale in which Gertrude Stein creates herself as a legendary figure, given to outrageous bragging and superhuman abilities. The parallels between Stein's autobiography and the tall tale are more than superficial, for the fundamental device of her autobiography—pretending to be someone else writing about her own exploits—is a prime characteristic of the tall tale. Richard Hauck writes, in his discussion of "The Teller in the Tall Tale," that a prime characteristic of the written tall tale is the author's pretense to be little more than a recorder of the story, a member of the audience listening to the story rather than its author. As a result, the real focus is often the psychology of the teller rather than the actual events of the tall tale. The teller's function is "to prove to strangers that this event, this hero, this locality, exceeds all their expectations. . . . It is the teller who is the manipulator of appearances and the creator of myth."[76]

Taking on the role of both teller and subject, Gertrude Stein presents herself as a great American folk hero, living on the frontier of narrative innovation and the literary establishment. Although her claims to genius are sometimes meant to be taken seriously, in the autobiography they are usually written in a self-mocking manner, suitable to a tall tale. For instance, although Stein wrote in *What Are Masterpieces?* that "the essence of being a genius is to be able to talk and listen to listen while talking and talk while listening,"[77] in *The Autobiography of Alice B. Toklas* she quotes Matisse as saying, "when you listen so carefully to me and so attentively. . . [you] do not hear a word I say" (15), thus undercutting her claim. Other physical and mental tests for genius, described in a self-deprecating fashion, include her ability to read "anything and everything" (974) and her power to outstare the sun: "She could even lie in the sun and look straight up into a summer noon sun, she said it rested her eyes and head" (55). To Carl Van Vechten, she appeared at first omniscient. He was "naturally bewildered" by her apparent ability to see into his mind when, on their first meeting, she "began to tease [him] by dropping a word here and there of intimate knowledge of his past life" (137). Her knowledge came, not from omniscience, but from a meeting with Van Vechten's wife the night before. Although she made a number of errors in recalling the past, Stein explained them away in *Everybody's Autobiography* by saying, "And so I know what a genius is, a genius is some one who does not have to remember the two hundred years that everybody else has to remember."[78]

Stein's exaggerations of her own importance are not so much ironic as humorous. If "it is characteristic of anything except itself," observed Oliver Evans, "the quality of Gertrude Stein's humor is characteristically American—and frontier American at that. It is 'Western' rather than 'Eastern' humor."[79] For all of her eccentric behavior as a bohemian in Paris, Gertrude Stein had at base a strong attraction for Americana, whether singing her favorite song, "On the Trail of the Lonesome Pine," playing the role of rugged western individualist with Toklas as sidekick, or "swapping tall tales with Westerners who occasionally visited her" in Paris.[80]

Describing the blend of fact and fiction common to the stories published in the New York *Spirit of the Times* from 1831 to 1861, Hauck writes, "That *Spirit* writers should make reporting and lying absolutely indistinguishable in style was characteristic of the kind of tale telling that the western traveler knew best."[81] Hauck's description of the characteristic blend of truth and lie common to the tall tale is also suggestive of the dadaesque quality of the American expatriate experience in the 1920s, not to mention the perennial paradox of the autobiographer, whose writing always lies on the frontier.

SHERWOOD ANDERSON

"Lies My Father Told Me"

3

[The world of the imagination] is also the world of dreams, in which the artist is relieved of the world of necessity. It is a world of "lies," of the kind that enlarge the real and grotesquely disfigure the truth.—Frederick J. Hoffman

That Gertrude Stein should select Sherwood Anderson from all of the Americans in Paris to be one of her personal favorites is odd enough, given the vast differences in their backgrounds, but even more surprising are their constant high praise for each other's writing and their repeated insistence on each other as literary influences. Stein asked Anderson to write an introduction to her *Geography and Plays*, carried on a lifelong correspondence with him long after breaking with Picasso and Hemingway, wrote positive reviews of his least successful books, and published two maudlin pieces: "Idem the Same—A Valentine to Sherwood Anderson" and "Sherwood's Sweetness."[1]

A number of parallels exist between the two writers: both published multiple autobiographies; had an experimental bent, particularly in terms of the rhythm of sentences; professed disdain for financial fame; and admired Ulysses S. Grant, at one time even planning to collaborate on a book about him. Although Anderson is in general perceptive about his own literary reputation, calling himself finally "a minor figure among the world's artists,"[2] he once allowed himself to indulge in Stein's claim to genius. "It must be that I am a genius as it is only the genius who can be as cruel as I was then. You see I take the genius to be a man who has something to settle with himself and I presume that I did at that time feel that there was something in me trying to aim itself against the enemy—society" (*Memoirs*, 258).

Anderson also shares with Stein a tendency toward androgyny, though his is clearly of a different degree and nature than is Stein's. The following physical description of him in 1924 helps to illustrate their mutual attraction: "When Sherwood first came to New Orleans he looked like an old mother, his face, I mean, very like that of Gertrude Stein. . . . It was the expression of a nice old woman, not effeminate but strong."[3] Echoing Stein's famous anecdote of Picasso's portrait of her, Anderson's earliest autobiographical sketch includes a story of a portrait of himself painted by William Hollandsworth; of this painting Anderson, commented, "This portrait, I am sure, does not look much like me, but the artist has caught in it the very spirit of my mother."[4]

Gertrude Stein also had a direct influence on Anderson's decision to return to autobiographical writing. Having written *A Story Teller's Story* in 1924 and *Tar: A Midwest Childhood* in 1926, he was stimulated by the popular and critical success of the serialization of *The Autobiography of Alice B. Toklas* in the *Atlantic Monthly* to begin what eventually became *Sherwood Anderson's Memoirs* (*Memoirs*, xvi). Apparently writing without irony, Anderson notes in a diary entry that his memoirs (which he first thought of as a third-person narrative, called either "I Build My House" or "Rudolph's Book of Days") would be "something like Stein's book but more honest" (*Memoirs*, xvii). Whether his *Memoirs* and the two major autobiographical works before it are more honest than *The Autobiography of Alice B. Toklas* is a complex question.

An initial problem involves deciding exactly how to classify his three books. Except for the posthumously titled *Sherwood Anderson's Memoirs*, none of his autobiographical books carries Anderson's name in its title. *A Story Teller's Story* seems at first the most like a traditional autobiography, but its title indicates that Anderson thought of it as a story, both in the sense of being a narrative and in the childlike sense of story as a synonym for fib. Particularly for literary lives, the tendency to structure life itself as a narrative is strong. Although Benjamin Franklin is the most obvious example in this regard—referring to his life as a book, a first edition with errata rather than mistakes—all autobiographies, as Fleishman writes, "resemble lives not in the sense that they are a close representative of them but because they are stories of that which is itself a story. . . . Life—indeed, the idea of a life—is already structured as a narrative."[5]

That life is a story is obvious from the familiar question "What's your story?" that we recognize immediately as a request for a brief autobiography, not as a call for anecdotes. Although the word *story* also serves as a synonym for lie, especially for children, there seems to be a common understanding that stories partake of a truth-value different from that of other forms of communication. Among the most familiar kinds of stories are fishing stories, war stories, bragging stories, and tall tales—all designed to appeal by a deliberate, built-in stretching of the truth that would never be classified as lying because no deception is really intended. Variations on this strategy include the delineations made by such natural storytellers as Nate Shaw, the invented name used in Theodore Rosengarten's *All God's Dangers* for Ned Cross, a black sharecropper in Alabama whose ground rules included a distinction between "what was told for the truth and what was told to entertain."[6]

Clearly, Anderson meant his autobiographical writing to entertain, as evidenced by the double use of the word story in the title of his first autobiography. Speaking of an incident recounted in *A Story Teller's Story*, Anderson describes the autobiographical act as being capricious:

> I had decided to perform a certain act and at the same time began laughing at myself, not thinking I would be foolish enough to attempt it. One of these conflicts between myself, as I live in my fancy, and myself as I exist in fact, that have been going on in me since I was a child had now started. It is the sort of thing that makes autobiography, even of the half playful sort I am now attempting, so difficult to manage.[7]

Termed "false in its feeling, its thought, and its composition" by Irving Howe, *A Story Teller's Story* has attracted a bewildering variety of critical labels, most of which reflect critics' difficulty with its deceptions in form and content.[8] Anderson's first titles were *Straws* and *A Modernist Notebook*, the latter an indication of the work's organization into four books consisting of a series of sections labeled "Notes." Gertrude Stein called it "not a story of events but of existence."[9] Others have named it "fictional autobiography," "semi-autobiography," "impressionistic autobiography," "pseudo-autobiography," "spiritual autobiography," "parable," as well as "misnamed autobiography," "romance," "confession," and "essay collection."[10] The book has been compared to Adams's *The Education of Henry Adams*, Mark Twain's *Autobiography*, and Marcel Proust's *Remembrances of Things Past*.[11] Adding to the generic confusion, the Viking Compass edition of *A Story Teller's Story* subtitles it *Memoirs of Youth and Middle Age*.

The second of Sherwood Anderson's autobiographical works, *Tar: A Midwest Childhood*, published when the author was fifty, is written in the third person, but as in Conrad Aiken's *Ushant*, a key to the characters is easily established. The critical edition of *Tar* includes a table of the real Andersons and their counterparts in the fictional Moorehead family. Anderson uses the real names of his children for three of the Moorehead siblings, leaves some characters with their real names (such as Jim Moore, who also appears in *Memoirs*), and admits openly in the foreword that he has used a "writer's trick" by creating "a Tar Moorehead to stand for myself."[12] Anderson continues: "It was only after I had created Tar Moorehead . . . that I could sit down before my sheets and feel at ease. It was only then I faced myself, accepted myself. 'If you are a born liar . . . why not be what you are?' I said to myself, and having said it, I at once began writing with a new feeling of comfort" (*Tar*, 10). This second autobiographical work, which was initially written in the first person, received its own array of critical names. The author usually refers to *Tar* as his childhood book, a term that Richard Coe proposes in *When the Grass Was Taller* for a form he calls "an autonomous literary genre: the 'Autobiography of Childhood and Adolescence,' called *jugenderinnerungen* in German, *souvenirs d'enfance* in French."[13]

Tar's generic confusions are furthered by the inclusion in the critical edition of the book of the actual diaries, edited by William Sutton, of Anderson's parents and by the fact that chapter 12 is Anderson's famous short story "Death in the Woods," with the fictional name "Tar" substituting for the "I" who narrated the story when it was published separately.

The book that began as an account of Anderson's building of Ripshin, his handmade house in Virginia, and that was finally titled *Sherwood Anderson's Memoirs: A Critical Edition* was written intermittently in various forms, under several titles, from 1933 until his death in 1941. Parts of the final version were begun as short stories and portions of novels; other sections were published as essays, presented in public lectures, or cut from the manuscript and published in other volumes.

Sherwood Anderson's Memoirs was originally published in 1942 in a completely unreliable edition edited by his lifelong friend Paul Rosenfeld and Anderson's fourth wife, Eleanor Copenhaver Anderson. Working with multiple versions of handwritten pages, conflicting outlines, and more than three thousand manuscript pages, Rosenfeld, though well meaning, not only completely rearranged Anderson's material but also rewrote some of his sentences, taking portions from anywhere in the manuscript and combining them in any way he wished. Fortunately, Ray Lewis White's completely reedited version, published in 1969, restores as closely as possible the original material as Anderson wrote it. Though the book does include numerous sketches of the author's wide circle of friends—from his childhood in rural Ohio, through the Chicago Renaissance, to his acquaintances among American writers, including Faulkner, Hemingway, Wolfe, and Dreiser—*Sherwood Anderson's Memoirs* is not precisely a memoir because its primary focus remains on Anderson. Although Max Grossman referred to *Memoirs* as "a case book"[14] and Rex Burbank argued that "*Memoirs* should be read and judged as a work of fiction rather than a piece of personal history,"[15] Anderson seems to have thought of it as autobiography.

Anderson describes an early section as "a sort of carrying on of *A Story Teller's Story* into a later-day experience" (*Memoirs*, xvii). As early as 1936, he wrote to Maxwell Perkins, with whom he was negotiating about the memoirs, "I would ask you, there at Scribner's, not to reveal that it is so frankly autobiographical" (*Memoirs*, xvii). Two years before his death, Anderson wrote of his memoirs, "The idea is really . . . to do an autobiography in a new way, not in the life of the teller but in lives that touch his life" (*Memoirs*, xxiv). Although that plan might have been carried out if Anderson had lived to see the book into print, *Sherwood Anderson's Memoirs*, as it stands in the critical edition, is as much autobiography as it is anything else.

The variety of generic labels attached to *A Story Teller's Story*, *Tar*, and *Sherwood Anderson's Memoirs* becomes more than a mere problem in classification, if A. O. J. Cockshut's distinction between reading autobiography and memoir is valid. According to Cockshut, we either read autobiography as art, paying slight attention to interior false notes and citing external mistakes in footnotes, or we read as a historian would read a record, using all available sources for verification. "It would seem, on the whole," Cockshut concludes, "that autobiography lends itself naturally to the first kind of reading, and memoir to the second."[16] Because Anderson combines autobiography and memoir in each of his three major personal narratives, many incidents being repeated in all three in slightly different versions, and consistently thought of himself as a storyteller, I believe that his autobiographies must be read in both of the ways proposed by Cockshut, particularly because Anderson's truthfulness has often been questioned.

"Advertisements for Myself"

When I was young I could remember anything whether it happened or not.
—Mark Twain

One of the reasons Anderson's autobiographies added little to either his commercial or his literary fame is that early reviewers and critics, working without the current sophisticated autobiographical theories, relied too much on Anderson's prefatory comments about his being a liar and failed to see how much and what kind of truth he was after. Thomas Couser is partially correct when he remarks that any incident from an author's life can become autobiography or fiction and that the difference lies "in the signals the author sends about the nature of his narrative," but in some cases, such as Anderson's, the signals themselves are deliberately unreliable although not necessarily dishonest.[17] For instance, Anderson's subtitle to *A Story Teller's Story* shows that he thought of the book as the story of his "journey through his own imaginative world and through the world of facts." Throughout all of his autobiographies, he constantly relates his personal preference for the world of the fancy.

> To the imaginative man in the modern world something becomes, from the first, sharply defined. Life splits itself into two sections and, no matter how long one may live or where one may live, the two ends continue to dangle, fluttering about in the empty air. To which of the two lives, lived within the one body, are you to give yourself? . . . There is the life of fancy . . . or the world of facts. . . . In the world of fancy . . . no man is ugly. Man is only ugly in fact. Ah, there is the difficulty! [*Story*, 59–60]

The distinction that he is making here is not between truth and lie, or between fiction and nonfiction, but between separate spheres of reality. Fancy for Anderson suggests imaginative and compassionate understanding of the beauty within the most grotesque of human actions, whereas fact is inhabited by "the Puritan, the reformer who scolds at the Puritans, the dry intellectuals, all who desire to uplift" (*Story*, 59).

The connection between telling stories, writing autobiographies, and lying is more explicit in Anderson's foreword to *Tar*: "I have a confession to make. I am a story teller starting to tell a story and cannot be expected to tell the truth. Truth is impossible to me" (*Tar*, 5). In the foreword to *Memoirs*, he makes virtually the same point: "Facts elude me. I cannot remember dates. When I try to deal in facts at once I begin to lie. I can't help it" (*Memoirs*, 21). Anderson goes on in *Tar*'s foreword to warn his readers not to trust storytellers, including himself:

> The teller of tales, as you must all know, lives in a world of his own. He is one thing, as you see him walking in the street, going to church, into a friend's house, or into a restaurant, and quite another fellow when he sits down to write. While he is a writer nothing happens but that it is changed by his fancy and his fancy is always at work. Really, you should never trust such a man. Do

not put him on the witness stand during a trial for your life—or for money—and be very careful never to believe what he says under any circumstances. [*Tar*, 7]

Failing to heed this warning, some critics have insisted on taking what Anderson wrote in his autobiographies as literal truth and then judging these books unacceptable because he did what he said he would do—allow fancy to modulate fact. Many readers have dispensed with the Anderson autobiographies because they failed to realize that, as Thomas Cooley puts it, "often inconsistencies in the record are considered more revealing than consensus."[18] Some of Anderson's critics and readers have accepted only his claim that the storyteller is unreliable when writing, while failing to heed his plea never to believe the writer "under any circumstances." Because Anderson's personal narratives are prefaced with warnings about his lack of fidelity to fact, is it fair for generations of commentators to continue to say of him, as Clarence Gohdes did, "like all good yarn spinners, he was a princely liar"?[19]

Anderson's open admissions of prevarication raise a number of important questions: should we trust a professed liar's confession of lying? How much is he lying about the degree of his lies? What is his rhetorical strategy in confronting us with confessions of deception? Sissela Bok asks, "What is the use of prefacing a lie by consulting with those one plans to deceive? . . . It would certainly be self-defeating to preface any one lie by consultation with the dupe. But it is not at all self-defeating to discuss deceptive policies beforehand, nor to warn the deceived themselves."[20] This strategy allows Anderson to provide his readers with clear warnings of the rules of the game. Unfortunately, many readers have taken his warnings so literally that they often see lies where none were intended and where none are present.

Sherwood Anderson's cavalier way with facts, his predilection for story over history, his manipulation in print of people's characters, and his insistence that if some of the people who appear in his books did not actually say the words ascribed to them, then they should have—all of these combine to present a truer picture of Anderson than a straightforward, factual biography could. The picture is made truer when we consider that he was as unreliable with factual truth in his actual life. Stark Young, for example, tries to explain the particular amalgam of the confidence man and the naïf, the poseur and the innocent, that made up the actual man:

Sherwood Anderson was a combination, impossible to convey in words to anyone who never saw him, of the straightforward and contrived, of simple and disarming sincerity and elaborate, canny pose. As well as I knew him—and for a time in the early twenties, I saw him almost every day—I was never sure when he was leaving off one and passing into the other; I am not sure that he always knew himself just when he was posing. I am speaking of something inner, far within, not merely of telling the truth or not telling it.[21]

In 1927, Percy Boynton called Anderson "an ornate and disinterested liar," and later Maxwell Geismar described Anderson's autobiographical voice as "enigmatic, disturbing, [a] half-honest and half-exhibitionistic light which Anderson insists on turning upon himself . . . this foxy publicity man turned fumbling poet."[22]

The words "foxy publicity man" echo a phrase that Anderson repeatedly used in self-description: "In all my after years I shall have to struggle against a tendency toward slickness and plausibility in myself" (*Story*, 17–18). He later wrote, "I have always, from the beginning, been a rather foxy man, with a foxiness at times approaching slickness" (*Memoirs*, 12), explaining that this slickness often took the form, as his private secretary revealed, of "playing the innocent . . . [making himself] appear naive" (*Memoirs*, 14). Variations on the adjectives foxy, slick, and plausible appear constantly in Anderson's personal narratives, as well as in his letters, often as confessions of a tendency in himself that he abhorred and that was especially emblematic of the self who worked for nearly twenty years in advertising and publicity work for the world of business.

Although he often tells the truth about his public and autobiographical persona, Anderson writes so candidly that many critics refuse to take his words at face value. Often, he was naive. Often, he was unaware that he was simultaneously playing the roles of provincial determined to outwit the fakery of the carnival sideshow and smooth-talking barker trying to dupe the rubes. Anderson appears to have been in his life the person he comes across as in his autobiographies— a peculiar combination, on the one hand, of the literary bohemian wearing orange scarves for ties, electrifying the literati of Chicago and New York, and, on the other, the primitive storyteller, happiest as a townsman and editor of folksy Appalachian newspapers.

In his earliest autobiographical statement, a 1918 publicity essay for his first novel, *Windy McPherson's Son* (1916), Anderson writes, "To my amazement, I found that on paper I was entirely honest and

sincere—a really likeable, clear headed, decent fellow" (*Story*, 347). **47**
Both sincere and honest, and usually authentic, he is often unreliable,
and both his life story and his life's stories are filled with an array of *Sherwood*
misrepresentation, duplicity, and exaggeration. When he calls himself *Anderson*
honest and sincere, he does not mean accurate and literal. He wants
the figure called Sherwood Anderson in the autobiographical stories
to appear sincere about his dissembling. Lionel Trilling, in his *Sincerity and Authenticity*, describes this effect:

> Society requires of us that we present ourselves as being sincere,
> and the most efficacious way of satisfying this demand is to see to
> it that we really are sincere, that we really are what we want our
> community to know we are. In short, we play the role of being
> ourselves, we sincerely act the part of the sincere person, with the
> result that a judgement may be passed upon our sincerity that is
> not authentic.[23]

Generations of readers have judged Anderson insincere and dishonest because of the candor with which he reveals his distortions of
fact, thereby chiding him for the lies whose existence is only known
through his own admissions. They fail to see how open he is about
such subjects as androgyny, meanness, his relations with women, or
his devotion to the world of business before he became an artist.

Observations about Anderson's penchant for embroidering are present in countless personal reminiscences of those who knew him. Irving Howe notes that "from Anderson's autobiographical volumes
it's possible to extract almost everything but reliable information."[24]
Henry Miller says that Anderson made life more lifelike, a comment
that parallels Richard Thomas's observation about the well-known
photograph by Alfred Stieglitz that is reproduced on the cover of Viking Press's *The Portable Anderson*: "The photograph . . . does not in
fact show Anderson as he looked most of the time; it illustrates the
way reality, or the illusion of reality, can elicit a subjective response
from the viewer. . . . What Sherwood was after was 'a reality so subtle
. . . that it becomes more real than reality.'"[25]

Karl Anderson, Sherwood's older brother, tells the story of interrupting him to make a factual correction as Sherwood was telling a
family story. Irving, another brother, responded, "Let him alone,
Karl. . . . I'd like to hear him tell it again to see what it would be like
this time."[26] Like traditional storytellers of tall tales or folk stories,
Anderson never thought anyone would expect him to try to set down
the literal truth. Another traditional Ohio writer, folklorist Jack Matthews, has observed, "The art of the story teller is that of a socially

acceptable lie."[27] Because Anderson thought of himself as a storyteller, working in the guise of a story writer, he emphasized the dramatic, public performance of his work. For example, in a section of his *Notebook* entitled "Notes out of a Man's Life," Anderson wrote, "I am sort of a showman. If it were possible, I would like to be a quiet retiring gentleman, concealing everything from my fellows."[28] This declaration, like most of what he wrote or said, is both a straightforward statement and a complex subterfuge. Just as Gertrude Stein did in claiming that she was writing *The Autobiography of Alice B. Toklas* as simply as Defoe wrote *Robinson Crusoe*, Anderson in this passage is actually explaining his story-telling method on two levels. He was a showman, a vaudeville performer, who thought of storytelling as magicians think of their art. To Anderson, readers and family members who questioned the literal accuracy of his stories were like untutored yokels at a traveling magician's performance—always screaming that it was a trick, that no woman was actually sawed in half, all the while demanding to know how the trick was done.

Occasionally, Anderson's brothers object to the ways in which he portrayed family members, but unlike Mary McCarthy, who sometimes admits that her accounts of family life were less than exact and that her siblings were right, Anderson professes not to understand his brothers' objections. For example, he repeatedly presents his maternal grandmother as Italian. Although he genuinely may have thought she was Italian when he wrote *A Story Teller's Story*, he knew she was German by the time the other autobiographies were published. In regard to *A Story Teller's Story*, Anderson had written to Karl, "I didn't try to set down obvious facts, and tried to get the spirit of something."[29] Still Karl objected to the change in nationality:

> "But she was German," said Karl. . . . "And so she was maybe to you," [replied Anderson]. I am sure that . . . it was difficult for my brothers to understand my position. If I choose to have an Italian, rather than a German, grandmother, what is it to you? If you prefer that your own grandmother be an old German, all right. Shall a man who has spent all of his life creating people not have the privilege of creating his grandmother?[30]

Although the grandmother's nationality matters little except to the family, the distinction is crucial to the author. Anderson says that he made her Italian because he "fancied the notion of having" to add to his northern blood "some of the warm blood of the South."[31] This consistent misrepresentation of his grandmother's origins provides us with an accurate picture of what Sherwood Anderson was like and how he fit into his family.

In a letter to the *Encyclopedia of American Biography* in which he attempted to correct the misunderstanding, Karl Anderson eventually came to see that the fancy should take precedence over fact: "I think it is inadvisable to change her nationality to German. Sherwood called her that [Italian] so often. I think he got that from an obsession my sister, Stella, had as a young woman. Stella and I like my mother were of latin coloration. In a while she held tenaciously to the thought that we had Italian blood in us."[32] Feeling pressure from family members to be more accurate but still unable to submit totally, Sherwood wrote in 1938 to Mary Helen Dinsmoor, who was writing a thesis on his life as reflected in his works: "I tried to make a picture of my maternal grandmother in *A Story Teller's Story*. She was from Austria and had come to this country at an early age. I have the impression that she came from that part of Austria nearest Italy and was Italian."[33]

Anderson's grandmother's place of birth is beside the point; the fact that he had such a strong compulsion to move her birthplace—as Alice Toklas wanted to alter Gertrude Stein's—becomes in itself an important point. Another kind of truth is also behind Anderson's misrepresentation, for as Ben Hecht reports, "There is no Italian blood in Sherwood . . . but for years I have never seen a hurdy-gurdy man with a monkey or a village tonsorial expert that wasn't the spitting image of Sherwood."[34] Anderson's manipulation of his grandmother's origins, so typical of all of his distortions, presents finally an authentic version of a writer who is interested in appearing as a new type of American, as an adult who is never really curious about his ancestors and as a child who learned family stories from a father notorious for making them up.

Interestingly, when Anderson depicts his sister Stella in *Memoirs*, the autobiographical situation is reversed. Describing a preacher giving a eulogy for Stella, who had become intensely religious following "a visitation from Jesus" (He apparently came into her bed to comfort her), Anderson writes:

One by one the preacher began and told the story of our lives. . . . The story went on and on, we her brothers turning occasionally to stare at each other. . . . And so we buried my sister and I was curious. I went, after a time, to see the preacher. "Where did you get that story?" I asked and he said that he had got it from a pamphlet . . . printed and distributed by some tract society. It

Sherwood
Anderson

was called "The Story of a Christian Life." It was, he said, a pamphlet written by my sister herself. [*Memoirs*, 140]

Although many of Anderson's remembrances seem less like lies, more like stories, nevertheless, he was unreliable in incident after incident in terms of factual recall when these remembrances are considered in context. For example, James Feibleman, in "Memories of Sherwood Anderson," recounts a story that he heard the author tell about a trip to Rotterdam for a socialist convention. Anderson said that he sailed on the *Titanic* but missed the conference, when actually he had spoken, on the problems of the writer in America, to the World Congress against the War that was held in Amsterdam. Feibleman remarks that Anderson's claim to have sailed on the *Titanic* was illustrative of his natural way with stories: "It was the only name of an ocean liner that he knew which had some particular story attached to it. . . . The truth is that he was not trying to deceive either himself or me; his logic was not the logic of fact, it was the logic of symbolism."[35]

Perhaps the clearest example of Anderson's attitude toward the real and the imagined occurs in the following account, taken from his *Notebook*, that demonstrates how his imagination worked. After telling a tender story of himself and an unnamed woman meeting in a park, he comments on his autobiographical act: "Even now as I sit writing of the woman, my hand, that plays back and forth on the paper, shakes with the memory of her." He ends the story with these questions:

> What matters if my hands tremble and I have forgotten to eat? What matter if the woman in the park later got lost in the rush of Chicago? What matter if I never saw such a woman, if I merely walked alone in the windswept park? What matter if I never in all my life knew such a woman? Is my story for all these reasons the less true? Is the moment in which I looked down into the loveliness of a woman's eyes less a part of my life because it happened in fancy?[36]

The reader is left to decide whether the woman in the park was real or imagined or both. A strong undertone in the story suggests that Anderson is hiding something about the meeting by presenting the series of "what matter" questions at the end. However, the story still rings true, despite his attempts to undercut its veracity, and among its most powerful truths is Sherwood Anderson's belief in story.

Because Anderson was untrained academically, many readers have assumed that he was clumsy or unaware of his subtle conflation of fact

and fiction. His identification with small towns and his deceptively
simple style have deceived critics who accepted similar manipulations
from writers such as Henry James, in part because the more sophisticated James was thought capable of such subtlety. When, for example,
James was questioned about the accuracy of a letter from his brother
William—an actual letter that he had distorted in *Notes of a Son and
Brother* by omitting some things William had written—he replied that
although the letter was inaccurate such inaccuracy was justifiable because he wanted "to do his best" for William and because "I daresay
I did instinctively regard it at last as *my* truth, to do with what I
would."[37] James's misquotation of actual letters, even though they
occur in an autobiographical context, is not unlike Dreiser's inclusion
of both real and fictional letters from the historical victim to the fictional victim in *An American Tragedy* or Norman Mailer's use of actual letters in *An Executioner's Song*.

According to Adeline Tintner, Henry James's autobiography was
told by "a narrator who was unreliable in terms of textual accuracy but
totally reliable in terms of detecting the growth and education of his
own consciousness, totally responsible to his own truth."[38] Similarly,
Sherwood Anderson's version of his life lays claim, not to a factual
past, but to a usable personal past that suited a storyteller's present.

The Anderson Legend

The autobiographer, unless he feigns amnesia, is not simply his own biographer.
—Lynd Forguson

Nowhere is the tendency to misunderstand Anderson's responsibility
to his own truth as strong as in the critical response to the series of
events that have become known as the Anderson legend. Lionel Trilling, so clear about the complexities of sincerity and authenticity in his
book of that name, based part of his assessment of Anderson's writing
on the Anderson legend, which Trilling seems to have accepted literally: "At the age of forty-five, as everyone knows, he found himself the
manager of a small paint factory in Elyria, Ohio; one day, in the very
middle of a sentence he was dictating, he walked out of the factory and
gave himself to literature and truth."[39] For Trilling, the writer's escape from Elyria became an event above which Anderson could never
rise. Ben Hecht, admitting that he "believed almost nothing" of the
Anderson legend, nevertheless continued to embroider the story in

print: "He had wandered for several months through cornfields and prairies, a victim of amnesia. He had arrived on foot in Chicago wearing a shaggy beard and still uncertain of his identity, but nevertheless landed a job immediately as a copy writer."[40] Trilling's inflating of Anderson's actual age of thirty-six and Hecht's changing of four days into several months are typical of the exaggerations that have become attached to the legend over the years.

Although Anderson usually seems to have presented the legend as legend, its power as a myth of the American artist has been so strong that generations of readers, writers, and critics have continued to accept and to emphasize the most romantic aspects of the story. The major function of *A Story Teller's Story*, according to Ray Lewis White, was to add "authenticity to his 'legends'"—namely, "the impoverished childhood, the exotic father and the suffering mother, the absorption in business life and the romantic revolt against that life and the entrance of the 'untutored Midwestern story teller' into the avant-garde literary circles of Chicago" (*Story*, xi). White's use of the word *authentic* is particularly important, for the power of the authentic has replaced that of the factual as the major argument of theorists of autobiography. Roy Pascal stresses the autobiographer's need for his or her "own truth" over what might actually have happened; Philippe Lejeune excuses factual discrepancies by arguing that fidelity to the whole narrative as it is being written takes precedence over absolute literal re-creation of the past. Both views are well summarized by Shirley Neuman: "Whether we opt for truth to the inner self or for fidelity to the experience of the narrative as a whole, we are substituting the concept of authenticity for that of verifiable truth or even sincerity."[41]

Sherwood Anderson is not as interested in literalness about his life as he is in authenticity about its myths. Even though he was frequently misleading about the items on the legend list, Anderson was not lying because he made it clear from the outset that his truth is different from that of the biographer or the journalist; he was at work on authentication of legends rather than on the presentation of history. Horace Gregory asserts that the "'real Anderson' is seen more clearly in the legendary episodes of the autobiographies than when he employs too consciously the pronoun 'I.'"[42]

The degree of deception in each of the five separate components of the Anderson legend differs in proportion to the importance of each myth to the author. His impoverished childhood and his position as untutored American artist seem to be fairly accurate. The escape from

Elyria and rejection of the business world are somewhat less accurate,

and finally his portrait of his parents is even more fictional, though
still representative of the truth. A close look at each of the legends,
making distinctions between what Anderson actually wrote in his
autobiographies and how the legends were embellished by others, reveals that the author was far more truthful than generally supposed.

Gerald Marriner claims, in "Sherwood Anderson: The Myth of the
Artist," that Anderson is guilty of "distorting the facts of his life" and
of "outright deceit," but often Marriner's assumptions are themselves
distortions.[43] For example, Marriner argues that Anderson distorts
the poverty of his childhood: "While the family's economic position
was at times difficult, it seldom if ever reached the proportions which
Anderson portrayed. Rather, it seems that his boyhood recollections
were based on one particularly harsh winter during which the family
knew actual want."[44] Marriner's argument is too much a quibble over
exactly what constituted poverty to a midwestern boy in the last quarter of the nineteenth century. William Sutton, whose exhaustive research is the most extensive source of information on Anderson's life,
sums up the situation by saying: "The poverty of the Anderson family
was not abject. A woman who knew the family well has said that the
family was 'aristocratically poor'. . . . The soundest view . . . seems
to be that conditions, though at times difficult, were seldom if ever
desperate."[45]

Anderson's actual descriptions of childhood poverty are consonant
with Sutton's evaluation. *A Story Teller's Story* opens with these words:
"In all of the towns . . . of my own Mid-American boyhood there was
no such thing as poverty, as I myself saw it and knew it later in our
great American . . . cities. My own family was poor but of what did
our poverty consist?" (*Story*, 5). Later he adds, "If her husband, the
father of the boys, is a no-account and cannot bring money home—
the money that would feed and clothe her children in comfort—one
feels it does not matter too much" (*Story*, 12). The question, "Of what
did our poverty consist?," is never answered, and the statement, "It
does not matter too much," is played down. In these instances, he is
not exaggerating his childhood poverty, though elsewhere he details
economic conditions in terms that are less than neutral. Later in this
first autobiography, in reference to the "actual flesh and blood family"
that his father "has left behind in an Ohio village," Anderson writes,
"It is not suffering too much. One need not waste too much sympathy
on his family. Although he was never . . . 'a good provider' . . . I, at
least, would be loath to trade him for a more provident shrewd and

thoughtful father" (*Story*, 38). Often Anderson's statements about childhood poverty are designed to comment on his father's nature more than on the actual living conditions of the family.

In the second autobiography, *Tar*, Anderson represents the family poverty much as in the first. He describes a procession of houses into which the family constantly moved as an indication that they could not always pay their rent but adds, "to a mind like Tar's—the truth always washed by the colors being brushed on by his fancy—houses in which he lived as a child could not be definitely placed" (*Tar*, 30). Again, a deliberate underplaying of poverty occurs: "The Moore-heads were poor and were getting every year poorer but that Tar did not know" (*Tar*, 58–59).

The second element in the Anderson legend is the idea that the author was unschooled in literature and yet was able to write effort-lessly. Marriner suggests that Anderson overemphasizes his lack of formal education; in some cases, the opposite is true. Anderson's schooling included very sporadic attendance in elementary school (only three days his third year), a total of nine months in high school, followed by one business course at the Lewis Institute and a one-year high school equivalency course at Wittenberg Academy, a preparatory school for Wittenberg College.[46] In later years, Anderson sometimes gave the impression that he had attended Wittenberg College, a falsi-fication only slightly more justified when the college awarded him an honorary doctorate. In *Memoirs*, Anderson dissembles by saying, "I had managed to get in a winter at college. . . . It was . . . a small Lu-theran college. It was called Wittenberg" (*Memoirs*, 198). As further evidence of Anderson's untruthfulness about his natural literary gifts, Marriner remarks that "he pored over his manuscripts, revising and rewriting. 'Hands,' the story of which he said, 'No word of it ever changed,' was revised extensively."[47] Anderson does exaggerate about the composition of this story; however, he tells the essential truth. Compared to other, earlier writing efforts, the composition of "Hands" was different because, in Anderson's words, it was his first "authentic tale" (*Memoirs*, 237).

William L. Phillips's meticulous analysis of the *Winesburg, Ohio* manuscript, which is in the Newberry Library's Sherwood Anderson Collection, resulted in this comment about "Hands": "It is likely that the story was written in one frenzied rush of the pencil. . . . and in this respect Anderson's comment that 'no word of it ever changed' is cor-rect; the story was 'grasped whole.' "[48] Anderson did make a number of changes in the manuscript—some words were crossed out as he wrote, some were inserted later—but he was not trying to mislead in

his remarks about the story's composition. "Hands" was always his
example of his first "authentic" story, by which he meant that it was
written all at one time with its few changes inserted later.

The escape from Elyria is the most well known aspect of the Anderson legend. His feelings of being unclean because of using words to advertise commercial products led Anderson to his decision to quit the business world and to disassociate himself from "the corrupt unspeakable thing that had happened to tale telling in America. . . . This matter of buying and selling" (*Story*, 223). Numerous expressions of distaste for the world of advertising, which he called prostitution, led up to Anderson's explanation of the moment of escape from Elyria. Although critics often focus on just the moment itself, Anderson emphasizes "the history of the moment," prefacing his explanation of the escape with these words: "The whole struggle I am trying to describe, and that I am confident will be closer to the understanding of most Americans than anything else I have ever written, was accompanied by a kind of mocking laughter at myself and my own seriousness of it all" (*Story*, 224). Anderson repeatedly represents himself as a liar in his advertising period: "I don't mean to say that my ideas were clean. I kept thinking up little schemes and putting them into operation at the same time I was preaching to myself and others against such schemes."[49]

Against the background of physical revulsion and shame over lies devised as an advertiser, Anderson begins the story of his break from Elyria, describing himself interrupting dictation to his secretary and walking out the door after having said these words: "My feet are cold wet and heavy from long wading in a river. Now I shall go walk on dry land" (*Story*, 226). To this point, his escape is accurately reported. William Sutton notes that Anderson's secretary remembers words such as those quoted above, and Anderson's letters of the period contain similar references to rivers and a search for dry land. A note to his first wife, Cornelia Anderson, which apparently was sent while he was aimlessly wandering the countryside, contains a similar image. "Cornelia: There is a bridge over a river with cross-ties before it. When I come to that I'll be all right. I'll write all day in the sun and the wind will blow through my hair."[50]

Anderson's less-than-exact remarks about his walkout take the form of half claiming that his escape was a deliberate fabrication on his part, that he only pretended to be slightly insane to justify his action. Sutton's documentation, which includes a letter Anderson wrote during the lost four days before he was discovered in Cleveland, indicates that Anderson was severely disoriented. The proper psychological definition of his breakdown is still conjecture. Sutton terms it as "probably easiest to designate as amnesia"; a business associate referred to it as "a case of lost identity."[51] According to Kim Townsend, Anderson's most recent biographer, "The term that comes closest to describing Anderson's condition is 'fugue state,' a state of flight, something like those Anderson had experienced as a youth when parts of his body, or the landscape, or his very life, seemed to float away."[52]

Irving Howe calls Anderson's claim that the break from business was "partly genuine and partly feigned" untrue, adding that Karl Anderson had reported that "there was nothing deliberate about the breakdown" and that Sherwood later told Margaret Anderson, editor of the *Little Review*, that his break with reality was "conscious aphasia."[53] In a letter to Marietta Finley, Anderson describes the whole episode as "an experience that ended in a convulsion that touched the edge of insanity."[54] Whatever happened exactly, to accuse the autobiographer of duplicity for failing to remember the exact events of a mental breakdown, for forgetting an episode of amnesia, hardly seems fair. Precisely how much of the breakdown was preplanned, how much accidental, is impossible for anyone, then or now, to determine. That an actual nervous breakdown might have occurred does not preclude Anderson's pretending to be slightly insane before he lost his sense of self.

The accuracy of this bizarre episode must be read in the context in which it was written. Anderson's version of his departure from the Anderson Manufacturing Company, of which he was president, occurs in a section of *A Story Teller's Story* that focuses on his anonymous return to Elyria two years after the actual moment of escape. Considering the break a supreme moment in his life, representative of the revolt from the world of business by all American artists, he also refers to the episode as "melodramatic and even silly enough" (*Story*, 218). A contemporary newspaper account in the *Elyria Evening Telegram* reports that "Anderson was surprised to awaken and find himself in a hospital and was inclined to consider his four days wandering a joke," thus giving credence to the idea that the author took his escape less than seriously at the time.[55] Referring to his return to Elyria—his "autobiography revisited"—as an attempt "to confront myself with myself" (*Story*, 218), Anderson casts his account into the form of a memory once removed.

"The myth which pictures Sherwood Anderson walking out of his office in the midst of dictating a letter is historically false but symbolically true," writes Howard Mumford Jones.[56] David D. Anderson expresses a similar view: "His accounts of his departure from his business career are pure fiction, accounts that are at once rational and

mystic, contrived and intuitive."[57] But "pure fiction" is as hard to
achieve as "pure autobiography," and Anderson's escape story is not
historically literal. Instead, it is a half-ironic account of an ambiguous
event that, only years later, came to symbolize for Sherwood Anderson the exact moment when he realized that he would transfer his
predilection for lying from the world of advertisements, where his
false words struck him as unhealthy, to the world of storytelling,
where deliberate elaborations and loose factual interpretation are inherent to the genre. As John Steinbeck observes through a fictional
character in *East of Eden*: "The difference between a lie and a story is
that a story utilizes the trappings and appearance of truth for the listener as well as the teller. A story has in it neither gain nor loss. But a
lie is a device for profit and escape."[58] Anderson writes that the idea
came to him to pretend to be deranged, but his actual words about the
escape hardly seem designed for gain: "Whether at the moment I
merely became shrewd and crafty or whether I really became tempo-
rarily insane I shall never quite know" (*Story*, 226).

The final component of the Anderson legend consists of his parental portraits. For Irving Howe, "the legend was not far from the actuality" when Anderson dealt with his adult life, when memories could
be made congruent with "the conception he had created of himself."
But in writing about his boyhood, particularly about his parents, "he
fell not merely into contradiction to fact but also into gaping inconsistencies within the legend itself."[59] Anderson's portraits of his mother
and father are sometimes romanticized, sometimes inaccurate, but
these distortions, which are both less frequent and less serious than
generally thought, are not only understandable but in many cases justified by his frequent warnings that he is not striving for literal accuracy. In the foreword to *Tar*, for instance, he notes,

> Like everyone else in the world I had so thoroughly recreated my
> childhood, in my own fancy, that Truth was utterly lost. And now
> for a confession. I have a love of confessions. I do not remember
> the face of my own mother, of my own father. My wife is in the
> next room as I sit writing, but I do not remember what she looks
> like. My wife is to me an idea, my mother, my sons, my friends
> are ideas. My fancy is a wall between myself and Truth. [*Tar*, 9]

His usual slickness at work again, Anderson only confesses that he
likes to confess and that he cannot help using his parents and friends,
in autobiography and in life, as ideas. Anderson is being less than
literal here; his mother's face was constantly before him as he wrote,

her framed picture on his desk or visible on the wall above his head in the photograph titled "The Memoirist," which is published in *Memoirs*.

Although usually crediting his father, Irwin Anderson, as the father of his own story-telling tendencies, Sherwood Anderson often depicts the creative act in motherly terms. His words demonstrate the profound influence of his mother on his creativity. He often refers to his tales as though they were his children in need of the clothing that his real father was at times unable to provide. "The tales that continually came to me . . . could, of course, not become tales until I had clothed them. Having . . . got the tone of a tale, I was like a woman who has just become impregnated. Something was growing inside me. Later, at night, when I lay in my bed, I could feel the heels of my tale kicking against the walls of my body" (*Story*, 260). Symbolically impregnated by his father's imagination, Anderson delivers stories that have a clear patrimony, a well-nourished form, and a genetic tendency toward lying. *Winesburg, Ohio* is dedicated to his mother, "whose keen observations of the life about her first awoke" in Anderson "the hunger to see beneath the surface of lives"; his autobiographies are dedicated on every page to his father, who was, "in some inscrutable way, appointed to be the bearer of lovely things to obscure people" (*Story*, 28). Together, these phrases describe Sherwood Anderson's characteristic tone and subject, revealing that his decision or compulsion to become a writer came from both parents. From this dual heritage, the storyteller distances himself: "To the tale teller, you must understand, the telling of the tale is the cutting of the natal cord" (*Story*, 93).

Anderson portrays his mother as a long-suffering woman whose silences were an indication of deep thought and whose early death was the result of a hard childhood as a bound girl coupled with the task of washing clothes in cold weather to make money because of her improvident husband. Anderson hints, in *A Story Teller's Story*, that his mother died at the age of thirty by saying, "A family of five boys and two girls—a mother who is to die, outworn and done for at thirty" (*Story*, 21). His words, however, are carefully chosen so that he can equivocate about her age at the moment of death. Emma Smith Anderson died on 10 May 1895 at the age of forty-three. With his self-claimed foxiness with words, Anderson has used the advertiser's trick of implying one thing while saying another: his mother was worn out at thirty, though she died thirteen years later. In *Tar*, his mother's life and death are similarly presented, but there he includes as his mother's confidant the figure of Doctor Reefy, a fictional character from *Winesburg, Ohio*. Rather than exaggerating her death, he writes in *Tar*, "The coming of death to Tar Moorehead's mother was without special dramatic intensity. She died in the night and only Doctor Reefy was with her. There was no death-bed scene" (*Tar*, 204).

Although no deathbed scene occurs in his first two autobiographies, Anderson invents one for *Memoirs*. He writes that his mother, who he now claims died at thirty-five, told her children on her deathbed, "'I do not fear to leave you. You are of the stuff of which kings are made'" (*Memoirs*, 242). With the next sentence, however, he confesses that he has just made up his mother's words. "What nonsense! The poor woman couldn't have said that but she did say something that fixed a certain impression in our minds, of that I am quite sure" (*Memoirs*, 242). A few paragraphs later, Anderson ironically congratulates himself for having revealed his earlier duplicity, though he still wants to cling to the possibility that he was not lying in the first place. "If my mother on her death bed had not got that off about kings (and I have the grace to doubt it, the imagination is a tricky thing) but if she had surely I was on the way to being at least one of the smaller American kings. I was in house paint. Why not the American house paint king?" (*Memoirs*, 244).

The following description of Emma Smith Anderson from *A Story Teller's Story* is reflective of both the author's and the son's psychological and artistic needs:

> Mother was tall and slender and had once been beautiful. She had been a bound girl in a farmer's family when she married father, the improvident young dandy. There was Italian blood in her veins and her origin was something of a mystery. Perhaps we never cared to solve it—wanted it to remain a mystery. It is so wonderfully comforting to think of one's mother as a dark beautiful and somewhat mysterious woman. [*Story*, 8]

This miniature biography is a classic example of Anderson's substitution of his truth for factual truth. In a strict accounting, this statement contains at least four misrepresentations—that his mother was beautiful, a bound girl, Italian, and of mysterious origin. A closer examination reveals that all four are true in psychological and narrative senses, although ambiguous at best when taken in the world of fact. Taken in their context, these are memories of an adult, whose mother died when he was eighteen, trying to imagine how he felt about her as a child.

Whether Emma Smith Anderson was beautiful is a matter of taste, as virtually all mothers are beautiful to their children; however, she does not seem to be especially beautiful by conventional standards, judging by available photographs. Whether she was a bound girl depends on what that term signifies. Although Ray Lewis White argues that "there is no evidence that Emma was ever a 'bound girl'" (*Tar*, 130), White's placing of quotation marks around the term suggests his uneasiness with exact definition. According to William Sutton, Anderson's mother "went into the Faris house at the age of nine . . . and stayed there continuously until her marriage."[60] Because the relationship between Emma and the Faris family was pleasant, according to all accounts, including Emma's diary, critics have consistently claimed that Anderson invented the idea that his mother was bound out. But the fact remains that Emma's own mother, who worked in another farm house for little more than room and board, could not support her children who consequently were forced to work for other families most of their lives in a contract for survival as binding as a written bond. As Townsend notes: "To him she was a 'bound girl.' She was oppressed, stifled, long-suffering. She was kept, kept from living life fully by the burden of her many children."[61] Emma Smith was not Italian, but her mother's German heritage seemed ambiguously "foreign" to the young Anderson, who admits that he liked to perpetuate the mystery of his mother's origin.

Although Anderson's feelings about his mother are valuable, his relationship with his father emerges as the most important theme in all three of his autobiographies, for it links the author's lying, his specific occupational choice of storyteller over writer as a means of self-identification, and even his escape from Elyria. Throughout the autobiographies, Anderson elaborates on his father's portrait, consistently drawing the same profile; Irwin McLain Anderson is a "ruined dandy from the South" (*Story*, 5), "a lovable improvident fellow" (*Tar*, 106), disliked by his son, the young boy, for failing to support the family but loved by Anderson, the man, for Irwin's legacy as a teller of tales. The overall picture mellows as the author matures, but everywhere the son suggests that his mother's death was partially brought about by his father's drinking, lack of a steady job, and cavalier attitude toward family responsibility. Much of the legend of Anderson's hatred for his father is based, not on the autobiographies, but on the first novel *Windy McPherson's Son*, in which the father's worst characteristics are exaggerated. "The realization of the fact that his father was a confirmed liar and braggart had for years cast a shadow over his days," says Sam McPherson, the Sherwood Anderson figure in the novel.[62]

By the time Anderson tells his father's story autobiographically, these views have softened considerably. Like Geoffrey Wolff, whose duplicitous father is the subject of Geoffrey's biography *The Duke of*

Deception, Anderson comes to admit that his father's improvident behavior, unreliability, and family falsehoods were not only good material for life stories but also an important ingredient in his own character. Anderson is never quite as detached about his father's lies as is Wolff, who writes:

> But there is a kind of truth that should be within reach of a participant in the events of his narrative, however difficult that truth may be to grasp. It is the kind of truth that can be won by a willingness to distinguish between what a writer feels he should have felt at a particular moment, and what he really felt. As I learned to make that distinction, uneasily, I learned again what I had forgotten, that I had in many ways a happy childhood, that it had been fun to be my father's son.[63]

Rather than distinguishing between what he felt and what he should have felt, Anderson presents both, often contemporaneously with what he is feeling as he writes. A characteristic Anderson strategy is to present an impression that is immediately questioned but left intact: "However, I again find myself plunging forward into a more advanced and sophisticated point of view than could have been held by the boy, beginning to remake his own life more to his own liking by plunging into a fanciful life. I shall be blamed" (*Story*, 94). Here the author reveals that his lifelong tendency to embroider and to invent a self was characteristic at an early age and, therefore, not as blameworthy as he thought because this tendency presents a true picture of his inner self. He later notes, "As I now sit writing, I am most doubtful of all of the veracity of this impression I am trying to give of myself as a boy" (*Story*, 98), illustrating Roy Pascal's classic definition of an autobiographer as a person "wrestling with the truth."[64]

Joan Henley writes of Anderson, "The autobiographical persona has worked out a way of asserting, and, at the same time, qualifying, his significance. This position is also reflected in the prominence of questions, as opposed to statements, in the narrative."[65] In addition to questions, Anderson frequently qualifies his statements; on nearly every page appear such disclaimers as "it could be that," "perhaps," "I think," "I wonder if I am now romanticizing," "it is hard to get a clear sequence of events in such a history as this I am trying to write," and "now it seems to me." Sometimes Anderson even presents disclaimers before, rather than after, a narrative. "Could I then have had all the thoughts I am about to attribute to myself? Probably not. But these notes make no pretense of being a record of fact. That isn't their object" (*Story*, 76).

The bitterest depiction of Anderson's father occurs when his son is young. The following passage, representative of many, attempts to explain why the son was so disappointed in his father: "A boy wants something very special from his father. You are always hearing it said that fathers want their sons to be what they feel they cannot themselves be but I tell you it also works the other way. I know that, as a small boy, I wanted my father to be a certain thing he was not, could not be. I wanted him to be a proud silent dignified one" (*Memoirs*, 78).

The scenes in which the son chafes at his father's undignified bearing are mostly those where the father is telling stories, and telling them badly. For the storyteller, the father's stories are embarrassing because "the tales he told would never hold water" (*Tar*, 36). "For him there was no such thing as a fact" (*Story*, 6), notes the son, adding that "most of the stories he told were lies" (*Memoirs*, 79). The son's objection to his father's lying is at the heart of this father-son relationship.

When Sherwood Anderson says that his father's stories "would never hold water," he means two things. The first is that his father's lies made the man look foolish because of easily detectable factual errors. Of those who heard the stories, Anderson writes, "I think now they all knew he was lying but they seemed to like him just the same. As a boy that was what I couldn't understand" (*Memoirs*, 80). But there is a deeper significance as well. As a professional storyteller-to-be, the young Anderson disliked the lack of craft in his father's stories—they would not hold water because they were not well made, because, to use one of the author's favorite words, they were not plausible. Not that his father lied, but that he did not lie well enough bothered the son. His father was only a tale teller who could never achieve the status of storyteller, nor ultimately become a story writer.

Anderson's first writing grew directly out of his disappointment with his father's story-telling ability. Of his own fledgling attempts, he says, "That first tale of mine . . . grew out of dissatisfaction with my father and a desire to invent another to take his place. And professional jealousy may have had something to do with it. He had been strutting about long enough" (*Story*, 72). Later in the retelling of one of his father's favorite stories, Anderson says, "I am too good a son to my father to leave such a tale hanging forever, thus, in the air" (*Story*, 45). Much of his ameliorating attitude toward his father came from the realization that his father was unaware of the possibility of being a storyteller by profession rather than by avocation. "I am the tale teller," says Anderson; "I am the one destined to follow the little

crooked words of men's search through the uncharted paths of the
forest of fancy. What my father should have been I am to become"
(*Story*, 18). The idea that his father's worst tendencies were the direct
result of not knowing that he himself was a tale teller underlies Anderson's personal narratives: "I was in my whole nature a tale teller. My
father had been one and his not knowing had destroyed him" (*Story*,
223).

The transformation of an inept tale-telling father into a story-telling son is the essential theme of *A Story Teller's Story*. As Henley
points out, this theme is directly tied to the father-son conflict:

> By characterizing himself as a "story teller" rather than a writer,
> Anderson links "all such fellows as father and myself" and signals
> the special significance of a motif that runs through the auto-
> biographies: "You grow more like your dad everyday." If the reli-
> gious accounts of vocation invoke a surrendering of the will to
> the Heavenly Father, Anderson's secular account involves an ac-
> ceptance of identity with his flesh-and-blood father.[66]

"I have perhaps lied now and then regarding the facts of his life,"
notes Sherwood Anderson of his father, "but have not lied about the
essence of it" (*Story*, 286). Although he remarks that "surely there was
something magnificent in my father's utter disregard for the facts of
life" (*Story*, 26), the inability to use facts in a more plausible way is his
chief complaint about his father. Anderson notes in the following unpublished passage labeled "from 'I Build My House' folder" in the
Newberry Library's Sherwood Anderson Collection, a passage that
apparently was once a part of the manuscript that grew into *Memoirs*:
"I think I had a great deal of contempt for my father and that it was
based primarily upon my contempt for him as a storyteller . . . his
natural talent always being corrupted by this everlasting laying it on
too thick."[67]

"Laying it on too thick" is a significant metaphor for a father whose
alternate trade was house painting, especially when used by a son who
was for a time president of a company distributing house paint. Sherwood Anderson often talks about his own particular writing ability in
painterly metaphors. For his father, who specialized in "graining"—
"The trick was to make pine look like oak, oak like cherry, cherry like
walnut" (*Memoirs*, 43)—painting was another form of lying. But the
father's brand of deception is particularly loathsome to the son:

> The boy who lives in the world of fact is to help his father put a
> priming coat on a new house. . . . In my day we used a dirty

yellow ochre for the purpose. The color satisfied no sensual part of myself. . . . It was used because it was cheap and later was to be covered up. . . . Ugly colors, buried away out of sight, have a way of remaining always in sight in the consciousness of the painter who has spread them. [*Story*, 94–95]

Anderson, who for a time was an amateur painter, was always attracted to the painter who worked from fancy. Like Lillian Hellman's pentimento metaphor, which will be significant in chapter 6, Anderson's figurative use of painting reflects his abiding interest in "the buried life," that essential strangeness hidden beneath the surface of human personality. In *A Story Teller's Story*, he records his delight when his brother Karl, who was a professional painter, brought him Gertrude Stein's *Tender Buttons*: "Here were words laid before me as if the painter had laid the color pans on the table in my presence. . . . Perhaps it was then I really fell in love with words. . . . The true painter revealed all of himself in every stroke of his brush (*Story*, 261–63).

Because his father was not a good storyteller and never realized that storytelling was his real calling, his father was unable to provide for his family or to discover ways to use his natural inclination to lie. Instead, Irwin Anderson became just a liar, when his real ability was as a storyteller, which would have been natural had he lived in an artistic world where lying and embroidering stories are hard to separate. Sherwood Anderson was almost caught in the same situation; however, he was able to escape from the house-painting business, a move he describes as "leaving my poor little factory, like an illegitimate child" (*Story*, 216). Maxwell Geismar, in pointing out many parallels between father and son, is inaccurate when he asks concerning Anderson, "Disavowing truth along with respectability . . . had he now not only taken over but out-done the parental image of an irresponsible story teller?"[68] Sherwood Anderson has outdone his father, but the son is far from irresponsible as a storyteller, though he uses his father's fondness for exaggerated stories as his own literary device.

Explanations can be given for some of Anderson's autobiographical irresponsibilities toward his father, such as his repeated habit of claiming that his father was from the South, usually from North Carolina (hence the name Tar from Tar Heel), even though he knew, as he notes in *Memoirs*, that Irwin Anderson was born "in a country town in Southern Ohio" (*Memoirs*, 79). His father's lifelong habit of claiming, Zelig-like, that he was born wherever his listener was is partially the reason why the son so often changed his father's birthplace. But

Karl Anderson remarks that his brother probably did not know where
their father was born, particularly while he was writing his first two
autobiographies, and that "these things were unimportant in Sherwood's mind."[69]

The most dramatic episode concerning his father occurs in the section of *Memoirs* called "Unforgotten" in which the father is shown in a
totally uncharacteristic, subdued way, silently bidding his son to swim
naked with him at night in a deserted pond on the edge of town:

> We had come in silence. . . . We were on a grassy bank at the
> pond's edge, when my father spoke, and in the darkness and rain
> his voice sounded strange. It was the only time during the eve-
> ning that he did speak to me. "Take off your clothes," he said and,
> still filled with wonder, I began to undress. There was a flash of
> lightning and I saw that he was already naked. [*Memoirs*, 83]

Images of nakedness recur throughout the autobiographies, as well as
the fiction, and usually signify an attempt at communication or self-
understanding rather than any overt sexual connotation. Led by his
father into the water, Anderson describes their semimystical experience, using water images reminiscent of those he spoke to his secretary just before his escape from Elyria:

> It was a large pond and I did not swim very well but he had put
> my hand on his shoulder. Still he did not speak but struck out at
> once into the darkness. . . . We swam thus in the darkness to the
> far edge of the pond. . . . He had become blood of my blood. I
> think I felt it. He the stronger swimmer and I the boy clinging to
> him in the darkness. [*Memoirs*, 84]

In this experience, which Anderson published separately as "Discovery of a Father" in the *Reader's Digest* "Most Unforgettable Char-
acter" format, he presents himself as a weak swimmer, learning from
his father how to move through the current with powerful strokes.[70]
Swimming has for Anderson a more figurative than literal meaning.
In *A Story Teller's Story*, he asks, "You must see that I am a swimmer
and have stripped myself of the clothes which are my ordinary life. . . .
I am a swimmer and am about to leap off into the sea of lives. . . . Will
I be able to swim there? Will I be able to keep my head above water?"
(*Story*, 230).

The lyrical swimming scene with his father more than atones for
the bitter attitude sometimes present in other descriptions of his father. "One of the strangest relationships in the world," he comments,
"is that between father and son. I know it now from having sons of my

own. I am hoping they do not turn out to be writers" (*Memoirs*, 76). Anderson ends the story of his father and the pond with this statement: "For the first time I had come to know that I was the son of my father. He was a story teller as I was to be. It may be that . . . I even laughed knowing that, no matter how much as a story teller I might be using him, I would never again be wanting another father" (*Memoirs*, 85).

Conclusion

I think each of us knows his own mystery with a knowing that precedes the origins of all knowledge. None of us ever gives it away. No one can. We envelope it with talk and hide it with deeds. Yet we always hope that somehow the others will know it is there, that a mystery in the other we cannot know will respond to a mystery in the self we cannot understand.—Kenneth Rexroth, *An Autobiographical Novel*

"It is really beside the point that Anderson's mother actually died on a Spring afternoon at the age of forty-two," writes Walter Rideout, "or that, as William Sutton has shown, Anderson's legendary walk-out from his paint 'factory' actually resulted from temporary mental breakdown more than from deliberate decision."[71] Although the actual season of death or the precise percentage of deliberation involved before his breakdown may be in themselves beside the point, the fact that these are the kinds of incidents responsible for perpetuating the idea of Anderson as untrustworthy makes them important to consider in detail. These and other incidents, often taken as evidence of the author's unreliability, are still not completely resolved, despite extensive detective work, principally by William Sutton, but also by such scholars as Ray Lewis White, David D. Anderson, Walter Rideout, and Kim Townsend.

Much of the caviling about the unreliability of the Anderson autobiographies stems from a lack of understanding of his techniques, a failure to believe his warnings, and a tendency, ironically enough, to believe his repeated claims that he was a liar. In actuality, Sherwood Anderson is ultimately fairly trustworthy; his autobiographies, especially self-revelatory. As Irving Howe perceptively notes:

Anderson was not, in any usual sense of the word, a liar. He was under no obligation to make life easy for future biographers, and he had, as he claimed for himself, the right to "arrange" his own past quite as he arranged the past of one of his fictional characters. But if his autobiographies cannot be read as records they can be taken as evidence, and if they often deviate from factual accuracy they as often penetrate to psychological truth.[72]

I agree with much of Howe's statement, though for me no autobiography should be "read as a record." But Howe is not as perceptive when he stresses factual errors and states that "*A Story Teller's Story* contains untruths which cannot be excused merely by saying that Anderson was uninterested in facts."[73] Despite the falsehoods, however, Anderson was fairly accurate, not just to psychological truth, but also to historicity. Given the vast number of episodes in the more than a thousand pages of his published autobiographical writings, the unreliability of the initial texts, the fact that the author usually worked only from memory (over a long period of time, and generally years after the events of which he wrote occurred), and coupled with his repeated warnings that he is above all a storyteller, Anderson's reputation as a liar is undeserved.

Most of the revisionist history done by those desiring to correct the untruths in Anderson's writing contains its own factual errors. Ray Lewis White, for example, working with all of the resources of the Newberry Library's Sherwood Anderson Collection, plus thousands of pages of manuscript, has still been charged with the same accusation so often made of Anderson—White's text is "faulty" and "the biographical footnotes contain a number of factual errors."[74] Many of William Sutton's factual corrections stem from such sources as interviews with residents of Clyde and Elyria, Ohio, talks and correspondence with Anderson's family members and acquaintances, the recently discovered diaries of his parents, newspaper stories, and historical documents such as county records—almost none of which Anderson had access to as he wrote.

Although Sutton's devotion of virtually his entire academic life to clarifying Anderson's story is invaluable, he has not judged his own sources with the same rigor that he applies to Anderson's autobiographical writing. Emma Smith Anderson's diary shows her to be, in Sutton's words, "just what her psychologically maimed fiction-writer son could least have afforded her to be: a healthy, rather immature older girl who was busily engaged in enjoying the surface realities of a rather routine country life" (*Tar*, 221). This depiction, however, is hardly justification for calling inaccurate her nonfiction-writing son's portraits of the woman she became. Because Irwin Anderson's diary suggests "a hard pious business man" is hardly sufficient reason to label Sherwood's portrait of him a "deviation from . . . reality" (*Tar*, 222). Sutton's reasoning, which is similar to numerous other critics', is misleading, and his amateur psychologizing is naive. The parents of the diaries were unmarried, with Emma still a teenager, Irwin in his midtwenties. The diaries themselves contain factual errors; for example, Emma Smith consistently calls her future husband "Irving" instead of "Irwin." Diary writing, as H. Porter Abbott has indicated, is sometimes as unreliable as any other form of autobiography, subject to the usual tension between design and truth.[75] Finally, all sources are narratives, with the same potential for fabrication as anything that Anderson ever wrote. As Robert Scholes, Carl H. Klaus, Michael Silverman, and Robert Kellogg have argued, "all knowing and all telling are subject to the conventions of art."[76]

Countless critical assessments of Sherwood Anderson's autobiographies have concluded that the factual errors in his writings have rendered them totally unreliable. However, Anderson's own critical evaluation is perhaps the most accurate. Speaking of his first autobiography within his last, he writes that *A Story Teller's Story* is "a book more or less, if not entirely, authentic. It has I think the true authenticity of a thing felt" (*Memoirs*, 238). With these words, Anderson foreshadows Alfred Kazin's comment that "the 'creative' stamp, the distinguishing imaginative organization of experience, is in autobiography supplied not by intention, but by the felt relation to the life data themselves."[77]

Sherwood Anderson meant for his life, particularly the parts that have become the Anderson legend, to stand as a mythic expression of the true artist in America. He repeatedly identified himself as a sort of modern Whitman:

> I am the American man. I think there is no doubt of it. I am just the mixture. . . . Behold in me the American man striving to become an artist, to become conscious of himself . . . and others, trying to have a good time and not fake a good time. . . . I am tremendously serious about it all, but at the same time I laugh constantly at myself for my own seriousness. . . . If you say the American man is not yet born, you lie. I am the type of the fellow. [*Story*, 222]

Like Richard Wright, whose *Black Boy* was meant—as I will show in the next chapter—to be the autobiography of a whole category of Americans, Sherwood Anderson thought of his life story as the tale of a type and never expected that his autobiographical writing would be examined minutely for factual errors. Instead, Anderson, who was above all else a storyteller, wanted to make the fullest use of the story of his life, rather than the life itself, to explain himself.

RICHARD WRIGHT 4
"Wearing the Mask"

An autobiography is the truest of all books; for while it inevitably consists mainly of extinctions of the truth, shirkings of the truth, partial revelations of the truth, with hardly an instance of plain straight truth, the remorseless truth is there, between the lines.—Mark Twain

Like the autobiographies of Gertrude Stein and Sherwood Anderson, Richard Wright's *Black Boy*, published in 1945, has confused readers because of its generic ambiguity. For many readers, the book is particularly honest, sincere, open, convincing, and accurate. But for others, *Black Boy* leaves a feeling of inauthenticity, a sense that the story or its author is not to be trusted. These conflicting reactions are best illustrated by the following representative observations by Ralph K. White and W. E. B. Du Bois. White, a psychologist, has identified "ruthless honesty" as "the outstanding quality which made the book not only moving but also intellectually satisfying."[1] But Du Bois notes that although "nothing that Richard Wright says is in itself unbelievable or impossible; it is the total picture that is not convincing."[2] Attempting to reconcile these opposing views, I wish to argue that both sides are correct; that the book is an especially truthful account of the black experience in America, even though the protagonist's story often does not ring true; and that this inability to tell the truth is Wright's major metaphor of self. A repeated pattern of misrepresentation becomes the author's way of making us believe that his personality, his family, his race—his whole childhood and youth— conspired to prevent him from hearing the truth, speaking the truth, or even being believed unless he lied.

For most readers, worries about *Black Boy*'s trustworthiness stem from questions of genre. Although the book was clearly not called "The Autobiography of Richard Wright," its subtitle—"A Record of Childhood and Youth"—does suggest autobiography with some claim to documentary accuracy. The following descriptions of *Black Boy* reflect the confusion of readers: biography, autobiographical story, fictionalized biography, masterpiece of romanced facts, sort of autobiography, pseudoautobiography, part-fiction/part-truth autobiography, autobiography with the quality of fiction, and case history.[3]

Some of these generic confusions were generated by Wright's statements about his intent. Although he meant the work to be a collective autobiography, a personalized record of countless black Americans growing up with a personal history of hunger, deprivation, and constant racism, he seems to have realized as he wrote that his own life was not a very characteristic one and that he was focusing as much on his particular problems as on a typical black childhood. Wright decided to write his life story after giving an autobiographical talk to a racially mixed audience at Fisk University in Nashville, Tennessee, in 1943. After the talk, Wright noted that he "had accidentally blundered into the secret black, hidden core of race relations in the United States. That core is this: nobody is ever expected to speak honestly about the problem. . . . And I learned that when the truth was plowed up in their faces, they shook and trembled and didn't know what to do."[4] A year later, Wright used the same metaphor when he wrote, "The hardest truth to me to plow up was in my own life."[5] But speaking honestly about a racism endemic throughout America was more complicated, for author and for reader, than Wright could have known, and a more delicate instrument than a plow would be needed for harvesting the past. Using truthfulness as his watchword, Wright began *Black Boy* as an attempt to correct the record of black history, including his personal one, which already consisted of a number of "biographies of the author" or "notes on contributors" that were written by himself in the third person, sometimes with exaggerated accounts of his youth. In several interviews, as well as in his "The Ethics of Living Jim Crow," an autobiographical sketch originally published in 1937 in *American Stuff: WPA Writers' Anthology*, Wright had already given an incorrect birth date and had begun to establish a history overemphasizing the negative aspects of his early life.[6]

Most revelatory about the conflict between his intentions and the actual writing of his personal narrative is the following observation by Wright from a newspaper article called "The Birth of *Black Boy*":

> The real hard terror of writing like this came when I found that writing of one's life was vastly different from speaking of it. I was rendering a close and emotionally connected account of my experience and the ease I had had in speaking from notes at Fisk would not come again. I found that to tell the truth is the hardest thing on earth, harder than fighting in a war, harder than taking part in a revolution. If you try, you will find that at times sweat will break upon you. You will find that even if you succeed in discounting the attitudes of others to you and your life, you must wrestle with yourself most of all, fight with yourself; for there will surge up in you a strong desire to alter facts, to dress up your

feelings. You'll find that there are many things that you don't want to admit about yourself and others. As your record shapes itself an awed wonder haunts you. And yet there is no more exciting an adventure than trying to be honest in this way. The clean, strong feeling that sweeps you when you've done it makes you know that.[7]

Although Wright seemed unsure of his book's generic identity, he never referred to *Black Boy* as autobiography. His original title, *American Hunger*, later used for the portion of his life story that began after leaving Memphis for Chicago, came after he had rejected *The Empty Box*, *Days of Famine*, *The Empty Houses*, *The Assassin*, *Bread and Water*, and *Black Confession*, all of which sound like titles for novels.[8] When his literary agent suggested the subtitle "The Biography of a Courageous Negro," Wright responded with "The Biography of an American Negro," then with eight other possibilities including "Coming of Age in the Black South," "A Record in Anguish," "A Study in Anguish," and "A Chronicle of Anxiety." Such titles indicate his feeling that the book he had written was less personal, more documentary—a study, a record, a chronicle, or even a biography—than autobiography.[9] Constance Webb reports that Wright was uneasy with the word autobiography, both because of "an inner distaste for revealing in first person instead of through a fictitious character the dread and fear and anguishing self-questioning of his life" and because he realized that he would write his story using "portions of his own childhood, stories told him by friends, things he had observed happening to others," and fictional techniques.[10]

Although some readers believe Wright gave in to the "strong desire to alter facts" and "to dress up" his feelings, the book's tendency to intermix fiction and facts is clearly part of both Wright's personal literary history and the Afro-American literary tradition in which he was writing. The form of *Black Boy* in part imitates the traditional slave narrative, a literary type that allowed for a high degree of fictionality in the cause of abolition.[11] A number of major works of literature by black Americans, such as Du Bois's *The Souls of Black Folks*, Toomer's *Cane*, and Johnson's *The Autobiography of an Ex-Coloured Man*, feature mixtures of genres; and Wright, simultaneously a poet, novelist, essayist, journalist, playwright, and actor, often used the same material in different genres. For example, "The Ethics of Living Jim Crow" first appeared as an essay and was later attached to the stories of *Uncle Tom's Children*, one of which, "Bright and Morning Star," is retold in *Black Boy* as a tale that held the protagonist in thrall, even though he "did not know if the story was factually true or not."[12] When "black boy" says that the story is emotionally true, he reflects exactly the kind of truth Wright wants his readers to respond to in *Black Boy*. Some of the characters in *Black Boy* have been given fictional names, whereas Bigger Thomas, the central character in the fictional *Native Son*, is the real name of one of Wright's acquaintances.[13] That he used real names in fiction and fictional names in nonfiction is typical of Richard Wright, who further confounded the usual distinctions between author and persona by playing the role of Bigger Thomas in the first film version of *Native Son*.

Richard Wright makes clear that *Black Boy* is not meant as a traditional autobiography by presenting much of the story in the form of dialogue marked with quotation marks, a technique that suggests the unusual degree of fiction within the story. Although critics often point to Wright's first novel, *Native Son* (1940), as the other half of *Black Boy*, another model for this autobiographical work was his more recently completed *Twelve Million Black Voices: A Folk History of the American Negro in the United States* (1941). Writing *Black Boy* in the spirit of folk history seemed a reasonable thing to do, and Wright apparently saw no hypocrisy in omitting personal details that did not contribute to what he was simultaneously thinking of as his own story and the story of millions of others. Wright's claim to be composing the autobiography of a generic black child is reinforced by the narrator's particular reaction to racism: "The things that influenced my conduct as a Negro did not have to happen to me directly; I needed but to hear of them to feel their full effects in the deepest layers of my consciousness" (190).

Roy Pascal may be right in asserting that "where a lie is the result of a calculated intention to appear right or important, danger is done to autobiographical truth" and that "the most frequent cause of failure in autobiography is an untruthfulness which arises from the desire to appear admirable."[14] However, most of the omission in *Black Boy* is designed not to make the persona appear admirable but to make Richard Wright into "black boy," to underplay his own family's middle-class ways and more positive values. Wright does not mention that his mother was a successful school teacher and that many of his friends were children of college faculty members; he omits most of his father's family background and his own sexual experiences. Also mainly left out are reactions from sensitive southern whites, including those of the Wall family to whom, we learn from Michel Fabre's biography, "he sometimes submitted his problems and plans . . . and soon con-

sidered their house a second home where he met with more understanding than from his own family."[15]

In addition to omissions, name changes, poetic interludes, and extensive dialogue, *Black Boy* is replete with questionable events that
biographical research has revealed to be exaggerated, inaccurate, mistaken, or invented. The section of Fabre's biography dealing with the
Black Boy years is characterized by constant disclaimers about the factuality of the story. Some omissions can be explained because the ur-
bane ex-Communist who began *Black Boy* "wanted to see himself as a
child of the proletariat," though "in reality he attached greater importance to the honorable position of his grandparents in their town than
he did to his peasant background."[16] Although these distortions are
acceptable to many, especially in light of Wright's intention of using
his life to show the effects of racism, numerous other manipulations
are less acceptable because they are more self-serving.

Most of these incidents are relatively minor and might be judged
unimportant; however, the misrepresentations in two of the book's
most important episodes—the high school graduation speech and the
story of Uncle Hoskins and the Mississippi River—might be less acceptable. "Black boy's" refusal to deliver the principal's graduation
speech rather than his own is apparently based on truth, but the version in *Black Boy* leaves out the important fact that Wright rewrote his
speech, cutting out more volatile passages, as a compromise.[17] The
story of Uncle Hoskins does not ring true, for how could a boy whose
life had been so violent to that point be scared of his uncle's relatively
harmless trick? He says of his Uncle Hoskins, "I never trusted him
after that. Whenever I saw his face the memory of my terror upon the
river would come back, vivid and strong, and it stood as a barrier
between us." One reason the tale feels false is that the whole story—
complete with the above revelations about Uncle Hoskins—actually
happened to Ralph Ellison, who told it to Richard Wright.[18]

For many critics, including Edward Margolies, these deliberate manipulations reduce *Black Boy*'s authenticity as autobiography because
they set up doubts about everything, the same doubts that resonate
through the remarks of black writers from Du Bois to Baldwin to
David Bradley, all of whom have persisted in taking *Black Boy*'s protagonist to be Richard Wright.[19] But, "Richard Wright is not the
same person as the hero of that book, not the same as 'I' or 'Richard'
or the 'Black boy,' not by several light years," argues James Olney, who
refers to the book's chief character as "black boy," explaining that "by
means of an encompassing and creative memory, Richard Wright

imagines it all, and he is as much the creator of the figure that he calls 'Richard' as he is of the figure that, in *Native Son*, he calls 'Bigger.'"[20] Olney's idea that the central figure be treated as a single person referred to as "black boy," a literary character representing the actual author both as a child and as an adult—the famous writer imagining himself as representative of inarticulate black children—is finally convincing. That seems to be what Richard Wright meant to do, what he said he had done, and what he did.

Unlike that of Janet Cooke, who was labeled a liar for inventing a black boy in a series of articles in the *Washington Post* on drug use, or of any of the other New Journalists mentioned in the introductory chapter, Richard Wright's approach is different: first, because he announces his intentions—in authorial statements external to the text and by title, quotation marks, use of symbolic and imagistic description, and well-organized plot—and second, because he is manipulating his own story, not someone else's. Ralph Ellison's review-essay on *Black Boy*, "Richard Wright's Blues," begins with the refrain, "If anybody ask you / 'who sing this song,' / Say it was ole [Black Boy] / done been here and gone,"[21] a blues singer's signature formula that clarifies two important facts about the book. First, the protagonist is a literary character named "black boy" who bears the same similarity to Richard Wright as the character Leadbelly, for example, does to the blues singer Huddie Ledbetter who sings about Leadbelly so often. Second, Ellison's refrain forewarns that the identity of the protagonist will be called into question by critics who will wonder who the elusive hero is and where he is going. Ellison sees *Black Boy* as a talking blues, but it is also a bebop jazz performance in which Wright uses his life as the melody on which to improvise.

Many critical objections to *Black Boy*'s methods of getting at the truth come from those who instinctively feel something strange about the work, not so much in its generic confusions as in its tone and in what Albert E. Stone, Jr., senses when he writes that "a proud and secret self presides over the text, covertly revealing itself through event, style, and metaphor."[22] When confronted with *Black Boy*'s deviations from absolute biographical truth, less-sophisticated readers, such as students, are seldom bothered. They sense that discrepancies uncovered by reading other texts have little bearing on the truth of the text at hand. Nevertheless, the same students often respond unfavorably to what they perceive as inauthenticity arising from within *Black Boy*. And part of their dislike of and distrust for "black boy" grows from the sense of our times that "narrative past . . . has lost its authenticating power," as Lionel Trilling observes. "Far from being an authenticating agent, indeed, it has become the very type of inauthenticity."[23] Caring little about the crossing of generic boundaries, students are disturbed by the idea that "life is susceptible of comprehension and thus of management," as Trilling further remarks.[24] In short, they are uncomfortable with *Black Boy*, not because it is not true, but because for them it does not ring true. They experience what Barrett John Mandel calls "dis-ease with the autobiography. It seems as if the author is lying (not, please, writing fiction), although readers cannot always easily put their finger on the lie."[25]

The lying that they sense centers on these three concerns: "black boy" is never wrong, falsely naive, and melodramatic, three characteristics of what Mandel refers to as autobiography in which "the ratification is negative—the light of now shines on the illusion the ego puts forth and reveals it as false."[26] Mandel believes that most autobiographers are basically honest, but those who are not give themselves away through tone: "Since the ego is in conflict with the truth, the reader very often gets that message. The author has created an illusion of an illusion. . . . The tone is forever slipping away from the content, giving itself away."[27] Although Mandel does not include *Black Boy* in the category of dishonest autobiographies, instead citing it as a typical reworking of the past, many critics have echoed the students' concerns.

For example, Robert Stepto finds fault with two early incidents in which "black boy" insists on the literal meaning of words: when the character pretends to believe his father's injunction to kill a noisy kitten and when he refuses ninety-seven cents for his dog because he wants a dollar. "The fact remains that *Black Boy* requires its readers to admire Wright's persona's remarkable and unassailable innocence in certain major episodes, and to condone his exploitation of that innocence in others," writes Stepto. "This, I think, is a poorly tailored seam, if not precisely a flaw, in *Black Boy*'s narrative strategy."[28] Rather than seeing these episodes, and others like them, as examples of bad faith or as rough edges in the narrative fabric, I see them as deliberate renderings of the terrible dilemma of black boys and of their need to dissemble about everything, especially about the nature of their naiveté. Wright's persona is confessing, not boasting. His family life and his difficulty with hypocrisy made lying at once a constant requirement for survival and a nearly impossible performance, especially for a poor liar whose tone gives him away.

The inability to lie properly, exhibited in countless scenes, is "black boy's" major problem in adjusting to black-white relationships in his youth. Asked by a potential white employer if he steals, "black boy" is incredulous: "Lady, if I was a thief, I'd never tell anybody" (160), he replies. *Black Boy* is filled with episodes in which its hero is unable to lie, forced to lie, caught between conflicting lies, not believed unless he lies. Poorly constructed lies are appropriate metaphors to portray a boy whose efforts to set the record straight are as frustrated as his grandfather's futile attempts to claim a navy pension. Falsehoods are an apt metaphor for the speech of a boy who distrusts everyone, including himself.

Black Boy's opening, in which Wright describes how his four-year-old self set his grandmother's house on fire out of boredom and experimentation, is cited by virtually every commentator as an allegory for the fear, rebellion, anxiety, and need for freedom of the hero, as well as for the motifs of fire, hunger, and underground retreat. After the fire, which destroys more than half of the house, the child delivers this recollection:

> I was lashed so hard and long that I lost consciousness. I was beaten out of my senses and later I found myself in bed, screaming, determined to run away. . . . I was lost in a fog of fear. A doctor was called—I was afterwards told—and he ordered that I be kept abed, that I be kept quiet, that my very life depended upon it. . . . Whenever I tried to sleep I would see huge wobbly white bags, like the full udders of cows, suspended from the ceiling above me. Later, as I grew worse, I could see the bags in the daytime with my eyes open and I was gripped by the fear that they were going to fall and drench me with some horrible liquid. . . . Time finally bore me away from the dangerous bags and I got well. But for a long time I was chastened whenever I remembered that my mother had come close to killing me. [13]

Albert E. Stone, Jr., perceptively notes that the last line of this passage represents "a striking reversal." "Where the reader expects a confession that the boy has tried (although inadvertently or unconsciously) to attack his own family, one finds the opposite. Such heavy rationalization clearly demands examination."[29] The adult autobiographer is not justifying setting houses on fire; rather, he is trying to show graphically and suddenly how distrustful a child of four had already become. The episode does not ring true because it is not necessarily literally true. In fact, Wright uses a contradictory description in "The Ethics of Living Jim Crow," written eight years earlier. Describing, in that essay, a cinder fight between white and black children, Wright claims he was cut by a broken milk bottle, rushed to the hospital by a kind neighbor, and later beaten by his mother until he "had a fever of

one hundred and two. . . . All that night I was delirious and could not
sleep. Each time I closed my eyes I saw monstrous white faces sus-
pended from the ceiling, leering at me."[30] The cinder fight is retold in
a later section of *Black Boy*, though in this version the hero's mother
takes him to the doctor and beats him less severely.

The old-time musician Lily May Ledford in Ellesa Clay High's *Past Titan Rock: Journeys into an Appalachian Valley*, says, "I never tell a story the same way twice, but I tell the truth."[31] Similarly, Richard Wright has borrowed the rhetoric of the oral historian in consciously fictionalizing the story of the burning house and his subsequent punishment, at the same time sending signals that he has done so. Wright wants the reader to feel that something is not quite right about the whole scene. That the three-year-old brother can see the folly of playing with fire when the four-year-old "black boy" cannot, that the reasons for setting the fire are as spurious as the explanation ("I had just wanted to see how the curtains would look when they burned" [11]), that the nightmarish description of white bags filled with foul liquid is obviously meant to be symbolic, and finally that the boy is chastened, not by his actions, but by the thought that his mother had come close to killing him—all of these signals are meant to paint a truthful picture of a boy who later came to hold "a conviction that the meaning of living came only when one was struggling to wring a meaning out of meaningless suffering" (112).

The opening scene suggests the whole atmosphere of the book—a desperate fear of meaningless visitations of violence without context, a life of deliberate misrepresentations of the truth and complete distrust of all people, a world in which "each event spoke with a cryptic tongue" (14). Throughout *Black Boy*, Wright presents a lonely figure whose life does not ring true because "that's the way things were between whites and blacks in the South; many of the most important things were never openly said; they were understated and left to seep through to one" (188). Thus all actions are tempered by a subtext, which is obvious to everyone, a strategy that the author claimed to have discovered when he delivered his Fisk University oration.

Whenever the narrator questions his mother about racial relationships, she is defensive and evasive. "I knew that there was something my mother was holding back," he notes. "She was not concealing facts, but feelings, attitudes, convictions which she did not want me to know" (58), a misrepresentation that disturbs "black boy" who later says, "My personality was lopsided; my knowledge of feeling was far greater than my knowledge of fact" (136). Although the narrator holds back or conceals facts, he is usually straightforward about emotional feelings, even though he can say, "The safety of my life in the South depended upon how well I concealed from all whites what I felt" (255). Worrying less about factual truth, Wright was determined to stress the emotional truth of southern life to counteract the stereo-typical myths shown in the song that prefaced *Uncle Tom's Children*: "Is it true what they say about Dixie? Does the sun really shine all the time?"[32]

One of the ironies of *Black Boy* is that the narrator's constant lying is emblematic of the truth that all black boys were required not only to lie but to lie about their lying. In the boxing match between "black boy" and a co-worker, this pattern is played out almost mathematically. The two black boys are coerced into a fight they both know is false, based on lies that are obvious to all. Much of the shamefulness of the whole situation is that they are forced to pretend that they are neither aware that the situation is false nor mindful that the whites know they know. These paradoxes are clearly analyzed in Roger Rosenblatt's "Black Autobiography: Life as the Death Weapon": "They had been goaded into a false and illogical act that somehow became logical and true. At the end of their fight, Wright and Harrison *did* hold a grudge against each other, just as their white supervisors had initially contended." As a result, "a lie became the truth and . . . two people who had thought they had known what the truth was wound up living the lie."[33]

Although personal and institutional racism was everywhere evident, southern whites generally maintained that they treated blacks more humanely than did northern whites, that they understood blacks and knew how to deal with them, and that they were friendly with blacks (as evidenced by their calling them by their first names)—all of which blacks were supposed to pretend they believed. Whites deliberately set up situations where blacks were forced to steal; not only did they like to be stolen from, but whites also forced blacks to lie by repeatedly asking them if they were thieves. "Whites placed a premium upon black deceit; they encouraged irresponsibility; and their rewards were bestowed upon us blacks in the degree that we could make them feel safe and superior" (219), notes the narrator. When he forgets to call a white co-worker named Pease "Mister," he is caught in a trap from which the usual escape is "a nervous cryptic smile" (208). The boy's attempt to lie his way out of the situation fails, despite his ingenuity in turning the false accusation into an ambiguous apology:

> If I had said: No, sir, Mr. Pease, I never called you *Pease*, I would by inference have been calling Reynolds a liar; and if I had

said: Yes, sir, Mr. Pease, I called you *Pease*, I would have been
pleading guilty to the worst insult that a Negro can offer to a
southern white man. I stood trying to think of a neutral course
that would resolve this quickly risen nightmare. . . .

"I don't remembering [*sic*] calling you *Pease*, Mr. Pease," I said
cautiously, "and if I did, I sure didn't mean . . ."

"You black sonofabitch! You called me *Pease*, then!" he spat,
rising and slapping me till I bent sideways over a bench. [209]

Episodes like this make clear that an inability to tell the truth does
not make black children into liars. Instead, the frequent descriptions
of the protagonist as a prevaricator reveal to white readers the way
blacks use lies to express truths, use, for example, the word *nigger*
to mean one thing to white listeners, another to black. The elaborate
system of signifying—of using words in exactly the opposite way
from white usage (bad for good, cool for hot), of wearing the mask to
cover emotions, of the lies behind black children's game of dozens—is
behind the motif of lying in *Black Boy*. Wright's metaphoric use of
lying is made more complex by his awareness that a history of misrepresentation of true feelings made it difficult for black people to be
certain when they were merely dissembling for protection, when they
were lying to each other, or to themselves.

"There are some elusive, profound, recondite things that men find
hard to say to other men," muses "black boy," "but with the Negro it is
the little things of life that become hard to say, for these tiny items
shape his destiny" (254). What sets the narrator apart from his black
contemporaries is his difficulty with the lying that they find so easy:
"In my dealing with whites I was conscious of the entirety of my relations with them, and they were conscious only of what was happening
at a given moment. I had to keep remembering what others took for
granted; I had to think out what others felt" (215).

The actual audience must narrow the gap between the narrative and
authorial audiences; the reader of *Black Boy* must strive to be like the
narrator of *Black Boy*, must keep what is happening at a particular
moment and the entire history of black-white relations—the content
and the context—together in his or her mind. Wright's context includes the need to speak simultaneously as an adult and as a child and
to remove everything from his story that, even if it happened to be
true, would allow white readers to maintain their distorted stereotype
of southern blacks. He was searching for a way to confess his personal
history of lying, forced on him by his childhood, while still demon-

strating that he could be trusted by both black and white. His solution is what Maya Angelou calls "African-bush secretiveness":

> "If you ask a Negro where he's been, he'll tell you where he's going." To understand this important information, it is necessary to know who uses this tactic and on whom it works. If an unaware person is told a part of the truth (it is imperative that the answer embody truth), he is satisfied that his query has been answered. If an aware person (one who himself uses the stratagem) is given an answer which is truthful but bears only slightly if at all on the question, he knows that the information he seeks is of a private nature and will not be handed to him willingly.[34]

What makes *Black Boy* compelling is its ability to remain autobiography despite its obvious subordination of historicity. Although a reader may not be aware of the complexities of "black boy's" "African-bush" slanting of the truth or know about the book's fictionalizing, something, nevertheless, is unmistakably autobiographical about *Black Boy* that convinces even the unaware. What makes this true is the way the author signifies his lying through rhetoric, appeals in writing to both black and white, as he was unable to do in his speech in Nashville. One of the most significant patterns of the lying in the book involves just such a distinction between speaking and writing.

Wright's claim to be speaking for the millions of inarticulate children of the South is ironically reinforced by the constant difficulty the narrator has with the spoken, as opposed to the printed, word. Although a love of reading actually saves "black boy," he is constantly threatened by speaking. Often out of synchronization, he speaks when he should be quiet or is unable to utter a word when questioned; his words slip unaware from his mouth, flow out against his will. Just as often, he is verbally paralyzed, unable to produce a phrase. Early in life, he questions himself—"What on earth was the matter with me. . . . Every word and gesture I made seemed to provoke hostility?" (158). He answers, toward the end of the book, "I knew what was wrong with me, but I could not correct it. The words and actions of white people were baffling signs to me" (215).

The problem with the spoken word begins with the narrator's killing a kitten because of the pretense of not reading his father's command as figurative and continues with the melodramatic description of himself begging drinks as a six-year-old child, memorizing obscenities taught to him in a bar. Later "black boy" learns "all the four-letter words describing physiological and sex functions" (32) and yet claims to be astonished, while being bathed by his grandmother, at her reaction to his command: "'When you get through, kiss back there,' I said, the words rolling softly but unpremeditatedly" (49). Wishing to recall those words, though only vaguely understanding why he is once again being punished so severely, "black boy" says, "None of the obscene words I had learned at school in Memphis had dealt with perversions of any sort, although I might have learned the words while loitering drunkenly in saloons" (53). This explanation is weak and unconvincing, especially given his earlier description of himself and other children stationing themselves for hours at the bottom of a series of outdoor toilets, observing the anatomies of their neighbors.

Forced to declare his belief in God by his family of Seventh-Day Adventists, "black boy" misspeaks again and again. "'I don't want to hurt God's feelings either,' I said, the words slipping irreverently from my lips before I was aware of their full meaning" (126). Trying to keep his grandmother from questioning him about religion, he hits upon the strategy of likening himself to Jacob, arguing that he would believe in God if he ever saw an angel. Although this plan is imagined with the purpose of "salving . . . Granny's frustrated feelings toward [him]" (128), the result is that his words are misconstrued. His grandmother thinks he has seen an angel, and "black boy" once again has "unwittingly committed an obscene act" (131). His explanation is another example of his difficulty with speaking as others did: "I must have spoken more loudly and harshly than was called for" (131).

Asked by a teacher to explain a schoolyard fight with two bullies, the protagonist says, "You're lying!," which causes the teacher to reply, even though "black boy" is right, "Don't you use that language in here" (137). Once again daydreaming, "black boy" interrupts his family's "arguing some obscure point of religious doctrine" with a remark that he says "must have sounded reekingly blasphemous" (147). This time his grandmother is in bed for six weeks, her back wrenched in attempting to slap her grandson for his statements. Again "black boy" is an innocent victim, beaten for not allowing his grandmother to slap him—his physical, like his verbal skills, out of rhythm with his family. He is slapped for asking his grandmother, on a later occasion, what his dying grandfather's last words were and for replying to the question "What time have you?" with "If it's a little fast or slow, it's not far wrong" (173). "Black boy's" poor sense of timing makes him feel unreal, as if he "had been slapped out of the human race" (210), and causes him to resemble Ellison's "invisible man" who believes that such a condition "gives one a slightly different sense of time, you're never quite on the beat. Sometimes you're ahead and sometimes behind. Instead of the swift and imperceptible flowing of time, you are aware of its nodes, those points where time stands still or from which it leaps ahead."[35] Suggestive of the sense of time essential to jazz, these words describe the narrator who is out of phase with everyone until he can control the timing of his life through the syncopated rhythms of *Black Boy*.

In light of this repeated pattern—swift physical reprisal delivered to the totally astonished narrator for speaking out of turn—the following justification for threatening his aunt with a knife is surprising: "I had often been painfully beaten, but almost always I had felt that the beatings were somehow right and sensible, that I was in the wrong" (118). This confession sounds false because "black boy" never seems to admit that he is blameworthy for anything. "Nowhere in the book are Wright's actions and thoughts reprehensible," objects Edward Margolies, echoing a number of others.[36] Robert Felgar makes a similar point when he remarks that "the reader does tire of his persistent self-pity and self-aggrandizement."[37] An early reviewer argues that "the simple law of averages would prevent any one boy from getting into as many situations as we have related in this story, and one senses with regret, that it is hard to know where biography leaves off and fiction begins."[38] What these critics see as foolish self-pity is most apparent in the heavily melodramatic description of the familiar playground game of crack-the-whip, which the narrator describes in life-or-death terms: "They played a wildcat game called popping-the-whip, a seemingly innocent diversion whose excitement came only in spurts, but spurts that could hurl one to the edge of death itself. . . . The whip grew taut as human flesh and bone could bear and I felt that my arm was being torn from its socket" (122). Here the author is depicting a children's game using the kind of rhetoric usually reserved for a slave narrative—a cruel overseer whipping a runaway slave "to the edge of death."

Wright's words are not self-pitying; instead, he is presenting a naive youth who was never good at lying or exaggerating. The misrepresentation is so obvious that only a particularly inept liar would attempt it, a child who did not want to be good at lying. Only an outsider, such as "black boy," to the established systems of lying by both races, a representative of the many black adolescents then coming of age— what Wright hoped would be a new generation of the children of Uncle Tom, no longer willing to accept the old lie that the best way to fight racism was to lie through both omission and commission— could fail to distinguish between melodrama and genuine oppression and could be so surprised at the power of his words.

Black Boy should not be read as historical truth, which strives to

report those incontrovertible facts that can be somehow corrobo-
rated, but as narrative truth. The story that Richard Wright creates in
Black Boy, whatever its value as an exact historical record, is important
both in telling us how the author remembers life in the pre-Depression South and in showing us what kind of person the author was in
order to have written his story as he did. Although he is often deliberately false to historical truth, he seldom deviates from narrative truth.
In *Black Boy*, Wright has made both the horrifyingly dramatic and the
ordinary events of his life fit into a pattern, shaped by a consistent,
metaphoric use of lying. "Interpretations are persuasive," argues Donald Spence, "not because of their evidential value but because of their
rhetorical appeal; conviction emerges because the fit is good, not because we have necessarily made contact with the past."[39]

In *Black Boy*, Wright creates a version of himself whose metaphor
for survival and for sustenance is falsehood. But the multiple lies of
the narrator, like the fibs of children trying to avoid what they see as
irrational punishment, are palpably obvious. These lies are not meant
to deceive; they are deliberately embarrassing in their transparency.
For the protagonist, whose home life was so warped that only when
he lied could he be believed, Alfred Kazin's dictum—"One writes to
make a home for oneself, on paper"[40]—is particularly true. The author's manipulations of genre and his metaphoric lies have produced
a book about which Du Bois's assessment is, in my judgment, exactly
backward: although much of what Richard Wright wrote is not literally true, the total picture is ultimately convincing, taken in context.
For all his lying, "black boy's" essential drive is for truth.

"I Do Believe Her Though I Know She Lies"

[Autobiography] is a construction, not a reconstruction; it is a made thing. So it fictionalizes even though it may not fabricate or "make up," invent out of "thin air," fabulate. But can anything come out of "thin air"? Can anything come of nothing? So the lies of the poet, both the lies in the interest of truth and the lies in the interest of lying, the art of lying are brilliantly revealing too.—Robert Sayre

Among the contemporary reviewers who struggled with the believability of *Black Boy* was Mary McCarthy, who had already begun to publish the autobiographical pieces that would be collected in 1957 as *Memories of a Catholic Girlhood*. Because she was writing her own autobiography at the time, McCarthy's assessment of Richard Wright in 1945 is particularly telling. She describes *Black Boy* as strained and melodramatic, exaggerated and distorted and, therefore, difficult to believe.[1] Her use of the word *exaggerated* is revealing, especially since she often confesses in *How I Grew*, her 1987 autobiography, that exaggeration and excessiveness were among her major vices as a child. But even more revealing are the following remarks in which she argues that Wright's persona structured his life to fit an invented identity:

> I myself cannot believe in some of the incidents. It is not that Wright invented or edited them for the purposes of this book, but that rather he invented and edited them while they were happening, that he encouraged them, directed them, pushed them this way and that, to conform to a pattern of persecution and revenge, a neurotic pattern of I-and-they, which was already at the age of four the blueprint of his personality. Long before he became a novelist, the young Richard Wright was making up a story, the story which was his actual life; and to the persons and events of that life he behaved as a childish *agent provocateur*.[2]

McCarthy's argument here is that *Black Boy* does not sound true because Richard Wright's life is too literary, too studied, too much a narrative, especially as a representative of "A Typical Negro," the title of her review. McCarthy's reading of *Black Boy* is a particularly accurate assessment of her own autobiographical stance. *Memories of a Catholic Girlhood* and *How I Grew*, with their numerous corrections, revisions, and republications, their attempts at distinguishing between the half-remembered, half-guessed, and half-true, are among our most valuable autobiographical texts precisely because of their pull between her need, on the one hand, both to use and to dismiss the Roman Catholic sacrament of penance and her need, on the other, to present an authentic portrait of a young girl with a profound love of scrupulous honesty who was given to constant lying.

McCarthy's treatment of her own childhood is not believable for a number of readers. "Something happens in my writing," McCarthy herself remarks. "I don't mean it to . . . a sort of swerve and swoop. . . . The description takes on a sort of extravagance—I don't know exactly how it happens."[3] As noted by Doris Grumbach, McCarthy's biographer, "The effect is highly emotive, like the religious chromos the author remembers so poignantly, and one finds oneself questioning the entire veracity of the memories."[4] Another reviewer comments about *Memories*: "Reading it there comes the feeling that Miss McCarthy must be holding back a great deal, for it would surely take greater abuse and hardships than she describes to inspire the tone she uses."[5] The most direct attack comes from an anonymous reviewer who writes, "Mary McCarthy wanted quite simply to lie about her experience, then make things all right by confessing the lie, while at the same time capitalizing on the fact that the reader would come upon the lie first, accept it as truth, and be impressed by it before he would come across the notes informing him that he had been duped."[6] Still another reviewer senses that something is missing from her confession: "In spite of her keen self-analysis and her evident desire to be honest, a faint disquieting hint of disingenuousness pervades the whole book as if something essential had been consciously or unconsciously suppressed."[7] Patricia Spacks also notices this sense of withholding, arguing that McCarthy's rhetoric conceals her profound need for love. "The security of love eludes her, nor can she ever confess directly her need for it," writes Spacks, who explains that "the autobiographer's apparent reluctance to admit openly her deep desire for love may be accounted for by the fact that the desire conflicts cruelly with the effort to control experience by understanding it, this memoir's more explicit theme."[8]

Part of what bothers these writers is the constant insistence in *Memories* that the author was a lying and quibbling child, which does not always ring true for two reasons. First, McCarthy is so strict in her interpretations, so hard on herself, that she exacts impossibly difficult standards, and second, in the first autobiography she is not confessing anything very bad. As a result, occasional lapses of memory occur over small details that are finally only important to Mary McCarthy.

The initial word in the title of her first autobiography indicates

that, for her, the autobiographical act is primarily motivated by
memory, but memory is particularly problematic for McCarthy because when she was six her parents died suddenly in an outbreak of
influenza. In the preface to *Memories of a Catholic Girlhood*, she explains why her lack of family makes writing autobiographically both
so difficult and so vital:

> *One great handicap to this task of recalling has been the fact of being
> an orphan. The chain of recollection—the collective memory of a
> family—has been broken. It is our parents, normally, who not only
> teach us our family history but who set us straight on our own child-
> hood recollections, telling us that* this *cannot have happened the way
> we think it did and that* that, *on the other hand, did occur, just as we
> remember it, in such and such a summer when So-and-So was our
> nurse.*[9]

One reason that Mary McCarthy cannot reconcile her adult self
with her memories of her childhood self is that her childhood was
characterized by an almost total absence of a sense of a personal history. Her great-grandfather *"seems to have been the only member of the
family who was alive to the interest of history"* (*Memories*, 6). Her maternal grandmother is characterized as a woman whose life story "was
kept, like her age, a secret from those closest to her" (*Memories*, 198);
her paternal grandmother had so little feeling for history that when
she died she *"left a fund to erect a chapel in her name in Texas, a state
with which she had no known connection"* (*Memories*, 80). Of her Uncle
Myers, McCarthy writes, *"It is as if Uncle Myers had contrived to filch
away the proof that he had existed corporeally"* (*Memories*, 85). In her
attempt to acquire a past, or to get beyond what she remembers of
her past, the author is unaware that her habitual lying and lack of a
history operate on her memory as a family paradigm, a concept that
Daniel Goleman describes as follows: "The family constructs a reality
through the joint schemas members come to share. . . . The topogra-
phy of a family's private universe is implicit in routines and rituals, as
well as in how members take in, interpret, and share (or don't share)
information."[10]

Lacking an authentic personal history, McCarthy—like Fitzgerald's
Jay Gatsby, who "sprang from his Platonic conception of himself"—
comes to realize that she must create her own identity in part: "Oh I
suppose everyone continues to be interested in the quest for self, but
what you feel when you're older, I think, is that . . . you really must
make the self. It's absolutely useless to look for it, you won't find it,
but it's possible in some sense to make it. I don't mean in the sense of

making a mask, a Yeatsian mask. But you finally begin in some sense to make and to choose the self you want."[11]

So important is lying to Mary McCarthy that Paul John Eakin describes it as a paradigm for her childhood: "Lying becomes a sign of her orphan condition, the making of fictions a function of her loss. . . . If *'this task of recalling'* is completed, if the broken link in *'the chain of recollection'* is repaired, then, at least in narrative, the orphan will repossess her missing parents."[12]

When *Memories of a Catholic Girlhood* is taken as a whole, including both the individual chapters and the italicized sections, a pattern emerges: the book is deliberately written as a parody of confession in all of confession's senses. McCarthy's first autobiography is an anti-confession that mocks both the Catholic sacrament of penance and the confessional form of autobiography that grew out of it. Her major metaphor of self is the act of lying, the inability to make a proper confession. Throughout the book she describes herself—like Hawthorne's Arthur Dimmesdale—as repeatedly thwarted in her attempts at telling the truth, constantly forced against her will to misrepresent. At the same time, the book functions as an actual confession in which a lapsed Catholic—caught between strong desires to reveal and to conceal, both from herself and from her readers—actually makes public some of her most private sins.

In the italicized preface and epilogues, McCarthy tries to make amends for the errors of her original misrepresentative versions of the past. Despite her open admissions of lying, McCarthy is no more unreliable than most autobiographers, who, according to William L. Howarth, are "all shameless liars and impersonators, slipping into disguises whenever, like Boswell, they need to walk some midnight Strand," because "they dissemble obviously, with that disarming candor that is honest about its own deceit."[13]

McCarthy might at first seem more unreliable than traditional autobiographers because she is caught in a complex rhetorical situation. She wishes to be scrupulously honest about her childhood but is constantly made aware, with each rewriting, that she has been misleading, that absolute honesty requires her to admit that she cannot be certain what she has invented and what actually happened. Although this difficulty is common to all autobiographers, it is particularly complicated for McCarthy because she is working in a confessional form that she also wishes to mock. She is simultaneously trying to confess and to undercut the act of confession. By calling her book *Memories of a Catholic Girlhood*, she specifically focuses attention on herself, less as

an individual and more as a generic Catholic girl, much as Richard
Wright meant to tell the story of a typical black childhood. And yet
among the most shocking of her confessions is that, in pretending to
lose her faith, she discovered that she actually had lost it. As a result,
these are the memories of a Catholic girlhood, written by an adult
who tells her readers openly that she lost her faith in Catholicism at an
early age. McCarthy could have called her book *Memories of a Lapsed
Catholic Girlhood*, but even that would not have been absolutely honest, since for much of her childhood she was devout, and since much
of the ritual and power of Catholicism has remained a strong force for
the lapsed adult.

"The Fact in Fiction"

Imagination and memory are but one thing, which for divers considerations hath
divers names.—John Hobbes

The initial problem with lying in *Memories of a Catholic Girlhood* involves genre. Like most of her autobiographical writing, *Memories of a
Catholic Girlhood* is a difficult book to classify, not only because of
its form and content, but also as a result of its publication history.
McCarthy's memories were published originally over an eleven-year
period—from 1946 to the book's publication in 1957. All but two
chapters were printed first in magazines as stories, and three appeared
in her *Cast a Cold Eye*. McCarthy's bibliographer, Sherli Goldman,
comments on the difficulty of fitting McCarthy's pieces into distinct
categories: "In its original form this bibliography had separate clas-
sifications for fiction and non-fiction. This led to problems. For example, 'Yellowstone Park,' which appears in the autobiographical *Memories of a Catholic Girlhood*, won an O'Henry short-story prize in
1957."[14] To some critics, such as Barbara McKenzie, the chapters of
Memories form "a collection of essays that set down certain themes
and attitudes that also sustain her fiction."[15] But others, such as Victor Lange, see the chapters not as essays but as fictionalized descriptions in which "each figure assumes in the telling a reality far more
complex and metaphorical than we have reason to expect in a work of
straight-forward autobiographical recollection."[16] The generic confusion about *Memories* is typical of virtually all of McCarthy's writing.
Doris Grumbach bases her biography of McCarthy on the "conviction that the fiction of Mary McCarthy is autobiographical to an ex-

traordinary degree in the widest sense of autobiography."[17] Grumbach clarifies her idea of the "widest sense of autobiography" when she states:

> Few writers in recent years have made such good use of autobiographical facts. Like a householder who puts every scrap of cloth or string or food to use, her autobiographical economy has been perfect; she seems to include in her fiction almost everything she remembers. If, in her use, she has "played" with the truth this is usually to the good. What results is not dreary, scrupulous, exact life history, but life history disseminated into all corners of the writer's products; autobiography as fiction, fiction drawing heavily upon autobiography.[18]

When Elisabeth Niebuhr asks McCarthy in a *Paris Review* interview if she objects to readers who see her books as romans à clef, McCarthy answers: "I suppose I really ask for it, in a way. . . . What I really do is take real plums and put them in an imaginary cake."[19] In this answer, McCarthy sounds as if she views her autobiographical writing as a highly fictionalized form with the kind of relation to real life that Marianne Moore demands of poetry—"Imaginary gardens with real toads in them."[20] But in her essay "Settling the Colonel's Hash," McCarthy takes an opposing view, arguing that *Harper's* is misleading when the magazine labels her "Artists in Uniform," published in its issue of March 1953, a story. However, she admits, "I myself would not know quite what to call it; it was a piece of reporting or a fragment of autobiography."[21] When readers, taking "Artists in Uniform" as fiction, suggest that such details as the author's dress and the colonel's lunch of hash have symbolic overtones, McCarthy answers that these details are not symbolic at all since the whole episode is meant as nonfiction:

> I had a sandwich; he had roast-beef hash. We both had an old-fashioned. The whole point of this "story" was that it really happened; it is written in the first person; I speak of myself in my own name, McCarthy; at the end, I mention my husband's name, Broadwater. When I was thinking about writing the story, I decided not to treat it fictionally; the chief interest, I felt, lay in the fact that it happened, in real life, last summer, to the writer herself.[22]

In a rebuttal called "Unsettling the Colonel's Hash: 'Fact' in Autobiography," Darrel Mansell wonders what difference McCarthy's declaration that "Artists in Uniform" is nonfiction should make in our interpretation of its language as symbolic:

> Are we supposed to believe that the word "hash" on a page of *Harper's* has potentially a symbolic meaning for about a year, then changes . . . because the author . . . wrote . . . that she remembers there existed real hash on a plate that she now identifies with the words "corned-beef hash" on page 47 of the March 1953 *Harper's*? Was there anything else on the real colonel's plate, a pickled pear omitted in the story but existing in reality, so that McCarthy is now in the state of reporting real hash that happened on an otherwise fictive plate? Can the rest of the plate be "symbolic" but not the hash? What if the station restaurant reports in and says it was lamb hash—can we then go back to symbolizing the word in the story?[23]

Mansell's hypothetical question about the specific type of hash becomes plausible when we notice that McCarthy writes in her rebuttal that the colonel had "roast-beef hash" but in the original story that "the waitress set down my sandwich and his corned-beef hash."[24] Of course, the transformation of corned beef to roast beef is of little importance to the story, where it does not seem to have much symbolic value in the first place. McCarthy's objection really seems to have been to forced symbol hunting rather than to symbolic interpretation altogether. But her insistence on the literal factuality of the meal is undercut by her error that dramatizes the natural fictionalizing of any autobiographical narrative, a fictionalizing caused by memory's tendency to remember what the artist wants it to remember. As McCarthy says of some "semi-fictional touches" in *Memories*: "I arranged actual events so as to make 'a good story' out of them. It is hard to overcome this temptation if you are in the habit of writing fiction; one does it automatically" (*Memories*, 164–65).

Even if her notion that a piece of writing should be analyzed one way if labeled fiction, another if called autobiography, were accepted, we would still be unsure how to proceed with much of her autobiographical writing. Sometimes she presents an episode from her life in both a fictionalized and a nonfictionalized version. For instance, some of the events recounted in the chapter of *Memories of a Catholic Girlhood* called "Yonder Peasant, Who Is He?" are repeated in the short story "Ghostly Father, I Confess" from *The Company She Keeps*. In "Yonder Peasant," the autobiographical character writes of McCarthy's real grandmother, Lizzie Sheridan McCarthy, "She did not visit our ménage or inquire into its practices. . . . She was liberal indeed with glasses and braces for the teeth. . . . She imagined us as surrounded by certain playthings she had once bestowed on us—a sandbox. . . . Years after the sand had spilled out of it and the roof had rotted away, she continued to ask tenderly after our lovely sand pile. . . . In the case of a brown beaver hat . . . she was clearly blinded to its matted nap" (*Memories*, 42–43). In "Ghostly Father," these same details are retold by the fictional Meg Sargent: "Then, after the flu was over, and mamma did not come home from the hospital, Aunt Clara had moved in. . . . The white sand darkened in the sandpile . . . and the pretty little girl who looked . . . so much like her mother was changed into a stringy, bowlegged child with glasses and braces on her teeth . . . and a brown beaver hat two sizes too big for her."[25]

These passages demonstrate the ease with which McCarthy slides between autobiographical fiction and fictionalized autobiography and explain her difficulty in sorting out her own writing. Discussing "Artists in Uniform," for instance, she writes, "Strangely enough, many of my readers preferred to think of this account as fiction. I still meet people who ask me, confidentially, 'That story of yours about the colonel—was it really true?'"[26] In "To the Reader," the preface to *Memories of a Catholic Girlhood*, she expresses a similar surprise about readers' reactions to the previously published chapters: "*Some readers, finding them in a magazine, have taken them for stories. The assumption that I have 'made them up' is surprisingly prevalent, even among people who know me. . . . More than once . . . I have had a smiling stranger invite me to confess that 'Uncle Myers' was a hoax*" (*Memories*, 3).

McCarthy's protestations of surprise are odd in light of her admission that "*many a time, in the course of doing these memoirs, I have wished that I were writing fiction. The temptation to invent has been very strong, particularly where recollection is hazy and I remember the substance of an event but not the detail—the color of a dress, the pattern of a carpet, the placing of a picture. Sometimes I have yielded, as in the case of conversations*" (*Memories*, 3–4). The structure of *Memories*—alternating chapters of autobiographical narrative followed by chapters of italicized amplification (interchapters that discuss factual errors, modify false impressions, and introduce additional narrative material)—reveals the significant amount of fictionalizing present throughout the book. Every chapter except the last is followed by an italicized chapter that appears at first to be correcting the fictional record.

Throughout these italicized explanations, McCarthy tries to categorize her departures from the truth into such refined gradations as "highly fictional," "semi-fictional," and "pure fiction." But these terms belie her admission that "actually when you write about something you get mixed up afterwards about which version is true."[27] In pointing out minute discrepancies that we would never have found for ourselves, McCarthy is able to claim an extraordinary candor, and yet her explanations are so full of doubts that they confuse the issue further. Each chapter's epilogue discusses the relative degree of misrepresentation present in the chapter. The level of fictionalizing can be insignificant, as shown by the correction of minor points substantiated by documentation: "*We cannot have been sick that long. The newspaper accounts of my parents' death state that 'the children are recovering'*" (*Memories*, 47). The misrepresentation extends to open admissions of her inability to determine the chapter's fictiveness: "*This story is so true to our convent life that I find it almost impossible to sort out the guessed-at and the half-remembered from the undeniably real*" (*Memories*, 124). Writing about "The Blackguard," a chapter the author calls "*highly fictionalized*," she says, "*In short, the story is true in substance, but the details have been invented or guessed at*" (*Memories*, 97). Of "The Figures in the Clock," McCarthy notes that "*there are some semi-fictional touches here*" (*Memories*, 164), and she gives as an example the following admission about the teacher who caught her sneaking in a bathroom window: "*I think it was Miss Gowrie who caught me, but I am not positive. Sometimes I feel it was and sometimes I feel it wasn't*" (*Memories*, 165).

Because we are told that Miss Gowrie is a fictional name and that a strong possibility exists that the author subordinated a strict accounting of what actually happened to the need to make a better story, simply classifying this story, and the whole of *Memories of a Catholic Girlhood* of which it is a representative sample, as self-conscious fiction is at first tempting. But in her second autobiography, *How I Grew*, published thirty years later, McCarthy affirms that the fictional Miss Gowrie was actually a real woman named Miss Mackay. Although still uncertain about the incident of coming in the bathroom window on graduation eve, McCarthy continues to hold out for the possibility that it was Miss Mackay who caught her.

At the end of the nonitalicized portion of the chapter "A Tin Butterfly," which was originally published in the *New Yorker* in 1951, McCarthy apparently reevaluates the story of the tin butterfly by adding: "Six or seven years later . . . I stopped in Minneapolis to see my brothers. . . . It was then that my brother Preston told me that on the famous night of the butterfly, he had seen Uncle Myers steal into the dining room from the den and lift the tablecloth, with the tin butterfly in his hand" (*Memories*, 80). This addendum to the story has the same function of clarification and authentification as the italicized interchapters. But this story also has an epilogue, written in 1957 at the time her writings were collected into *Memories of a Catholic Girlhood*. This second epilogue throws the entire situation into doubt:

> *About the tin butterfly episode, I must make a more serious correction or at least express a doubt. An awful suspicion occurred to me as I was reading it over the other day. I suddenly remembered that in college I had started writing a play on this subject. Could the idea that Uncle Myers put the butterfly at my place have been suggested to me by my teacher? . . . After a struggle with my conscience . . . I sent for Kevin and consulted him about my doubts. He remembers the butterfly episode itself. . . . He remembers the scene on Uncle Louis' screened porch when we four, reunited, talked about Uncle Myers. But he does not remember Preston's saying that Uncle Myers put the butterfly there. Preston, consulted by long-distance telephone, does not remember either saying it or seeing it. . . . But this is all conjecture; I do not know, really, whether I took the course in Playwriting before or after the night on Uncle Louis' porch. The most likely thing, I fear, is that I fused two memories. Mea Culpa. . . . But who did put the butterfly by my place? It may have been Uncle Myers after all. Even if no one saw him. [Memories, 82–83]*

McCarthy's confession, complete with a mea culpa, implies "a more serious correction," "a doubt," an "awful suspicion," and suggests that the entire family has trouble remembering the most memorable indication of Uncle Myers's cruelty. At the same time, she gains credit for honesty in admitting these doubts and manages to suggest at the end that she may have been right all along. According to Paul John Eakin, the two versions of the tin butterfly story, as well as the whole book, are not to be taken as competing testimonies, or as alternate endings to the story. Instead, the two versions represent "a series of earlier recallings . . . a series of prototypes for the autobiographical act." For Eakin, the presence of fiction within autobiography is "an ineluctable fact of the life of the consciousness" and, therefore, a "central feature"[28] of the truth of a life transformed into a story, an echo of Philip Roth's statement: "We are all writing fictitious versions of our lives all the time, contradictory but mutually entangling stories that however subtly or grossly falsified constitute our hold on reality and are the closest thing we have to truth."[29] Applying this reasoning to McCarthy's story, Eakin argues that McCarthy's fictionalizing adds rather than subtracts from her truthfulness: "The making of fictions, moreover, is central to McCarthy's identity, in her character early on

as a problem liar, and eventually as a writer, and it forms a critical part
of the mass of autobiographical fact that she is dealing with."[30]

In picturing her brother and herself trying with *"burning interest"*
to reconstruct their past, *"like two amateur archaeologists, falling on any*
new scrap of evidence, trying to fit it in, questioning our relations, belabor-
ing our own memories" (*Memories*, 6), McCarthy has chosen an apt
metaphor. For in reading through her book, we become aware of the
chronological acquisition of deeper and deeper layers of her history.
Like an archaeologist—whose knowledge of ancient civilizations in-
creases with time for discovery, each level of knowledge modified by
the uncovering of another layer—so McCarthy in her epilogues appears to be getting closer and closer to the truth. These corrections of
earlier corrections, however, raise as many questions as they answer,
for in addition to the confession of specific errors in the chapter each
follows, each section also includes a narrative of new memories. Her
autobiographical situation is particularly complicated because she reveals things that turn out not to be true but has nothing with which to
replace them. This absence of verifiable memories, coupled with an
intense need for verification, frequently causes problems of tone.

Consequently, *Memories* is filled with qualifications and corrections: *"I think I remember but I am not positive"*; *"or did someone tell me*
this story?"; *"I do not think this was true"*; *"I have the feeling of 'remem-*
bering,' as though I had always known it"; *"the prize of a dime (no, a*
nickel)"; *"I now think"*; *"so far as I know"*; *"But this cannot be right"*;
"Possibly so, but I never heard this from any member of the family"; "as far
as I could make out"; "I forget the details"; and finally, "according to
one informant."[31] Similar disclaimers, checks, and balances occur
throughout *How I Grew*: "But stop! That cannot be true"; "I hardly
know how to tell this"; "Maybe I have imagined the whole thing"; "I
am guessing, of course"; "If I reconstruct it right"; "But no"; "and
now comes another hiatus in my memory"; "But wait!"; and countless others.[32]

McCarthy's corrections of the text, within the text, are also an accurately written representation of the way she actually speaks. As Elisabeth Niebuhr notes about her interview with the author, "While Miss
McCarthy's conversation was remarkably fluent and articulate, she
would nevertheless often interrupt herself, with a kind of nervous
carefulness, in order to reword or qualify a phrase, sometimes even
impatiently destroying it and starting again in the effort to express
herself as exactly as possible."[33] All of these hesitations are designed to
persuade the reader that all the author seeks is to relate what really
happened. The very fact that she questions the accuracy of the smallest

detail suggests that, for the most part, the substance of her book is scrupulously true to history. Her claim that her story is substantially true, even though it might sound like a lie, is one of many such claims in the book where a major theme is the lie, or false confession.

Good and Bad Confessions

The person who confesses is lying and fleeing the real truth, which is nothing, or contorted, and in general blurred.—Paul Valéry

Confessing and the lie are one and the same. In order to be able to confess, one tells lies.—Franz Kafka

In addition to generic confusions, lies in McCarthy's autobiographies are directly connected to the idea of confession. McCarthy's title stresses that her first autobiography is of a Catholic girlhood, although much of the story is actually set outside of the strictly Catholic part of her youth. In the Roman Catholic sense, confession refers to the central act of the sacrament of penance, auricular confession or exomologesis, a public "avowal of sin made either to God or to man."[34] Although Catholics often use the word *confession* to refer to the sacrament of penance, confession, according to church teaching, is only one of the distinct elements of penance: confession, contrition, satisfaction, plus the absolution of a priest.[35] To receive forgiveness for one's sins, the penitent must list sins by kind and number; express a sincere sorrow for the sins and make a firm resolve not to commit them again; and finally, make satisfaction, that is perform whatever penance is assigned by the priest in order to receive absolution. By this strict standard, both *Memories of a Catholic Girlhood* and *How I Grew* are what Catholics often call "bad" confessions, defined by the church as sacrilegious confession:

A confession is said to be sacrilegious when a penitent conceals in bad faith one or more mortal sins, or the kind of sins he has committed, or the number of times he has committed them, or if he knows himself to be without genuine sorrow for one or more mortal sins, even though his confession of them is in other respects satisfactory. In his subsequent confession such a penitent must not only make a good confession of all the sins that formed a necessary part of the previous confession, but must also make mention of the sacrilegious confession itself.[36]

If *Memories of a Catholic Girlhood* is read in light of this definition, the book is clearly a sacrilegious confession, a term that signifies Mc-Carthy's autobiographical situation. She wishes to publicly present memories of herself as a Catholic girl, memories that focus on venial sins, such as lying, and the mortal sin of losing her faith—which she compounds by having lied about it first—and yet the adult who is confessing no longer remembers all of her sins, does not really feel a sense of contrition, in fact is partially motivated by a desire to boast rather than to express sorrow, and yet finds herself, inexplicably, drawn to the Catholic form of confession as a means with which to accomplish these complex tasks. To further complicate her performance, McCarthy is drawn to frankness, the willingness to say openly what is often understood being a hallmark of her character. As Elizabeth Hardwick notes about McCarthy's lifelong habit of making outspoken remarks: "Taken together, they display a candor that might slip from any honest woman occasionally, but never from one honest woman so often. The shock, in the end, is the consistency of her candor."[37]

Although McCarthy repeatedly confesses her lies, she does not appear to feel remorse for them. Instead, she seems to boast of her inventiveness. Perhaps this tone can be excused as part of the genre, for as Alfred Kazin reminds us, "If the confession is an attempt to ward off a curse, writing it out is also a boast,"[38] a fact that is reflected in the two meanings of exomologesis: confessing one's sins or boasting of God's greatness.

If *Memories of a Catholic Girlhood* can be taken as a kind of literary sacrilegious confession, its sequel, *How I Grew*, might be seen as an instance of a general confession, defined as "the repetition of all or many of one's past confessions. A penitent may be under obligation to make such a confession because of a series of sacrilegious confessions made in the past."[39] Although the second autobiography eventually covers McCarthy's life from her entrance into Vassar through her first marriage, it also goes back to her Catholic girlhood, covering much of the same ground as her first. What McCarthy is actually confessing is a difficulty with reconciling her love of truth and fact, plus her predilection for candor, with the incontrovertible fact that as a child she was a problem liar.

For the adult autobiographer, working through an understanding of her lying with every autobiographical act, simultaneously boasting and confessing through a bad confession her triumph over losing her faith, all the while demonstrating on every page the influence of

Catholicism, both of her autobiographies are confessions in another sense of the word: "Confession originally was used to designate the burial-place of a confessor or martyr . . . the new resting place to which the remains of a martyr had been transplanted."[40] The connection between confession and burial place is inherent in Paul de Man's well-known essay "Autobiography as De-facement," which uses Wordsworth's *Essays on Epitaphs* to illustrate the argument that autobiographical and biographical persona are so "disfaced" and "disfigured" that they could be said to "die," their personal narratives becoming a kind of epitaph.[41]

In thus placing an epitaph over her girlhood self—here lies (in both senses of the word) Mary McCarthy—the author is both deliberately mocking the two meanings of confession I have been discussing and making profound use of the form. Eugene Stelzig reminds us that confession involves both exposure and concealment: "Nietzsche's assumption that deep truths are in need of the mask also holds true for the confessional imagination."[42] Mary McCarthy's autobiographical desires are just such a contradiction; she fears something invisible about herself that others can see, yet only in revealing what only she can see in her innermost self can she hope to understand what is on the surface visible to others.

In addition to mocking confession as the Catholic sacrament of penance, and in its earlier meaning as a martyr's new burial site, *Memories of a Catholic Girlhood* also mocks confession as an autobiographical genre. As anticonfession, the book takes almost exactly the opposite form from confession as defined by Georg Misch: "This form of the autobiography is determined by this systematization of sins; the facts are arrayed in accordance with this, furnished with theological explanations of the gravity of the various lapses, and contrasted with the pious figures of parents and grandparents. The whole is surrounded and interspersed with self-accusations and expressions of remorse."[43] McCarthy mocks this form in her *Memories of a Catholic Girlhood* that are arranged in accordance with sins committed against her, or sins she was forced to commit. These accounts are furnished with theological explanations of her sins' lack of gravity and contrasted with the sacrilegious figures of surrogate parents and grandparents. The whole is surrounded and interspersed with epilogues devoted to self-justifications and misleading self-accusations and a nearly complete lack of remorse.

In an article on Tennyson's *In Memoriam*, W. David Shaw defines the autobiographical confession in terms of a number of characteristics, the first of which is the rhetorical need "to persuade the reader of some truth." According to Shaw, "The privacy of 'confession' is never far removed from the publicity of 'profession.'" What seem like mere facts, at the start, are moderated by a second person until, by the conclusion, they have evolved through a "pattern of conversion" so that "the conclusion seems the natural outcome of the opening," and the whole confession thus becomes open ended. Shaw's final characteristic is that theme follows form: "With the addition of 'confession' to 'profession,' or experience to doctrine, the 'what' becomes a 'how,' as the very manner of the author's 'confession' enacts the truths to be professed."[44]

In many ways, McCarthy's confession parodies these characteristics. Her autobiography uses rhetoric "to persuade the reader of some truth," but the effect is the opposite; she often seems to be trying to convince the reader that truth is impossible to attain. Her book's facts do sometimes take on prototypical qualities. The title reinforces her idea that these memories are of a Catholic girlhood in general, and she writes that *"'Yonder Peasant' . . . is not really concerned with individuals. It is, primarily, an angry indictment of privilege for its treatment of the underprivileged, a single, breathless, voluble speech on the subject of human indifference"* (*Memories*, 49). But her experiences of human indifference are hardly typical of most Catholic girlhoods, and her denunciation of Catholicism is not the usual "typological truth." In the italicized section of "C'est le Premier Pas Qui Coûte" following her revelation of a loss of faith, McCarthy acts as a second person mediating her own anticonversion. Her concluding chapter is open ended, for "Ask Me No Questions" is the only chapter without an italicized rebuttal. Yet this chapter is also circular because it retraces McCarthy's childhood through her increasingly more complicated perceptions of her grandmother. Because the words "Ask Me No Questions" are usually followed by "I'll Tell You No Lies," the final chapter leads readers back to where they began, unable to decide how to take the final confession. Finally, the book echoes Shaw's tenth attribute of confession because its form, a contradictory mock confession, duplicates its theme of false or bad confession.

For Mary McCarthy, "confession itself," as Eakin demonstrates, "offers an equivocal model for the expression of autobiographical truth, involving as it does in McCarthy's case the partly involuntary, partly voluntary, public performance of a lie about one's self."[45] This familiar pattern recurs throughout her writing. The prototypical McCarthy character confesses to indiscretions that are especially shocking, both for their candor and for the cosmopolitan tone of the confession that somehow suggests that the author is both penitent and confessor. Eleanor Widner identifies the contradictory rhetoric of the typical McCarthy confession when she describes the author's need "to cry simultaneously *mea culpa* and 'How great I am,' in a fusion of personal attitude and public image."[46]

"Lies like Truth"

There are no whole truths; all truths are half-truths. It is trying to treat them as whole truths that plays the devil.—Alfred North Whitehead

In chapter after chapter, McCarthy describes herself in situations where she is required to lie by societal pressures. Often this theme is furthered by episodes in which she tries to tell the truth but no one will believe her. On the first page of her preface, she expresses mock amazement that earlier versions of her memories were taken as fiction: "*I do not understand the reason for these doubts; I have read about far worse men than my cruel uncle in the newspapers. . . . Can it be that the public takes for granted that anything written by a professional writer is* eo ipso *untrue? The professional writer is looked on perhaps as a 'storyteller,' like a child who has fallen into that habit and is mechanically chidden by his parents even when he protests that* this time *he is telling the truth*" (*Memories*, 3). This is certainly a disingenuous statement, an innocent protestation that the author is being forced by an uninformed public into playing the role of the little boy who cried wolf, when actually the bulk of the book to follow confesses over and over that, when the author was a child, she told so many "stories," so many lies, that the adult cannot distinguish them.

All the layers of misstatement, correction, and further correction, the multitude of false episodes left as originally printed, despite subsequent evidence that they are untrue, are designed to support her vision of a childhood of which she says, "My whole life was a lie, it often appeared to me, from beginning to end" (*Memories*, 173). Patricia Spacks writes that "the form and style of *Memories of a Catholic Girlhood* largely define its meaning, as the book constantly calls attention to its own artifice, manipulating the reader's doubts about whether 'true' autobiography is possible."[47]

Although she repeatedly tries to separate truth and hearsay, McCarthy is actually only remaining true to her conception of herself as the daughter of a family of natural liars, clinging to a part of her lost family history. "*There was mendacity, somewhere, in the McCarthy blood*" (*Memories*, 11), she observes. Speaking of her romantic father, she

adds, *"Most of my memories of him are colored, I fear, by an untruthfulness*
that I must have caught from him, like one of the colds that ran round the
family" (*Memories*, 11). Excusing her predilection for lying as an inherited trait, McCarthy often points out that her falsehoods are an
essential part of her childish personality.

When her grandfather checks on the identity of the father of her
teenage friend in the chapter called "Yellowstone Park," the young
McCarthy is actually surprised that she has told the truth:

> For in my representations to my grandparents, I always had the
> sensation of lying. Whatever I told them was usually so blurred
> and glossed, in the effort to meet their approval . . . that except
> when answering a direct question I hardly knew whether what I
> was saying was true or false. I really tried, or so I thought, to
> avoid lying, but it seemed to me that they forced it on me by the
> difference in their vision of things, so that I was always transpos-
> ing reality for them into terms they could understand. [*Memories*,
> 172]

For the adult author, who has formed an identity for her self based in
part on absolute honesty, these confessions are particularly painful.
McCarthy constantly resorts to such qualifications as "the sensation of
lying," "my representations," "their vision of things," and "transpos-
ing reality," when the author as a child was simply lying, as all children
do, and for the usual reasons. According to Elizabeth Kamarck Minnich in "Why Not Lie?," "One sure mark of a lie, personal, social or
political, is not just that it doesn't correspond to reality, our usual
definition of a lie, but that there is effort put into making reality correspond to it. Lies are our effort to make things go the way we want
them to."[48]

McCarthy's confessions of lying have an odd perspective. Often,
she overemphasizes the smallest prevarication, blaming herself for the
slightest accidental misrepresentation, and yet on other occasions, she
expends enormous energy in complicated attempts at proving that she
is not at fault. For instance, in the chapter called "C'est le Premier Pas
Qui Coûte," she excuses her habit of lying by noting that she was
punished for telling the truth when she directed "spiteful taunts" at
a rival: "I never broke any of the rules, and was it my fault if she
blubbered when I applied, perfectly accurately, a term I had heard
mothers whisper—*nouveau riche*?" (*Memories*, 108). In a later chapter
"Names," she depicts herself again forced to lie because of the sensi-
bilities of others. Because the nuns in her boarding school mistake a
cut leg for the onset of menstruation and refuse to believe her protes-

tations of truth, McCarthy is forced to reopen the cut on her leg every month. As a consequence, she is forced to lie. Once again, she has an excuse: "It was not my fault; they had forced me into it; nevertheless, it was I who would look silly—worse than silly; half mad—if the truth ever came to light" (*Memories*, 135). Part of her tone is an authentic rendering of that classic cry of childhood—"not my fault"—and part is an ironic confession. If she really thought that the revelation of her forced subterfuge about menstruation would make her look half-mad, she would never have mentioned it in the first place. Her protestations are often meant to be taken ironically, like her insistence that she was humiliated by the nickname C. Y. E. and would never tell anyone how much it bothered her, all the while revealing to her readers the particulars of its acquisition.

Because no one will believe her when she tells the truth, McCarthy's life becomes characterized by the act of lying. "There I was, a walking mass of lies, pretending to be a Catholic and going to confession when really I had lost my faith, and pretending to have monthly periods by cutting myself with nail scissors; yet all this had come about without my volition and even contrary to it" (*Memories*, 136). Similarly, in "The Figures in the Clock," she justifies her lying about having left the grounds of the school to meet a boy the night before graduation. Called to the principal's office, she says, "I saw that I could graduate after all if I would make the concession of lying. . . . The lie was a favor being asked of me. . . . I was going to equivocate, not for selfish reasons but in the interests of the community" (*Memories*, 162). Here she argues that she sacrificed integrity, "seeking a formula that would not compromise principle too greatly" (*Memories*, 162), so that the graduation ceremonies could continue on schedule with herself as one of the principal speakers. Like Richard Wright wrestling with his conscience before giving in to his high school principal, she sees her lie in this case as a hypocritical call for a positive moral action rather than as an easy way out.

In a later scene, she repeats this pattern. Having lied to her grandparents about spending a vacation in Yellowstone Park, she worries about amassing a "proper array of lies" to describe the park. "It was not the fear of being found out, even, that was troubling me," she argues, but a matter of etiquette: "I felt I owed my grandparents the courtesy of a well-put-together and decently documented lie" (*Memories*, 187–88). Like Sherwood Anderson, Mary McCarthy seeks integrity in the organic wholeness—the narrative truth of a well-made story—rather than in a literal rendition of what actually happened. In all of the episodes of lying in her first autobiography, only once does

McCarthy admit that she lied for self-protection or self-gain. In the last chapter, her grandmother catches McCarthy in a lie about having used her makeup. "I felt so guilty at what I had done that I would not admit that I had been 'into' her dressing table, even when confronted with the proof" (*Memories*, 228). Although she would not tell her grandmother the truth, she does admit the lie, without attempting to justify it, to the reader. But even this instance is part of an overall pattern of false confession, for it makes a lie of her earlier statement, "It was against my code of honor to lie when you were directly accused" (*Memories*, 161).

In "C'est le Premier Pas Qui Coûte," when she confesses her doubts to a priest who "sat with half-averted face, as priests do in the confessional" (*Memories*, 116), he does not believe that the questions of faith are really hers but suspects her of having read atheistic literature. In this anecdote, McCarthy implies that confessing the truth is pointless, since no one, not even the priest, ever believes her. But behind this protestation lies the fact that she had made a bad confession, pretending to lose her faith in order to gain popularity with her friends. And, as the title asserts, "It's the first step which costs," for she actually does lose her faith, which, ironically, makes her confession of having lost faith true. And now she must lie again, this time pretending to have regained faith, not out of a sense of responsibility to her own soul, but "as a public duty" in "a sense of obligation" to "satisfy Madame MacIllvra and Madame Barclay and my new friends" (*Memories*, 122).

The epilogue to "The Blackguard" includes still another scene in which the author's confession does not meet with approval. Trying to confess to a sin of impurity, she admits, "*I had been looking up words like 'breast' in the big school dictionary and in a medical book at home and discussing them with my fellow pupils*" (*Memories*, 100). But this apparently simple confession, according to McCarthy, is rejected by her confessor: "*'Is that all?' His voice sounded positively indignant. 'Yes, Father.' 'You mean to tell me that this is your only sin of impurity?' 'Yes.' Before I knew it, he had pronounced absolution, and the door of the confessional grate was shut almost with a bang, as though I had been imposing on his valuable time*" (*Memories*, 100). Again, McCarthy implies that a truthful confession is not acceptable and that lying for the sake of others' expectations is preferable.

This recurring pattern begins in the preface when she discusses her improper first Communion. Having broken her fast by drinking water, she elects to make a false Communion rather than fail "*the school and my class*" (*Memories*, 20). Not for herself, but for the sake of others, she is willing to lie: *"The sisters would be angry; my guardians would be angry"* (*Memories*, 20). As with other important rituals of her girlhood—menstruation, loss of faith, graduation, first sexual experience —her first Communion is a misrepresentation. This pattern of lying is metaphoric of her life: *"Every subsequent moral crisis of my life, moreover, has had precisely the pattern of this struggle over the first Communion; I have battled, usually without avail, against a temptation to do something which only I knew was bad, being swept on by a need to preserve outward appearances and to live up to other people's expectations of me"* (*Memories*, 20–21).

Throughout the epilogues, which have been called a "long apologia,"[49] McCarthy follows this pattern. These confessions, like the chapters they comment on, are designed to *"preserve outward appearances and to live up to other people's expectations."* Following her decision to make an improper first Communion, McCarthy says, *"I could not imagine that I could make a true repentance—the time to regret was now, before committing the sacrilege; afterwards, I could not be really sorry for I would have achieved what I had wanted"* (*Memories*, 20). Obviously, McCarthy is not being hypocritical here; she is not trying to quibble, to have it both ways; instead, she is confessing that as a child she valued popularity over faith, lost her faith at the first sign of doubt, constantly lied and then pretended that she had no choice, and was aware all the time that true contrition was not possible, given her self-knowledge. This series of confessions of an inability to make a proper penance is an admission that Mary McCarthy makes about her entire childhood. When readers questioned her about the truth of "Artists in Uniform," she replied that she was shocked that "it seemed to them perfectly natural that I would write a fabrication, in which I figured under my own name, and sign it, though in my eyes this would be like perjuring yourself in court or forging checks."[50]

That she would equate fabrication with perjury and forgery and yet confess repeatedly to lying constitutes the central paradox of her identity, a paradox that the writing of *Memories of a Catholic Girlhood* hopes to resolve. According to Eakin, for instance, the mystery she wishes to solve through public confession is the guilt and anger surrounding the sudden death of her parents.

> On the one hand, she constantly criticizes herself—as a child telling lies, as an autobiographer making fictions—for infidelities to the truth; on the other, she willingly conspires with her earlier selves in the invention of wish-fulfilling fiction. In this case nei-

ther memory nor imagination succeeds in dispelling the darkness that shrouds the primal event of death and loss.[51]

The darkness that surrounds her parents' death is the same darkness that obscures Mary McCarthy's life. The death of her parents; the suddenness with which she was transported into a completely different family, complete with new parents, in a new city, with a new house, and a new set of rituals; followed by the repeated abruptness with which she was rescued from this second set of parents, Aunt Margaret and Uncle Myers, and resettled into yet another house with a third set of parents and a completely different set of rituals—all of this raised grave doubts in her mind about her own history and consequently her own identity.

Like all autobiographers, she wants to write a story that will reconcile her self and her life, but unlike most authors, McCarthy cannot connect the two. For example, the adult autobiographer, reading her own letters, discovers that the feelings she remembers about her first days at Vassar are exactly the opposite of what she wrote. "This is alarming, above all to one who has set out to write her autobiography. It raises the awful question of whether there can be multiple truths or just one. About truth I have always been monotheistic. It has been an article of faith with me, going back to college days, that there is a truth and that it is knowable" (*How I Grew*, 199).

For an author who has lost her religious faith but couched her confession in a religious form, who has believed since her college days in the idea of a single, knowable truth but is baffled by the period before college when she was a self-characterized liar, Mary McCarthy finds herself in an untenable rhetorical position. According to George W. S. Trow, her position is endemic to the modern age: "In what does a search for new truth-configuration consist? I propose that it is an attempt to discover the true configuration of lies and truth that impressed itself on one's mind during the formation of one's personality. . . . What an apprehending man or woman often says today is: This configuration of lies and truth is truth to me."[52]

McCarthy has become a collection of her multiple childhood selves, for whom no particular configuration of lies and truth is satisfactory. No matter how many times she writes her story—going back over the same episodes, first in *Memories of a Catholic Girlhood* and later in *How I Grew*—she still cannot reach agreement with herself, still cannot understand how to fit together her memory and the few documents that remain from her childhood as an orphan.

McCarthy's constant search for identity, for a key to the past, for the secret about herself that she imagines everyone else can see, is summarized in the phrase "the word for mirror," which both Eakin and Gordon O. Taylor use as chapter titles.[53] Believing that her Jewish grandmother, Augusta Morganstern Preston, conceals a mystery that will explain everything about herself, McCarthy discovers in the last chapter of *Memories of a Catholic Girlhood* that her grandmother's secrets cannot be uncovered because the woman refuses to answer questions about the past and because, as the chapter title "Ask Me No Questions" indicates, the only answers she could give would be lies. McCarthy becomes aware of her grandmother's inability to help her in her search for self when Augusta Preston forgets the word for mirror. For Eakin, this is such an important moment that he contends, "the autobiographical act, we might say, is the attempt to find the word for mirror."[54]

But even if the word could be remembered, and a reversed image viewed, the reflection could never solve McCarthy's dilemma. As Michael Ignatieff explains, the photograph, "like a harshly lit mirror," undercuts memory's continuity. "As a record of our forgetting, the camera has played some part in engendering our characteristic modern suspicion about the self-deceiving ruses of our consciousness. Memory heals the scars of time. Photography documents the wounds."[55]

Her recurring attempts to confess childish lies, the better to convince us of her candor, reflect the discrepancy between the author whose girlhood persona was characterized as a problem liar and the adult whose friends constantly describe her as a ferocious truth teller. Dwight Macdonald describes McCarthy as "extremely scrupulous about the truth," a remark echoed by Elizabeth Hardwick who notes, "Mary is almost physically incapable of saying something she doesn't mean . . . almost bodily."[56] A large part of McCarthy's autobiographical problem is a persistent belief in the strength of facts, though in many ways the specific facts of her childhood are not as important as her use of them.

McCarthy claims in the preface to *Memories of a Catholic Girlhood* that she is trying to produce a kind of history. *"But all these people are real; they are not composite portraits. In the case of my near relations, I have given real names, and, whenever possible, I have done this with neighbors, servants, and friends of the family, for, to me, this record lays a claim to being historical—that is, much of it can be checked"* (*Memories*, 4). But she is more concerned with creating the feeling of history than actual history. As she comments in her well-known essay "The Fact in Fiction":

> This air of veracity is very important to the novel. We do really (I think) expect a novel to be true, not only true to itself, like a poem, or a statue, but true to actual life, which is right around the corner. . . . We not only make believe we believe a novel, but we do substantially believe it, as being continuous with real life, made of the same stuff, and the presence of fact in fiction, of dates and times and distances, is a kind of reassurance—a guarantee of credibility.[57]

Of course McCarthy is talking here of the novel, but her call for an "air of veracity," rather than actual veracity, applies as well to her personal narratives. In demanding an "air of veracity" in fiction and *a claim to being historical* for her autobiography, because *much of it can be checked*," McCarthy echoes Warner Berthoff's distinction between history and fiction: "Ideally, then, *history* is descriptive, and its problem is verification. *Fiction* is constitutive or inventive, and its problem is veracity. Both, as modes of narrative, are composed. But in the first case the order of the narrative is meant to reveal a pre-existent order of actuality; in the second, though the narrative may imitate the form of a history, it is known from the first to be a particular writer's invention."[58]

But in *Memories*, McCarthy clearly blends history and fiction and, therefore, blurs the need for verification and veracity. Her book both attempts to "imitate the form of a history" and claims to be history. She stuffs her account with historical facts that need to be checked, simultaneously admitting that, on the one hand, most of them can never be verified and, on the other, that many of her attempts at checking the facts have proven that her memory and her sense of artistic decorum might have subverted the historicity of the past.

How I Grew: "The Figure under the Carpet"

It requires a certain kind of talent, a certain kind of inwardness to look at the reverse of a tapestry, to know when and where to seek the figure under the carpet.—Leon Edel

At the conclusion of her review of *Black Boy*, McCarthy, describing Richard Wright, unconsciously reveals a most important aspect of her own autobiography's effect. "Of such people it is difficult to say whether their account of experience is true or false," she writes; "it is true in the sense that something very like it happened, and false in the sense that it did not happen to the narrator but that on the contrary the narrator happened to it."[59] This formulation, which at first appears to be the reverse of the normal teleological order, demonstrates McCarthy's misapprehension about identity formation. Because she has no parents to correct what she realizes are necessarily false recollections, she has come face to face, in writing and rewriting her autobiography, with direct evidence that her memory is faulty. Despite her love of truthfulness, she fails to realize that for everyone, not just orphans, the same reverse pattern of identity creation holds. Erik Erikson explains:

> By accepting some definition as to who he is, usually on the basis of a function in an economy, a place in the sequence of generations, and a status in the structure of society, the adult is able to selectively reconstruct his past in such a way that, step for step, it seems to have planned him, or better, he seems to have planned *it*. In this sense, psychologically we *do* choose our parents, our family history, and the history of our kings, heroes, and gods.[60]

For McCarthy, the quest for a self is apparently distinct from making an identity, a distinction best clarified by Norman Mailer's statement that "McCarthy's work has been a constant illustration to us that honor is a pose, a kind of scaffolding for identity—and identity is the central spiritual problem of our time."[61] For McCarthy, honor is a pose in the sense that the figure seen in a photograph has been posed, not in the sense that the figure is a poseur. Because she is so hard on herself, turning her famous cold eye inward, she fails to realize that honor is a pose for many people and that how we choose to pose, what we place in the foreground, tells us much about our identity. In *How I Grew*, McCarthy writes, "And now I perceive that it was all of a piece, consistent, that stage behavior of mine: on stage, unless I was actually speaking my assigned lines (i.e. 'acting'), I forgot that an audience can see me" (*How I Grew*, 23).

She seems unaware that much of our identity is on the surface, visible to others, hidden to ourselves, that identity is as much our reaction to others' reactions to our self-presentations as anything else. Her chief childhood fear—most clearly expressed in the chapter in *Memories* called "Names" and in its earlier version, "C. Y. E."—is that there is something obvious about her, not necessarily something negative, that everyone else can detect but that she cannot fathom. Her paradoxical quest for the truth through lies becomes an attempt to find

truth by coming at it from the underside. In *On Lies, Secrets, and Silence*, Adrienne Rich aptly comments:

> In speaking of lies, we come inevitably to the subject of truth.
> . . . There is no "the truth," "a truth"—truth is not one thing, or
> even a system. It is an increasing complexity. The pattern of the
> carpet is a surface. When we look closely, or when we become
> weavers, we learn of the tiny multiple threads unseen in the over-
> all pattern, the knots on the underside of the carpet.[62]

Reflecting on the self that existed before she made herself into a literary figure—the narrator of two autobiographies—McCarthy writes, "So I, who was not yet 'I,' had been painted over or given a coat of whitewash, maybe two or three times, till I was only a bumpiness, an extra thickness of the canvas" (*How I Grew*, 161). In this painterly metaphor, strikingly similar to Lillian Hellman's well-known concept of pentimento, McCarthy persists in imagining that posing, painting, whitewashing, and writing are lies because they are on the surface, an idea directly contradicted by her friend, Hannah Arendt: "Could it be that appearances are there not for the sake of the life process but, on the contrary, that the life process is there for the sake of appearance? Since we live in an appearing world is it not much more plausible that the relevant and the meaningful in this world of ours should be located precisely on the surface?"[63]

McCarthy's phrase "a bumpiness . . . of the canvas" is one of a whole series of images that run throughout her autobiographies, images of carpets, weaving, and knitting, literal and figurative patterns, all having in common a sense of interruption in the pattern that simultaneously reveals the pattern (the figure in the carpet) and suggests the key to the pattern (the underlying truth). When McCarthy describes herself as a bump in the canvas, she echoes "the bulge in the carpet" at her grandmother's home, "a bell [her grandmother] stepped on when she wanted the maid to come in" (*Memories*, 199). "The bulge in the carpet" parallels "her gloves, which had bumps in them (made by her rings, I discovered later)," and her "enchanted house, which was full of bulges too" (*Memories*, 201).

McCarthy's attempt to create a story to provide an answer for her autobiographical problems centers around this grandmother in the enchanted house. She calls her grandmother "*the key*" and writes that "*the sense of a mystery back of the story I had already told traced itself more and more to the figure of my grandmother*" (*Memories*, 193). Apparently, "*the story I had already told*" refers to all of *Memories of a Catholic Girl-*

hood up to the last chapter. The mystery behind the story is yet another instance of McCarthy's chief worry—something is strange about her upbringing that others can detect immediately. This mystery has to do with her grandmother's lack of a documented past: she does not wish to appear in photographs or, for that matter, in her granddaughter's books; in short, she wants to forget the word for mirror. Augusta Preston possesses, in its purest form, the common trait of both sides of the author's family—a repression of the past, a distrust of documentation, that is only overcome by the telling of stories. "My grandmother was a gifted *raconteuse*," writes McCarthy, "when she could be induced to tell one of her stories" (*Memories*, 216). Like Sherwood Anderson, Mary McCarthy counts storytelling (in both senses of the word) as a major family inheritance.

This grandmother, who holds the key to McCarthy's childhood memories, is unwilling to reveal even the tiniest details about the past, although she represents the only link to that innocent period before McCarthy's parents'—and her daughter's—death. This reluctance to mention the past is coupled with a curious concentration on the smallest fact in the present: "The part was always greater to her than the whole, and some of the things she noticed would have escaped the attention of anyone but a phrenologist" (*Memories*, 213). And like a phrenologist, seeking clues in the bumps in the carpet, McCarthy returns to her grandmother's house to find the bulge no longer there.

> One Sunday, perhaps the last time we went there, we could not find the bulge at all, and I remember the strange, scary feeling this gave me, as though I had been dreaming or making up a story and there had never been any bulge or bell in the first place. It did not occur to us that the bell must have been removed to keep us from annoying the maid, and the mystery of its disappearance used to plague me, long after we had left Seattle, like some maddening puzzle. I would lie awake in my new bed, thinking about the bell and wishing I could be given another chance to look for it. Five years later, when I was brought back to that house to live, a girl of eleven, I had the great joy, the vindication, of finding the bell just where I thought it should be, between her feet and mine. [*Memories*, 199–200]

In contrast to Augusta Preston, the author's other grandmother, Lizzie Sheridan McCarthy, is described as being generous with memories of Mary's parents, Tess and Roy McCarthy. "These memories doled out by our grandmother became our secret treasures; we never spoke of them to each other but hoarded them, each against the rest, in the miserly fastnesses of our hearts" (*Memories*, 45). McCarthy describes the effect of her paternal grandmother's dispensing of these memories by saying, "her mind embroidered the bare tapestry of our lives" (*Memories*, 43). This weaving metaphor echoes the following statement about memory from Goethe:

> Whatever we encounter that is great, beautiful, significant, need not be remembered from outside, need not be hunted up and laid hold of, as it were. Rather, from the beginning, it must be woven into the fabric of our inmost self, must become one with it, create a new and better self in us and thus live and become a productive force in ourselves. There is no past that one is allowed to long for.[64]

Having stated in her earlier autobiography that she is through with the quest for identity, content with making a self, the author of *How I Grew*, now thirty years older, frequently describes that art of self-invention through a weaving motif. This pattern begins, in *How I Grew*, with an unfinished story:

> When he died, my father . . . had been reading me a long fairy tale that we never finished. It was about seven brothers who were changed into ravens and their little sister, left behind when they flew away, who was given the task of knitting seven little shirts if she wanted them to change back into human shape again. At the place we stopped reading, she had failed to finish one little sleeve. [*How I Grew*, 4]

This anecdote, which presents the family in a story-telling situation left unresolved, suggests McCarthy's autobiographical situation— her memories are always embroidered, but no matter how carefully she attempts to weave the facts, her fairy tale past always remains unraveled.

Throughout *How I Grew*, she struggles with digressions, fighting her narrative impulse that keeps telling personal stories not directly tied to her ostensible theme—the education of Mary McCarthy. "Yet losing the thread (or seeming to) has given me time to wonder about the truth of what I was saying" (*How I Grew*, 9), she notes, an expression of a pattern echoed in the later comment "I arrived among my Sacred Heart contemporaries like a dropped stitch in time and in some ways I never caught up" (*How I Grew*, 26). Of the death of her first lover, she writes, "His passing . . . would leave a little rip or tear in the fabric of my life not easily rewoven" (*How I Grew*, 86). Among her most important intellectual influences was Ted (Ethel) Rosenberg, who was "sweet on my grandmother [Augusta Preston]" and characterized by the "weaving of romances, as though to cover the nudity of everybody's life" (*How I Grew*, 57).

This last instance of the weaving pattern is especially significant because of its suggestion that covering nakedness is part of the purpose of weaving stories out of the material of our lives. According to Martha Lifson, the allegorical quest for the secret self, like McCarthy's attempts to penetrate her grandmother's masks of clothing and make-up, is comprised of equal parts of attraction and repulsion:

> When the self is undressed, it appears naked to both the creator and the reader. Thus at the very point of attempting to be most revealing and most honest, at the very point of success as a teller of stories about the self, the autobiographer is faced with too much unveiling. The self is now so bare that paradoxically it becomes unauthentic, either because the completely revealed is akin to the disguised and inauthentic (too shocking, extreme, and excessively demanding of attention), or because the completed and therefore rigid self is fake and threatening as a self in process, ever presented in veils and images, is not. For modern writers especially, it is the unfinished, the in-process, the writing itself that seems to convey the truth.[65]

Although McCarthy sees her grandmother Preston as the clue to her autobiography's impasses—the whole difficulty of being forced into constant lying, fusions of memories, unfinishable fictions, because of an inability to get any factual answers about the past—*Memories of a Catholic Girlhood* ends with the revelation that nothing is really behind the grandmother's masks. The secret that is revealed on the night Aunt Rosie dies, when Augusta Preston is most open and vulnerable to McCarthy, is that her grandmother "had never really cared for anyone but her sister" (*Memories*, 243), a discovery that is perceived in the "intellectual part" of McCarthy's mind as merely an awareness that "some sort of revelation had taken place" (*Memories*, 243). Because McCarthy says of her grandmother, "I never saw her undressed" (*Memories*, 226), the awful spectacle of this carefully concealed woman (for whom a botched face-lift counted as a major tragedy) writhing on the bed, "her yellow batiste nightgown . . . pulled up, revealing her thighs" (*Memories*, 242), seems a particularly important moment. However, as Lifson argues, and McCarthy demonstrates, the most authentic way to see Augusta Preston is not when she is naked but when all of her masks are in place, for the only revelation that occurs, when she is naked, is that an unknowable revelation has occurred and that the central figure of McCarthy's Catholic girlhood is of little help, since this figure is most revelatory on the surface and, yet, has forgotten the word for mirror.

Another clue to this important last chapter of *Memories of a Catholic Girlhood* is embedded in its title, "Ask Me No Questions," that hints at the Catholic teaching about lying often called mental reservation—the use of equivocation and ambiguity to withhold truth. "In the strict sense [mental reservation] means giving utterance to only part of one's judgment while retaining in mind or whispering inaudibly another part necessary to make the statement objectively truthful."[66] McCarthy practiced this technique when she was questioned by the principal of the Annie Wright Seminary on the night before her graduation. In *How I Grew*, she describes that lie as *"suppressio veri"* (*How I Grew*, 165). The *New Catholic Encyclopedia* gives as an example of mental reservation the case of a formerly unfaithful wife who, having received penance for her adultery, is asked by her husband if she has been faithful. Her answer, "I am free from sin," is a truthful reply that suppresses the facts on the grounds that this is not the sort of question a husband ought to ask directly of a wife. Like priests who have heard a confession, other professionals are entitled by the church to practice mental reservation if they are asked questions whose answers they believe the questioner has no moral right to know.[67]

When we reread "Ask Me No Questions" with mental reservation in mind, we see that the revelation McCarthy has received from her grandmother, although impenetrable, is also helpful; she has learned that one way to conceal without lying is to suppress part of the truth through ambiguity and to couch her sentences in such a way that she is both revealing and concealing at the same time. This is a strategy attributed by Elizabeth Hardwick to all autobiographers: "In autobiography, self-exposure and self-justification are the same thing. It is this contradiction that gives the form its dramatic tension."[68]

Initially, the title of Mary McCarthy's second autobiography seems oddly childish, reminiscent of the increments of a child's growth posted on the bathroom door. McCarthy appears to have imagined this second autobiography as an intellectual history—the intellectual growth of Mary McCarthy. She begins with "I was born as a mind during 1925, my bodily birth having taken place in 1912" (*How I Grew*, 1), and spends a considerable amount of time enumerating such factual details as books read, courses taken, classmates at various schools, and favorite teachers. Among the lists of books is the childhood series *The Five Little Peppers and How They Grew*, which might have suggested the title. Another possible inspiration might have been "How It Went," the first section of her *The Seventeenth De-gree*. Yet another possibility is suggested by the following explana-tion from the interchapter to "Yellowstone Park": "*Also, in Medicine Springs, I was having to live up to a role that 'grew me up' overnight*" (*Memories*, 192). In this usage, growing up is equated with living up to a pose, the standard McCarthy position. At any rate, after reading *How I Grew*, we can see that Mary McCarthy's growth was as much spiritual as intellectual and that the title aptly describes a person who grows in ethical stature by her increasing willingness to make a good confession, as constituted by *How I Grew*.

What is immediately striking about the second autobiography, es-pecially if we come to it after having read the first, is its tone, which is more serious and less ironic. Again McCarthy struggles with mem-ory, but no longer is the problem of fictionalizing even mentioned. Again she is confessing—confessing this time in fact to a number of sins omitted from the first book. This time, however, the ironic mea culpa—the physical sign of the Act of Contrition required in any act of penance—is replaced with a more genuine sense of sorrow. She has grown in sorrow and understanding, even as her memories have grown less secure.

In *Memories of a Catholic Girlhood*, Mary McCarthy confesses that she cannot make a proper confession; in *How I Grew*, she confesses that her first book is false because of sins that she withheld—withheld from herself as well as from the reader. She confesses cleverness as a secret vice, excessiveness as a mistake, and a possible plagiarism, courting of approval, and false witness as venial sins. But the most important confession in the second autobiography is a serious strain of anti-Semitism that the adult author is only willing to admit to at the age of seventy-five, when secure in the knowledge that her life since college has provided ample penance for this mortal sin. In terms of confession, the author of *Memories* corresponds to the young girl, Mary, whose constant complaint is the lack of severity with which her sins are regarded: "*My sins, as I slowly discovered, weighed heavier on me than they did on my confessors*" (*Memories*, 20); "*And when I went to my weekly confession, I seldom got anything but the very lightest penance—those little Our Fathers and Hail Marys were almost a disappointment to me*" (*Memories*, 53). Her paradoxical complaint is with the looseness of the Catholic Church, its easy attitudes toward lying, its lack of se-verity toward sinners, as expressed in her wondering why she—"who yielded to every impulse, lied, boasted, betrayed—should, by virtue of regular attendance at the sacraments and the habit of easy penitence, be saved?" (*Memories*, 89). She was trying, in the act of writing her first autobiography, to confess to being a problem liar as a way to

express disdain toward the lying that she had absorbed from those
aspects of the Catholic Church she most associated with the McCar-
thys' kind of Catholicism: "*I never really liked the doctrine of Indul-
gences—the notion that you could say five Hail Marys and knock off a year
in Purgatory*" (*Memories*, 26).

This form of Catholicism, with its emphasis on the quibble, the
hypothetical question, and the equivocating standard, was particularly noxious to the young Mary because inherent in her makeup was a
love of the precise, the exact Latinate word, the absolute. As McCarthy relates in *How I Grew*: "I was a firm believer in absolutes: the lack
of shadings, of an in-between, made Asgard a more natural residence
than Mount Olympus for my mythic propensity, just as clear, concise
Latin was always more natural to me than Greek with all its 'small,
untranslatable words'" (*How I Grew*, 6).

In contrast to this young Mary, unhappy with the easiness of her
penance, the Mary of *How I Grew* is far more self-aware, far less naive,
and consequently far more conscious of the seriousness of those sins
that cannot be so easily atoned for by a lifetime of intellectual activity.
Where the interchapters of *Memories* quibble over impossibly fine distinctions between fact and fiction and attempt to correct memory's
lapses by force of will, the whole of *How I Grew*—which acts as an
interchapter to the first book—corrects the record on more serious
matters. Where the McCarthy of *Memories* is witty and flip, especially
about her constant lying, and only serious in the chapters about her
parents' death and in the chapter on her grandmother, the McCarthy
of *How I Grew* is serious throughout. The humor and wit of the first
book are revealed in the second to be deliberate attempts at dealing
with the memories of Uncle Myers and Aunt Margaret and the loss of
her parents. "Laughter is the great antidote for self-pity," she writes;
"yet probably it does tend to dry one's feelings out a little. . . . There is
no dampness in my emotions, and some moisture, I think, is needed
to produce the deeper, the tragic notes" (*How I Grew*, 17). This evo-
cation of emotional dryness suggests the following sentence from
Memories, which occurs just before she describes lying about her first
Communion: "*I knew myself, how I was and would be forever; such dry
self-knowledge is terrible*" (*Memories*, 20).

In contrast to her first autobiography, *How I Grew* is filled with
major confessions that make her childhood lies seem the most venial
of sins. Unfortunately for the adult autobiographer, these lies of
youth now obscure the past. In reviewing *How I Grew*, another Catholic autobiographer, Wilfrid Sheed, writes:

Lying must have been irresistibly attractive to a precocious, not particularly saintly child who had been shuttled between families, regions and schools, adopting new personas on the way like baggage labels, and, like many basically truthful people, Miss McCarthy took to it like a duck to water (it helps to know exactly what you're lying about). But those lies now constitute another exasperating scrim between herself and what she so desperately wants to remember. However knowingly and consciously the lie is told, it plants a seed of ambiguity, another version of truth is now at large in the world—which may be why the author was so hard on Miss Hellman. (To a reformed liar, lies are the ultimate menace, as booze is to the alcoholic.)[69]

In *Memories*, lies are confessed as venial sins and attributed primarily to forgetfulness and fictionalizing; in contrast, *How I Grew* is filled with remorse as she confesses the mortal sin of anti-Semitism, a sin the author cannot forget despite a memory given to "leakage or 'running' as of non-fast colors" (*How I Grew*, 20) in some cases, complete disassociation, "resulting in big patches of amnesia" (*How I Grew*, 48), in others. Her loss of memory is greatest in the following description of the precise moment in which she lost her virginity: "Of the actual penetration, I remember nothing; it was as if I had been given chloroform" (*How I Grew*, 77).

The sense of amnesia that McCarthy feels about her loss of virginity does not apply to the details surrounding it, so that the reader of the second autobiography becomes aware of one of the things withheld from the first book. McCarthy's grandfather's insistence on a strict watch over her activities with boys does not seem so quaint when we learn that "the young man with a Marmon roadster" who appears briefly in the "Yellowstone Park" chapter of *Memories* figures prominently as her first lover in *How I Grew*. Although not revealing this detail in *Memories* is certainly not lying, McCarthy is partially practicing mental reservation in representing herself later in "Yellowstone Park" as almost losing her virginity "the *very* first night, the *very* first man" (*Memories*, 182), neglecting to add that she had already lost her virginity at the age of fourteen.

In *How I Grew*, she frequently expresses remorse, as when she confesses that an unnamed sexual practice caused her to "cringe with shame to think of afterwards" (*How I Grew*, 156), or when she writes of a letter of recommendation from her Latin teacher, recently discovered in the files of the Vassar Committee on Admissions, "Reading that, how can I fail to feel like a worm?" (*How I Grew*, 170). Believing that Ethel Mackay was deceived because she could not have imagined the young McCarthy's indiscretions and lies, the adult McCarthy writes, "Invincible in her ignorance, she may have known me better than I knew myself. That is, *I* was deceived by the will-less, passive self I seemed to be living with, and Miss Mackay was not" (*How I Grew*, 170).

In this passage, as in a number of others in both autobiographies, McCarthy separates her childhood self into parts, suggestive of the mind-body split that so often occurs in *How I Grew*. She frequently has trouble recognizing herself in this condition. For example, she writes of herself as a public high school girl, "'I don't know that child'" (*How I Grew*, 48); however, of the existence of "*someone else* watching—what used to be called our conscience," she writes emphatically, "I believe that there is: I *know* that other person" (*How I Grew*, 104). And this strong conscience is what finally compels her to admit that she has suppressed a terrible fact about herself as a child and young adult: not only was she anti-Semitic, but this form of racism might actually have caused her to begin her career as a writer.

Reading over her earliest attempts at fiction, McCarthy half confesses that "it almost looks as if my impulse to write had had some relation to a juvenile anti-Semitic bias, to an anger which had to be directed against the Jewish quarter of me that I half-tried to disavow —a project all the more tempting in that 'it' did not show" (*How I Grew*, 102). In making this statement, with its characteristic half-revealing/half-concealing stance, McCarthy explains considerably more than she might realize: the constant worry that something hidden about her is immediately obvious to others and the far more important secret that she hoped to discover about Augusta Morganstern Preston are both connected to her youthful anti-Semitism, which has a particularly strong element of concern about physical appearance. Whether a person "looks Jewish," whether "it" shows, is an important aspect of many of her confessions on this subject.

When, in a passage cited earlier, she wrote that she was deceived by her will-less self, McCarthy is confessing to self-deception, a sin she particularly hates.

> So then did my impulse to write come out of my allowed quota of private, unvoiced anti-Semitism? I hope not. If it were true, I ought to quit writing. I prefer the explanation that a fierce dislike of self-deception had something to do with it. Moreover the nicer explanation is more convincing, I am relieved to see, in that self-deception remains, in my book, a major sin or vice whereas

any dislike of Jews I had as a girl has been, let us say, pretty well sublimated. [*How I Grew*, 103–4]

Not only is this an odd confession, turning self-deception into a mortal sin and reducing anti-Semitism to a minor infraction, but it is also especially revealing of the contrariness of the author's moral stances. For in her conscience, unlike the usual Freudian psychological model, what is remembered rather than what is suppressed is a sign of the most extreme guilt:

> When you have committed an action that you cannot bear to think about, that causes you to writhe in retrospect, do not seek to evade the memory: *make* yourself relive it, confront it repeatedly over and over, till finally, you will discover, through sheer repetition it loses its power to pain you. It works, I guarantee you, this sure-fire guilt-eradicator, like a homeopathic medicine—like in small doses applied to like. It works, but I am not sure that it is a good thing. . . . To flinch from such memories, simply suppress them, might have been healthier. Is it right to overcome self-disgust? [*How I Grew*, 156]

Again, McCarthy's life story suggests that, for her, what is on the surface can be as revealing as what is buried in layers of consciousness. Her objection to Richard Wright's inventing a self to live up to is actually a reflection of an innate desire to keep her own methods hidden. Like Wright's, McCarthy's life has been a constant effort to create separate identities, based, not on the suppression of negative qualities of the old self, but on deliberately exaggerated versions of the self planted by a highly self-conscious mind set on repeating youthful sins until they no longer have the power to cause guilt.

Although McCarthy seems sincerely to believe that her juvenile anti-Semitism has been sublimated, it actually appears as a regular motif in both autobiographies. She asks the reader directly not to "think that our school was anti-Semitic" because she remembers "the position was more delicate than that" (*How I Grew*, 103), but she is not persuasive and does not seem to see that delicacy in racism is not necessarily a positive quality. The McCarthy of *Memories*—who confesses to what she calls "a curious attitude" toward Jewishness in which "the crudest anti-Semitism ('Ikey-Mose-Abie,' I used to chant, under my breath, to myself in the convent) mingled with infatuation and with genuine tolerance and detachment" (*Memories*, 211)—becomes even more overtly anti-Jewish in *How I Grew*. She describes

Jewish acquaintances as "hook-nosed" (*How I Grew*, 103), with "frizzy

hair and pouting lips" (*How I Grew*, 216); she believes the reader will
be as startled as she is at the sudden recollection about her first high
school crush—"*Larry Judson was Jewish*" (*How I Grew*, 45). In college,
she confesses, her group's shock over discovering that a classmate was
Jewish causes the adult author much remorse: "Our mass refusal to
believe that she was Jewish made us look like a bunch of anti-Semites;
the common memory of that was an embarrassment. Who would not
feel the need to separate after such an experience?" (*How I Grew*, 217).

All of this confession resonates with a strange tone. Are these the
confessions of a woman so sure of herself, so convinced that she is not
now anti-Semitic, that she can casually repeat the anti-Semitism of her
youth? Or are these the remarks of an adult who still does not realize
the depth of her feelings about Jews? As a young woman, Mary Mc-
Carthy had a major break in her friendship with Hannah Arendt over
the following careless pro-Hitler remark: "She felt really sorry for
Hitler, he didn't know what was happening to him, he expected the
Jews to love him," a statement that Brock Brower in "Mary McCarthyism" describes as characteristic of McCarthy's "*enfant-terrible*
role."[70]

Her ambivalent attitude about anti-Semitism becomes particularly
important in regard to her grandmother's Jewishness, a subject about
which she practiced a severe form of mental reservation:

> It was as though I had forgotten the flock of Morgensterns in my
> family tree; out of sight, out of mind. By senior year this had
> changed. Doubtless the rise of Hitler had something to do with
> it. By senior year I was well aware of having a Jewish grand-
> mother and aware of it—let me be blunt—as something to hide. I
> excused myself by saying to my conscience that I could not fight
> on all fronts at once. [*How I Grew*, 217]

Not acknowledging publicly that her own grandmother was Jewish
became a particular intellectual problem when the author made
friends with a Jewish woman named Frani Blough. Blough's plans to
visit McCarthy's family in Seattle raised the worry that

> if she recognized my grandmother's Jewish traits—assuming
> they *were* recognizable—she would wonder at my never having
> mentioned that detail in the whole course of our friendship. . . .
> It would be useless to plead that the subject had never happened
> to come up, that if I had been asked, I would have told, which

was true: I would not have gone so far as to deny Augusta Preston, or, rather, her Jewishness, outright, like Peter in the garden.
[*How I Grew*, 219]

In this confession, as throughout both *Memories of a Catholic Girlhood* and *How I Grew*, Mary McCarthy presents for public consump-
tion her most private sins in a display of candor that simultaneously
reveals and conceals. She constantly claims that she wishes to hide the
very sins she tells us about in blunt detail, just as she proclaims her
hatred of her school nickname while unconsciously revealing how
much, even as an adult, as this country's most celebrated woman of
letters, she still would give to find out what it meant.

"Are You Now or Were You Ever?"

Everyone's memory is tricky and mine's a little trickier than most.—Lillian Hellman

When Mary McCarthy publicly named Lillian Hellman a liar, the resulting lawsuit seemed to suggest that the distinction between autobiographical truth and legal truth could be sustained in a courtroom. McCarthy's charge—which came in January 1980 in response to Dick Cavett asking her which writer she thought to be overrated—was, "I said in some interview that every word she writes is a lie, including 'and' and 'the.'"[1] Hellman responded with a lawsuit charging McCarthy with defamation. Although Hellman died before this legal dispute came to court, the initial victory was hers, for Justice Harold Baer ruled that McCarthy's motion to dismiss the suit on the grounds that her statements were expressions of opinion about a public figure was invalid. Judge Baer ruled that the strong statements seemed to fall "on the actionable side of the line . . . outside what has come to be known as the 'market place of ideas.'"[2]

The Lillian Hellman-Mary McCarthy feud is in several ways emblematic of the moral position each has taken toward lying and personal identity. When asked a question similar to the one Dick Cavett posed to McCarthy, Hellman replied that she did not want to talk about other writers because they have enough difficulties without her adding to them, an echo of her famous refusal before the House Committee on Un-American Activities (HCUA) to name names.[3] And yet her insistence on pursuing an expensive lawsuit because of McCarthy's half-serious remarks is characteristic both of her lifelong habit of taking the romantic moral stance—what Hellman calls "the honor child stuff" and often mocks in her memoirs—along with her predilection for engaging in lawsuits against those she thought of as enemies. Hellman was, for instance, one of four people who brought suit against Richard Nixon to produce the Watergate tapes.[4]

On the other hand, McCarthy's stand is revelatory of a history of anti-Hellman remarks, including her statement that the Hellman-written propaganda film *North Star* was "a tissue of falsehood woven of every variety of untruth."[5] In a 1946 review of Eugene O'Neill's *The Iceman Cometh*, McCarthy lumped Hellman with George Kaufman, Clifford Odets, and William Saroyan as writers of "oily virtuosity," and in a more recent interview with her brother Kevin, she

attacked Hellman for questioning in a talk to students at Sarah Lawrence College in 1948 John Dos Passos's political motives during the
Spanish civil war.[6]

In his published plea for a reconciliation of the two writers, Norman Mailer expresses the distinction between McCarthy and Hellman
in terms of honesty and identity. "To say that Lillian Hellman is dishonest is blarney," begins Mailer; "she was the only artist of the 1950's
whose remark before the House Committee on Un-American Activities is unforgettable. . . . She was also saying, by the force of her person and her work: 'Forget identity. You have it or you don't. There is
only honor, or lack of honor.'" Turning to McCarthy, Mailer remarks,
"McCarthy's work has been a constant illustration to us that honor is
a pose, a kind of scaffolding for identity."[7] Although clearly on Hellman's side, Mailer is perceptive in showing that McCarthy's claim was
spoken in the Irish spirit of blarney, a kind of overstated boasting
far different from lying. Mailer is really arguing that these two mem-
oirists approach memory from different perspectives. For McCarthy,
the whole idea of honor *is* a pose, which is not to say that she is dis-
honorable. As I argued in chapter 5, McCarthy's characteristic way of
using lies to get at her personal version of the truth about herself
consists of living up to a pose, building an identity.

In contrast, Lillian Hellman's emphasis on honor over identity as
something one either has or does not have reflects her basic orientation toward moral issues. In *Pentimento*, she expresses an early liberal
belief in environment over heredity to Caroline Ducky, one of several
black women from whom Hellman's moral code ultimately derives.
She asserts that her cousin Willy could not have possessed certain
traits at birth, to which Caroline Ducky replies, "That ain't early, the
day you push out, that's late."[8] Discussing Clifford Odets's testimony
before the HCUA in *Scoundrel Time*, Hellman again stresses innate
honor over created identity: "It's all been decided so long ago, when
you are very young, all mixed up with your childhood's definition of
pride or dignity" (*Three*, 664).

In comprehending Mary McCarthy, we are most successful when
we use her terms, when we join her search for identity and approach
her autobiography armed with Paul John Eakin's injunction: "Autobiography is better understood as a ceaseless process of identity formation in which new versions of the past evolve to meet the constantly changing requirements of the self in each successive present."[9]
But Lillian Hellman is a different person, and her autobiographical
personality is best understood by adopting her typical approach. For
Hellman, explaining the discrepancies in one's life by carefully modi-

fying over time is too easy. Hellman would not agree with Thomas Pynchon's claim that

> we can justify any apologia simply by calling life a successive re-
> jection of personalities. No apologia is any more than a romance
> —half a fiction—in which all the successive identities taken on
> and rejected by the writer as a function of linear time are treated
> as separate characters. The writing itself even constitutes another
> rejection, another "character" added to the past. So we do sell
> our souls: paying them away to history in little installments. It
> isn't so much to pay for eyes clear enough to see past the fiction
> of continuity, the fiction of cause and effect, the fiction of a hu-
> manized history endowed with "reason."[10]

For Hellman, selling our souls is too much to pay, is too much an
apologia that costs too much in moral interest. Instead, she demonstrates repeatedly that for her the rejection of "the fiction of continuity" is best achieved, not by life charged on the installment plan, but
by life charged with its most passionate meaning through repeated
presentations of self in contradictory stories whose lack of coherence
or reason parallels life's patterns. Never mind that the individual
memoirs contain contradictions or that in each successive memoir inconsistencies exist. As Linda Wagner-Martin argues, "Clearly, Hellman is using the process of autobiography both to explore her memories and to challenge the notion that recollection is a means to truth
(or, in the words of James Olney, autobiography is a 'monument of
the self as it is becoming')."[11]

Instead of using a technique such as McCarthy's made-identity, invented by the adult to explain her childhood to herself, Lillian Hellman's approach has been to thwart the process of identity formation
deliberately. Instead of arriving at the end of the autobiographical act
with the most current version of herself, she reverses the progression,
beginning with an "unfinished" self and ending with "maybe," moving, not toward a monument, but toward the destruction of a monument. Hellman's pattern—yes, no, maybe so—is constantly reflected
by her persona's movement, not toward a sense of reconciliation, of
having finally gotten down in writing what happened, but increasingly toward a conviction that, as she writes about her memories in
the introduction to *Three* (the collected and annotated version of *An
Unfinished Woman*, *Pentimento*, and *Scoundrel Time*), "Often parts of
them now seem to have been written by a woman I don't know very
well" (*Three*, 9). Hellman's sense of a discontinuity between her then
current self and the self who wrote her autobiographies is similar to

Florida Scott-Maxwell's assertion, toward the end of her life: "It has taken me all the time I've had to become myself, yet now that I am old there are times when I feel I am barely here, no room for me at all."[12]

Where McCarthy's method of self-presentation is identity continually refined in each revision, for Hellman the more natural method, as Wagner-Martin explains, is refraction: "We are forced to look at Hellman differently in each episode."[13] Her four autobiographical books are neither chronological nor of the same tone.

In addition to their literary fight, McCarthy and Hellman are linked in other ways. For instance, Elizabeth Janeway says of them, "These writers base their interpretations of women's needs and desires on standards that are essentially masculine, even if they are not conventionally so." Patricia Spacks is more accurate in linking the two as being set apart from other women because of their success in traditionally masculine-dominated worlds. Spacks describes their essential differences in terms that echo Mailer's: "McCarthy, using her artistry to understand her experience; Lillian Hellman, defining a heroism of endeavour."[14]

Where McCarthy avoids generic labels by calling her personal narratives *Memories of a Catholic Girlhood* and *How I Grew*, Hellman introduces a complication through her subtitles. *An Unfinished Woman* is "A Memoir," *Pentimento* is called "A Book of Portraits," and she refers to these two works plus *Scoundrel Time* as "memoir books" in *Maybe*, which is subtitled "A Story." Like McCarthy, she added italicized comments when her personal narratives were republished, leaving the original text alone. "I did not make changes in the books, although I was often tempted, because alteration seemed a kind of cheating" (*Three*, 5). In interviews, she insisted that she had not written autobiography. Of *An Unfinished Woman*, she has said, "No, no, it's not an autobiography at all. I've chosen the word memoir . . . because I couldn't find any other word that seemed to me right for it," an idea echoed in a later interview with Jan Albert where she says she has not written autobiography because "the word autobiography should be about yourself and have some space control."[15]

Hellman's four autobiographical books are actually hybrids of several forms of life-writing. The traditional distinction between autobiography and memoir is expressed by Roy Pascal, who admits that "no clear line can be drawn."

There is no autobiography that is not in some respects a memoir, and no memoir that is without autobiographical information; both are based on personal experience, chronological, and reflective. But there is a general difference in the direction of the au-

thor's attention. In the autobiography proper, attention is focused on the self, in the memoir or reminiscence on others.[16]

To the extent that her books focus on others, she has written memoirs, but memoirs with an individual twist. The traditional memoir is
often written by a less famous person who tells what it was like to have
been an observer of the famous. For this reason, political memoirs are
common. As Pascal explains, "When the author enters into the complex world of politics, he appears as only a small element, fitting into a
pattern . . . aware of a host of personalities and forces around him."[17]
But Hellman's focus is frequently the reverse; she is the famous person observing a series of obscure lives—relatives like Bethe, Willy,
Aunts Jenny and Hannah, and people not normally celebrated such as
Sophronia Mason, Helen Jackson, Jimsie, Caroline Ducky, Arthur
Cowan, and Sarah Cameron. Richard Poirier's introduction to *Three*
calls the book "essays in recollection" and "a gallery of people nearly
anonymous" (*Three*, viii).

Of her four autobiographies, *Scoundrel Time* is the more traditional
memoir in that it focuses on the famous with emphasis on an important historical moment, and yet it is hardly that simple since it does
not concentrate merely on the external. According to Marcus Bilson, the distinction between autobiography and memoir is not the
outward or inward focus of narration but "the length of time of the
narration and the dynamic nature of the author's represented self."[18]
Bilson's extended explanation brings us back to the problem of Hellman's presentation of self that, I believe, separates her from McCarthy. According to Bilson:

> In the autobiography, the self is a kinetic entity, always changing
> and evolving in a highly self-aware manner toward a goal or a
> sense of identity. . . . When the self stops changing and growing,
> an autobiography is over, and if the narrative continues, as Ben
> Franklin's does, a memoir begins, for the self represented is then
> a static being, no longer acting or acted upon in order to present
> the story of that self's growth.[19]

Although *Scoundrel Time* partly satisfies this definition, the book
does not remain firmly in the world of memoir because, for one reason, Hellman continues to discuss her changing opinion of her role in
the HCUA hearings. She refers to those hearings throughout *Pentimento*, especially in the chapter called "Dashiell Hammett," and in the
italicized defense of the charges that she was "pro-Stalinist," a defense

that was added between chapters 12 and 13 of *An Unfinished Woman* when this work was reprinted in *Three*. That she chose to place her defense to charges brought against *Scoundrel Time* within *An Unfinished Woman* is suggestive of her sense of self in flux, as is the statement on the final page of *Three*: "I am angrier now than I hope I will ever be again; more disturbed now than when it all took place" (*Three*, 726). Although *Scoundrel Time* is the most memoirlike of her books, its emphasis is, finally, not on Joseph McCarthy nor on Richard Nixon, not on the historic figures that usually delineate a memoir, but on herself, especially her loss of faith in liberalism because of what she saw as the failure of many intellectuals, particularly liberal anti-Communists, to act with honor.

An *Unfinished Woman* begins as classic autobiography, with the traditional recitation of the author's time and place of birth, parents' backgrounds, and childhood memories, all told in a straightforward chronological fashion. But the narrative is broken in chapter 8 with the introduction of large sections taken, apparently unedited, from diaries. Frequently Hellman comments on the diary entries, using brackets and dates to distinguish her words as they were originally recorded and as updated in 1968. In an italicized comment added to *Three*, she admits that the diary sections are sometimes false because they exclude the passion she felt, and yet she leaves them in because their falseness tells another kind of truth: she knew that they were false when she first entered them during the Spanish civil war but came to believe that they represented a lack of passion common to her generation's writing about Spain. By extension, they have come to suggest one explanation for multiple examples of failure to recognize fascism—on her part and on the part of others—in Germany, Spain, Russia, and America.

The testimony of later diaries and notebooks is often undercut. Hellman repeatedly asserts that the passion she felt—for Raya, her Russian translator-guide, and for an unnamed state department man whom she met during her visits to hospitals—is left out of the factual accounts recorded in various diaries. Further confusing the issue of genre, a number of accounts of her trips to Spain and Russia were published previously, sometimes as reportage, other times as stories.[20]

If the first two-thirds of *An Unfinished Woman* is autobiography supplemented by modified diary entries, the last third consists of what she refers to in *Pentimento* as portraits. "Dorothy Parker," "Helen," and "Dashiell Hammett" are biography, rather than autobiography, although the Hammett piece was originally called a memoir.[21] Like a traditional biographer, Hellman uses letters, newspaper clippings, magazine pieces, personal interviews, her own diaries and those of others, and her writer's book. Yet her choice of subjects (often obscure people about whom facts are impossible to obtain, for whom a logical story is impossible to tell), her constant admission that she is doubtful of the authenticity of her portraits, and the fact that each of her subjects is intimately related to her—all of these facts turn her biographies into partial autobiographies. Richard Poirier remarks that one of her favorite stories was Melville's "Bartleby the Scrivener," and Hellman, while a student at Columbia University, once contemplated writing a biography of Melville (*Three*, xx). Like the lawyer-narrator of "Bartleby," Hellman combines story, biography, autobiography, memoir, and obituary into a personal form of life-writing that best exposes the enigmatic nature of both life and the attempt to record it. Like this narrator, her frustration in putting life onto paper tells as much about the biographer as about the subject.

Like Gertrude Stein's, Hellman's autobiographical writing has produced a public protest, followed by a series of manifestos labeling the author a liar. Although many of her detractors have attacked with the quasi-legal tone common to the attacks on Stein, the extraliterary problems of her testimony before the HCUA and her lawsuit with McCarthy are complicating factors in Hellman's case. It is one thing to use the art of rhetoric in autobiography, another to lie in a courtroom. Had the McCarthy-Hellman suit been brought to trial, one wonders about the possibilities of calling literary critics to testify. Imagine what the HCUA, including future autobiographer Richard Nixon, would have made of Paul John Eakin's assertion that "twentieth-century autobiographers . . . readily accept the proposition that fiction and the fiction-making process are a central constituent of the truth of any life as it is lived and of any art devoted to the presentation of that life."[22]

The attacks on Hellman's veracity began with Martha Gellhorn's article "On Apocryphism" in the *Paris Review*, which argues that "apocryphal stories . . . among friends" are understandable and acceptable but that putting such stories into print after all witnesses to the apocryphal incident are dead is dangerously unfair. Gellhorn illustrates her argument with a lengthy rebuttal to both Hellman's *An Unfinished Woman* and Stephen Spender's interview on the art of poetry, which had appeared in a previous number of the *Paris Review*.[23] That Spender is included in Gellhorn's article is interesting since he is among those who have attacked Hellman's portrait of Julia in *Pentimento* as being, not only fictional, but also based on the life of Muriel Gardiner, author of an autobiography named *Code Name "Mary."*[24]

According to Hellman's biographer, William Wright, Mary McCarthy was responsible for pointing out to Gellhorn and Spender a number of discrepancies in *Pentimento*.

Samuel McCracken's "'Julia' and Other Fictions by Lillian Hellman," published in *Commentary*, is a lengthy argument that Julia is based on Gardiner, that Hellman's memoirs are so inaccurate that they have resulted in a minor "contaminating effect on our knowledge of our times," an effect made more important because the treatment of the issue of her lying "will tell us a good deal about the health, intellectual no less than moral, of our literary establishment."[25] Sidney Hook devotes a full chapter to Hellman, called "The Scoundrel in the Looking Glass," in his *Philosophy and Public Policy*, charging that in her memoirs "Lillian Hellman is an eager but unaccomplished liar" whose books are "a compound of falsity and deliberate obfuscation."[26]

Straightforward though these charges are, Hilton Kramer's attack is even more direct. In "The Life and Death of Lillian Hellman," which sounds like the title of a biography, he asserts that she is more than "a false and self-serving witness." For Kramer, "she stands exposed as a shameless liar" whose *Scoundrel Time* is "one of the most poisonous and dishonest testaments ever written by an American author," who "profoundly . . . misrepresented, distorted, and ignored the truth in writing the autobiographical trilogy" that he repeatedly refers to as "so-called memoirs." For Kramer, the book reviews of Hellman's autobiographies, along with the politically and personally motivated writing against Hellman by such authors as William Phillips, Diana Trilling, and William F. Buckley, plus the arguments and charges by Gellhorn, Gardiner, Spender, and McCracken constitute "a sweeping exposé of the falsehoods that formed the very fabric of Hellman's autobiographical writings."[27] Kramer's final judgment is that "the 'memoirs' that brought her wealth, fame, and honors of every sort are now shown to have been a fraud."[28] His charges stem partially from his lack of understanding of autobiographical truth and his confusion of the interrelated terms fiction, nonfiction, memoir, and autobiography.

That her attackers have made confusing claims is clear from a look at the key words in their attacks: Gellhorn sees Hellman as an apocryphiar, Spender thinks she is guilty of being a fiction writer and a plagiarist, and Kramer and Hook and the other right-wing anti-Communists escalate the literary charges one turn by naming her a liar and a perjurer. In contrast, left-wing anti-Communists with literary roots, such as Diana Trilling, correctly see part of the conflict as a problem in defining literary, rather than political, terms. Trilling writes of *Scoundrel Time*, "A narrative that should have commanded attention as a work of autobiography, one among several volumes in which Miss Hellman, an imaginative writer of established gift, looks back upon her past, is being read as a political revelation innocent of bias."[29] Throughout her counterargument, Diana Trilling—who also cites such literary sources as Lionel Trilling's introductions to his novel *The Middle of the Journey* and to Isaak Babel's stories—bases her remarks on the assumption that *Scoundrel Time* should be treated within its literary genre, "if Miss Hellman's narrative is to be properly assessed as historical reporting."[30]

Distinctions between historical reporting and personal narrative, as well as between true and false, fiction and nonfiction, and even fictive and fictitious fiction, are inherently complicated, even without reversals of previous political positions, the encroachment of time, the deliberate and accidental falsity of memory, and the differing requirements of veracity in various genres when seen from different points of view. Hellman writes halfway through *Maybe*: "It goes without saying that in their memoirs people should try to tell the truth as they see it or else what's the sense? Maybe time blurs or changes things for them. But you try, anyway."[31] But this assertion of trustworthiness—which includes a rhetorical appeal to veracity by admitting the possibility of failure of execution of the intention to tell the truth—occurs within a book that is labeled "A Story" and is printed in italics as an addition, in a manner similar to McCarthy's habit of adding italicized alterations to her text. *Maybe*'s generic situation is further confused by the book's physical appearance; the standard paperback edition continues the color scheme of *Three*—black cover, title in gold accented with red stripes—making *Maybe* seem to be part of the same package. Hellman posits her attempt at telling the truth in her autobiographical trilogy as being different from what she has done in *Maybe*:

> In the three memoir books I wrote, I tried very hard for the truth. I did try, but here I don't know much of what really happened and never tried to find out. In addition to the ordinary deceptions that you and others make in your life, time itself makes time fuzzy and meshes truth with half truth. But I can't seem to say it right. I am paying the penalty, I think, of a childish belief in absolutes, perhaps an equally childish rejection of them all. I guess I want to say how inattentive I was—most of us, I guess—to the whole damned stew. . . .

What I have written is the truth as I saw it, but the truth as
I saw it, of course, doesn't have much to do with the truth.
[*Maybe*, 50–51]

Hellman's admission of special doubt about her subjective version
of the truth versus the absolute truth of "what really happened" and
her distinction between the first three books and the last, in terms of
degree of congruence between "history" and "personal history," are
both unnecessary, according to Bilson, who persuasively argues that
all memoirs are subjective:

> The memorialist's real intention, despite all claims to being an
> objective observer, is to use this source for subjective ends—to
> embody his own moral vision of the past. It is not the memorial-
> ist's desire to present men and events as they were (although he
> invariably thinks he is doing so), but rather to represent them as
> they appeared to him, as he experienced them, and as he remem-
> bered them. The three verbs—"appear," "experience," and "re-
> member"—all involve the element of human subjectivity in per-
> ception and concomitantly the possibility of human error. The
> modern historian constantly wages a battle against such subjec-
> tivity and the possibility of error, however unsuccessfully: such
> a battle is a mandatory part of the methodology of his discipline.
> On the other hand, the memorialist accepts quite freely the sub-
> jectivity of his own perception as the *sine qua non* of his work;
> without it, his work would have little interest or meaning; it
> would not be memoir.[32]

Armed with the assumption that Lillian Hellman's four autobiographical works are literary documents, works of art that combine a
variety of life-writing's forms (autobiography, biography, memoir,
and diary), we can begin to analyze the contentions of her most an-
tagonistic critics that she is, at best, a tricky and disingenuous simpli-
fier, at worst, a fraudulent liar. The major charges against her autobiographies can be summarized as follows: she obscures her life by
chronological discontinuity and a tendency toward reticence; she lies
by omission because of her elliptical style and her too meticulous attention to surface finish; she is falsely modest and naive, manipulating
her position in history so that her political faults are diminished, her
personal heroism augmented; she misrepresents her historical position in terms of the HCUA and the split between anti-Communists
and anti-anti-Communists; and, most damning, she makes herself
look heroic by claiming to aid Julia when actually she took the idea for

Julia from another person's life. Although at times in her autobiographies Hellman is wrongheaded, inaccurate, less than forthcoming, misleading, annoyingly moralistic, and exasperatingly mean spirited, her autobiographies are ultimately exceptionally authentic portraits of America's greatest woman playwright, a woman whose life story has significance far beyond its literal events.

Because her major adverse critics have been political analysts, writing with a historian's approach, rather than literary critics well versed in contemporary autobiographical theory, her autobiographical writing has generally been misinterpreted, primarily because those who have criticized her have misunderstood her tone, failed to consider her four books as one unit, and overlooked the subtitles of her autobiographical performances. Those who have written favorably of Hellman's memoirs are primarily novelists and playwrights such as Marsha Norman, who says of Hellman, "I am not interested in the degree to which she told the literal truth. The literal truth is, for writers, only half the story."[33]

An Unfinished Woman

You are a gallant little liar. And I thank you for it.—Kurt Müller, *Watch on the Rhine*

Like Gertrude Stein in *The Autobiography of Alice B. Toklas*, Hellman reveals exactly what she means by her title, *An Unfinished Woman*, in the last sentences of her book: "I do regret that I have spent too much of my life trying to find what I called 'truth,' trying to find what I called 'sense.' I never knew what I meant by truth, never made the sense I hoped for. All I mean is that I left too much of me unfinished because I wasted too much time. However" (*Three*, 300). A number of readers have thought of the word *unfinished* in terms of such missing parts of the author's life as her testimony before the HCUA, her days in the theater, or the personal relationships she eventually covered in *Pentimento* and *Maybe*. In fact, large periods of her life are not included in this first book: 1931–35, 1942–44, and 1945–65. Others, praising her candor, have taken unfinished as a synonym for unvarnished, the direct statements of an author who, unlike Mary McCarthy, never went to finishing school. But for some, exemplified most strongly by Martha Gellhorn, unfinished is more properly a polite way of saying incomplete, inaccurate, and untrustworthy.

Gellhorn's lengthy diatribe appears in a section of the *Paris Review* labeled "Guerre de Plume" that features attacks and rebuttals. In general, Gellhorn's argument proceeds in two ways: first, a detailed, point-by-point refutation of virtually everything Hellman wrote about the Spanish civil war and Hemingway, who had of course been Gellhorn's husband, and, second, witty, often bitterly humorous, ad hominem attacks on the Hellman persona. Gellhorn's arguments against the Hellman of *An Unfinished Woman* are really expressions of a personal dislike, compounded by a misreading of the tone of the memoirs. For example, Gellhorn begins, "Goodness to Betsy . . . what an *important* lady. How marvelous for Miss Hellman to be Miss Hellman." Later she remarks, cruelly, "If Miss Hellman's beauty had matched her brains she would have been a more cuddly personality."[34]

The main thrust of Gellhorn's argument is that Hellman is an apocryphiar because most of the events she describes—dinners with Hemingway and others, air raids in Spain—could never have taken place. As proof, Gellhorn offers page after page of "documentation." She has checked newspapers, her own diaries, letters, and other sources and believes that Hellman's books are fabrications designed to make her presence in Spain seem important and noble. Unlike Carlos Baker's biography of Hemingway, which Gellhorn calls "The King James Version," Hellman's account is a confusion and distortion of the record. Throughout her own essay, however, Gellhorn reveals discrepancies between various newspaper accounts about the degree of danger or the numbers of bombs. She has checked the Society for Cultural Relations with the USSR in London—"ah research, research," she notes—and claims that Hellman could not have seen *Hamlet* in Moscow in 1937. But no amount of research is free of error. According to William Wright, McCarthy's research contradicts Gellhorn's in terms of the itinerary of the old *de Grasse*, the ship on which Hellman claims she brought Julia's body home.[35]

Much of Gellhorn's argument is based on differences between *An Unfinished Woman* and *Pentimento* in terms of dates and places. Before her attack is over, Gellhorn claims that Spender is also an apocryphiar, as well as all Hemingway scholars, and, finally, Hemingway himself, who "became a shameful embarrassing apocryphiar about himself."[36] Although Gellhorn's article might be dismissed as the bitter remarks of a woman with an obvious bias, both her ideas and her research methods have been taken over by others, such as Samuel McCracken and Hilton Kramer, in defense of Mary McCarthy in her charge that Lillian Hellman was a liar.

Stephen Spender refutes the Gellhorn attack by arguing directly, "I am sorry that Martha Gellhorn is having trouble with her memory.

. . . However, she should not exploit her oblivion for the purpose of calling me a liar." Spender adds that although Gellhorn was generally mistaken, probably unintentionally, he had in one case conflated one date with another.[37] A defense for Hellman, however, is more complex. Hellman prefaces the reprinted version of *An Unfinished Woman* with this explanation: "*What a word is truth. Slippery, tricky, unreliable. I tried in these books to tell the truth. I did not fool with facts. But, of course, that is a shallow definition of the truth. I see now, in rereading, that I kept much from myself, not always, but sometimes*" (*Three*, 9). The words "fool with facts" are ambiguous; they could mean, "I didn't deliberately alter any facts so far as I'm aware" or, alternately, "I didn't bother to check up on facts, to worry much about exactness of date and location." This last sense is echoed by her later comments in the "Dashiell Hammett" portrait:

> Thirty years is a long time, I guess, and yet as I come now to write about them the memories skip about and make no pattern and I know only certain of them are to be trusted. I know about that first meeting and the next, and there are many other pictures and sounds, but they are out of order and out of time, and I don't seem to want to put them into place. (I could have done a research job, I have on other people, but I didn't want to do one on Hammett, or to be a bookkeeper of my own life.) [*Three*, 279]

Actually, Hellman is misleading here. Although she has certainly not attempted scholarly research appropriate to a professional biographer—the kind of meticulous historical research that filled her notebooks for *Watch on the Rhine*—she did take two trips to Russia in preparation for writing *An Unfinished Woman.* For the portrait of Hammett, she wrote to eleven people who were with him in the Aleutians; of the eight who answered, seven claimed that he was in places he never could have been at times that are, in Hellman's words, "checkably inaccurate."[38] Being checkably accurate is not the point of Hellman's books, a fact that she has never hidden. Throughout all four of her autobiographies, she constantly reminds us—as directly as McCarthy does in *Memories of a Catholic Girlhood*—that she is not striving for fidelity to fact. Her books are replete with disclaimers: "perhaps," "maybe," "'in those days' I have written, and will leave here," "that's the way I remember it," and, of course, the "however" that ends her first book. Among the many admissions of doubt about factual details, particularly important is the following disclaimer from *Maybe*, which shows that her not being a bookkeeper of her own life presents an accurate picture of what Hellman was really like:

It's no news that each of us has our own reasons for pretending, denying, affirming what was there and never there. And sometimes, of course, we have really forgotten. In my case, I have often forgotten what was important, what mattered to me most, what made me take an action that changed my life. And then, in time, people and reasons were lost in deep summer grass. I have tried to explain this, often to people who were hurt by my forgetfulness, but they do not understand, nor can I expect them to. It is not pleasant to be forgotten. By now it doesn't worry me as much, but it has changed life and taken away parts of belief I would like to have back. [*Maybe*, 64–65]

In addition to the simple problem of memory's duplicity, another answer to Gellhorn's attack is that she misunderstands Hellman's tone. In Gellhorn's reading of *An Unfinished Woman*, which parallels many other people's, Hellman is falsely noble, or excessively long suffering without noticing the plight of those around her. In short, to Gellhorn, Lillian Hellman is too much on stage: "She is the shining heroine who overcomes hardships, hunger, fear, danger—down stage center—in a tormented country."[39] Those who see the Hellman persona in these terms have failed to realize the ironic, tongue-in-cheek style that Hellman so often adopts when she tries to hide her embarrassment and ineptness and simultaneously keep up the cool, unemotional, tough-guy stance she so admired in Hammett. In a voice that is not always successful, she often pretends to be pretending, as when she opens her "biography" of Hammett by writing, "And so this will be no attempt at a biography of Samuel Dashiell Hammett, born in St. Mary's County, Maryland, on May 27, 1894" (*Three*, 276).

In one sense, she is right; the chapter that follows is not biography since it follows too closely the "Bartleby the Scrivener" pattern, focusing as much on Hellman as on Hammett. The piece in question is not really biography because it was first presented as an introduction to Hammett's collected writings and, in its appearance in *An Unfinished Woman*, it takes on many of the characteristics of an elegiac eulogy. And yet, it is biography, both because it begins with biography's customary facts about the birth of its subject and, because in writing it as she has, Hellman validates Hammett's claim that her biography of him—in a manner similar to Stein's *The Autobiography of Alice B. Toklas*—"would turn out to be the history of Lillian Hellman with an occasional reference to a friend called Hammett" (*Three*, 276).

When Hellman begins her "biography" of Hammett by asserting, "I will never write that biography because I cannot write about my closest, my most beloved friend" (*Three*, 276), she is writing both

ironically and seriously at the same time. Obviously, she is beginning that biography and echoing Stein's "lie" in referring to a lifelong lover as a "friend."

Anthony Brandt's definition of irony is particularly applicable to Hellman's use: "Irony affords a way of noticeably backing off from what one says so that it is clear that one probably doesn't mean it, at least not wholeheartedly, but that needn't mean that one means the opposite, either; in any case both parties know that what's going on superficially, in one's words, is not what's going on underneath."[40]

Gellhorn has made two errors: she confuses irony with sarcasm and fails to realize that irony, although often flippant, can be used as a rhetorical device with the most serious of purposes. Hellman's portrayal of herself in *An Unfinished Woman*, like the Henry Adams of *The Education of Henry Adams*, is of a relative failure. Much of what Gellhorn sees as boasting self-importance is actually intended to be self-deprecating. As a young girl, Hellman assimilated certain moral stances: "I was taught, also, that if you gave, you did it without piety and didn't boast about it" (*Three*, 28). This inherited trait is combined in the author with Hammett's characteristically understated code: "Hammett's form of boasting was always to make fun of trouble or pain" (*Three*, 283).

Hammett, who like Sherwood Anderson was once involved with the advertising world, summarizes his calculated, understated advertising style as follows: "Meiosis . . . has nothing to do with modesty or moderation in speech as such. . . . It is a rhetorical trick, the employment of understatement, not to deceive, but to increase the impression made on the reader or hearer. In using it the object is, not to be believed, but to be disbelieved to one's advantage."[41] Together, these related forms of inverted bragging become important ingredients in the Hellman-Hammett persona, resulting in a unique form of nonboasting about boasting, making mainly negative claims for personal bravery. Although certainly bordering on lying, particularly when used in advertising, Hellman's meiosis is intended, not to deceive, but to underplay her naturally bold personality. As Pascal tells us, in contrast to overwriting, "The untruth of under-writing is of course much more bearable, since it is allied with qualities of modesty or shyness that in their turn win our sympathy."[42]

Hellman is aware of her understating tendency: "Is it age, or was it always my nature, to take a bad time, block out the good times, until any success became an accident and failure seemed the only truth?" (*Three*, 211). But she is apparently not aware that her constant self-deprecating sometimes comes across in reverse. For instance, Gell-horn cites, as an example of Hellman's conceit, her explanation for not going to the press office in Valencia, although asked to return: "I . . . had two telephone calls . . . suggesting I come back to the office and meet people who might like to meet me," writes Hellman, "and have not gone. This is nothing new: part the need to make people come to me, part not wanting to seem important" (*Three*, 95). These words, from a diary entry written thirty-two years before publication of *An Unfinished Woman*, are included both to show her candor and to amplify the author's general presentation of herself, not as a heroic figure, but as an inept radical, unsure of how to act, but always aware of the irony of her position as an American woman playwright whose passionate antifascism constantly placed her in awkward positions near the battlefront, unable to do anything concrete to help.

"Not wanting to seem important" is followed in the passage attacked by Gellhorn with the following words that Gellhorn omitted: "But then why have I come here, what will I see, or do, what good will I be to these people as I eat their food or use their cars or lie on a bed reading Julian Green? I settle it by going for a walk" (*Three*, 95). The tone is intended half-ironically. It is the same tone used throughout Hammett's *The Thin Man*, in which Nora Charles, who was based on Lillian Hellman, is always in the way of the real detective, stumbling onto clues accidentally, solving part of the mystery while pretending to be asleep. Hellman's whole stay in Spain might, at first reading, seem nothing but a series of ineffectual dinner parties, liberal posing designed for furthering legends and generating literary materials, when actually her description is intended as an ironic depiction of her political naiveté and her personal frustration over her ineffectiveness. When, at the end of one party, she is repeatedly asked to convey the importance of the antifascist fight to the president of the United States, she replies that "it didn't matter what people like me said or thought. They were silent for a second and then a woman applauded politely and everybody went to bed" (*Three*, 100). This is not boasting; rather, it is an honest admission of her inability to affect political action, a revelation of her inefficacy, punctuated by the unenthusiastic clapping of a single person.

Throughout *An Unfinished Woman*, Hellman undercuts her effectiveness through a repeated pattern of accidents and sicknesses. Ironically, she uses the traditional device of Hollywood—the twisted ankle—to signify heroism for women. Like so many movie heroines being carried, in the strong arms of a man, from burning buildings or being pulled, by a quicker, thinking man, out of quicksand, Hellman

is constantly awkward, stumbling through her autobiography, twist-
ing her ankle just at the wrong time. Her first memory, as a child,
of the persistent anger she so often attributes to herself—what other
people see as the quality that makes her a "difficult woman"—is undercut by an ankle injury: "I tried to get up from the couch, but one
ankle turned and I sat down again, knowing for the first time the
rampage that could be caused in me by anger. . . . I knew that soon
after I was moving up the staircase, that I slipped and fell a few steps"
(*Three*, 31). This episode, like so many to follow, ends in her vomiting.

Back in Spain, she records in her diary the following description of
her actions after an aerial bombardment: "(The planes had been around
all afternoon and the mess was new and looked hot.) The filthy indig-
nity of destruction, I thought, is the real immorality, as I slipped and
turned my ankle" (*Three*, 98–99). Questioned at yet another dinner
party about the passionate emotion that she had derived from her stay
in Spain—emotion that she says she had "little right to . . . from so
short and relatively safe a visit" (*Three*, 130)—she responds with the
same pattern. "My life, all I felt in Spain, is going out in drip-drops, in
nonsense, and I suddenly was in the kind of rampage anger that I have
known all my life" (*Three*, 132). As a result, she "slipped to the floor,
had a painful ankle and didn't care" (*Three*, 132). On this occasion,
her ankle is broken, and years later, en route to Moscow, she notes, "I
turned my once-broken ankle in the ice ruts" (*Three*, 141).

In addition to the constant ankle accidents, as well as many other
physical injuries, including the cut knee she received after falling from
a taxi (a story described in *Three* in the prefatory "On Reading
Again"), Hellman's picture of herself in action is often accompanied
by humiliating physical details—tears, excessive sweat, frequent diz-
ziness, and vomiting. She is constantly clumsy, falling off running
boards of cars (*Three*, 107), "falling over and over again" while walking in new boots in Moscow (*Three*, 194), stupidly giving away her
position on the Russian front line by allowing the sun to reflect off
field glasses (*Three*, 170), confessing "two minor accidents and once I
killed a rabbit" while driving home to Hollywoodland (*Three*, 70),
and always depicting herself as acting incoherently: "(As others grow
more intelligent under stress, I grow heavy, as if I were an animal on a
chain)" (*Three*, 166).

Because Hellman reminds her readers that much of her heroic
stance when faced with fear is a pretense, she signals that her frequent
clumsiness is not ironic, is not meant to glorify herself. From the first
paragraph of *An Unfinished Woman*, when she says, "Even as a small
child I disliked myself for the fear and showed off against it" (*Three*,

13), through her depiction of her generation as being "pretend cool" (*Three*, 45), to her admission that in terms of money she "cared so much, in fact, that I pretended not to care" (*Three*, 190), Lillian Hellman repeatedly undercuts the Hammettesque hard-boiled detective style so often attributed to her. Caught between the masculine standard for heroic action, especially at time of war—the Hammett-Hemingway grace under pressure—and its traditional feminine counterpart of fainting and feistiness, Hellman adopts a personal style somewhere in-between, an impassioned form of action in which, angry beyond control, she is hampered by traditional feminine physical weakness with a masculine twist, a literal turn, or trope: an ankle turned, not out of weakness, but in anger, almost deliberately, in an attempt to demonstrate her ability to fluctuate between the male and female worlds.

In *The Female Imagination*, Patricia Spacks reports that a personal visit from Hellman made students at Wellesley College nervous because "she didn't fit the established categories. If she exemplifies the possibilities of independence . . . she also suggests unexpected dangers and qualification."[43] The reaction of Spacks's students to a literal Lillian Hellman reinforces the view of the autobiographical Hellman as an antiheroic figure, who undercuts her heroism with irony and simultaneously seeks to gain the reader's admiration for her honesty. Spacks is accurate in arguing that "Hellman exemplifies in her memoir, *An Unfinished Woman*, the degree to which feminine freedom may depend on ignorance, derive from fantasy, and produce paradoxical limitations."[44]

However, I disagree with Spacks's argument that Hellman is unaware of "an ironic edge" and lacks self-understanding. Hemingway praises Hellman's determination to broadcast an antifascist appeal, despite the physical dangers, by saying, "So you have *cojones* after all" (*Three*, 112–13), which echoes Regina Giddens's famous closing lines from Hellman's *The Little Foxes*: "So you've got spirit after all. Most of the rest are made of sugar water" (*Three*, 14). These words are not, as Spacks suggests, taken wholeheartedly as a compliment. That Hellman is aware of the irony of both compliments is clear from her continued depiction of Hemingway in *An Unfinished Woman* as a poseur and from her description of her Uncle Jake, who originally spoke the lines from *The Little Foxes*, as "a man of great force, given . . . to breaking the spirit of people for the pleasure of the exercise" (*Three*, 14). Spacks continues her argument by noting of Hellman, "Her central effort has been to create, for her own benefit as well as for others, a character to meet masculine standards." Spacks concludes with the belief that "Lillian Hellman's work has been to make a self, rejecting in the process many traditional concomitants of femininity."[45]

Virtually every published interview with Hellman reports that her physical bearing was surprisingly feminine. Although she pictures her own body movements as stumbling and jerky, she is seen by others of both sexes as being, unconsciously, gracefully seductive. Jane Fonda, who plays Lillian Hellman in the movie version of the "Julia" section of *Pentimento*, describes her as "flirtatious and feminine and sensual."[46] In a *New Yorker* profile, Margaret Case Harriman says of her, "Actually Lillian Hellman is neither cute nor tough. For a woman with militant undercurrents, her surface behavior is more often mild than not, and she is genuinely feminine to a degree that borders on the wacky."[47]

In actual life, Hellman seems to have combined the apparently contradictory traits of physical gracefulness and a lack of coordination that rendered her clumsy in numerous physical activities. She is described as unable to open a safe or shoot a gun—aiming at a flying duck, she hit a wild lilac bush; aiming at a large deer right in front of her, she hit a dogwood tree behind her. Her sense of geography is often amiss, as is her sense of direction. Essential to understanding the tone of *An Unfinished Woman*, as well as her other autobiographies, is a realization of this combination of grace and awkwardness, a combination that is paralleled in Hellman's personality and that often manifests itself in an apparently boastful tone when modesty is intended, a form of self-mockery that sometimes appears to be the opposite, a character trait that renders her an unfinished, rather than a completed, woman.

Pentimento: My Julia

Harke newes, o envy, thou shalt heare descry'd
My *Julia*; who as yet was ne'r envy'd.
To vomit gall in slander, swell her vaines
With calumny, that hell it selfe disdaines,
Is her continuall practice; does her best.
          —John Donne

An Unfinished Woman is a book marked by a recurring tone of regret, an insistence on wasted energy, a series of incomplete stories that fail to fit. In the minds of those who see Lillian Hellman as a liar, her description of analysis under Gregory Zilboorg might serve to characterize the whole effort: "It seems mingy and not the whole truth" (*Three*, 226). From her perspective, the book is an unsuccessful attempt to present the whole truth; from her antagonists' point of view, however, little separates a fragmentary truth, or a half-truth, from a lie.

Pentimento, in contrast, has a positive tone. This second autobiography, which acts as the missing half of the first, or its subtext, helps to alleviate the negative tone of the initial try. *Pentimento* fills in gaps and explains reasons for their existence, although maintaining the earlier book's insistence on memory's fallibility and the impossibility of completely understanding any event. As a title, *Pentimento* is particularly apt, containing a metaphor for Hellman's autobiographical act. The book begins with an extended definition of its title:

> Old paint on canvas, as it ages, sometimes becomes transparent. When that happens it is possible, in some pictures, to see the original lines: a tree will show through a woman's dress, a child makes way for a dog, a large boat is no longer on an open sea. That is called pentimento because the painter "repented," changed his mind. Perhaps it would be as well to say that the old conception, replaced by a later choice, is a way of seeing and then seeing again. [*Three*, 309]

In using this painterly term, combined with the subtitle *A Book of Portraits*, Hellman emphasizes the biographical, rather than the autobiographical, nature of her effort. And in *Pentimento*, she has managed to produce portraits that constantly reflect on the photographer, self-portraits in a convex mirror.

Like the title *An Unfinished Woman*, which suggests getting beneath the surface, *Pentimento* invokes a sense of transparency, a revision. But as is the case with most of Hellman's work, she has used an artistic term in an individual way. In the world of art history, pentimento suggests an effort by the artist to cover up a portion of the original painting, to obliterate a mistake. The artist has "repented" in the act of creation, realized the error, and apparently hidden it from view. The discovery of pentimenti represents an invasion of the artistic process, a failure of the medium to convey the message, an accidental parallel to the use of the x-ray machine to determine a painting's authenticity.

In contrast, what Hellman has done is a kind of reverse pentimento; she has simultaneously layered old and new paint, deliberately exposed the pentimenti behind her portraits. Where a painter repents at failure and covers it up, Hellman has repented over having covered up failure. Instead of realizing an error and attempting to hide it, she has deliberately created a context in which both old and new coexist. Examples include her consistent pattern of mixed tenses, such as "the letter said, says now" (*Three*, 311), or "I thought, I think now" (*Three*, 511), and her constant use of extended parenthetical statements that undercut the sentences they follow. In one sense, Hellman's diaries and writer's book are the original works of art that over time have come to seem inaccurate—hence her frequent comments about their untrustworthiness—but the errors have been superimposed rather than composed, though sometimes one diary entry is quoted within another. Hellman's pentimento comparison is not meant to refer just to the autobiographical act; for her, pentimento becomes a metaphor for memory, an analogy to the particular difficulty of artistically remembering a life, telling the truth despite the mendacity of memory.

Hellman's particular use of pentimento as a metaphor can be more easily understood by looking at its use in the autobiographies. For instance, in her preface to *Three*, she writes, *"What didn't I see during the time of work that I now see more clearly? . . . Or what did I see in the past that I could not now duplicate?"* (*Three*, 4). A more physical pentimento occurs when, en route to Madrid, Hellman encounters a Spanish woman who examines her hair:

> "You do something to your hair?"
> "Sometimes I have it bleached."
> "What color you born with?"
> "I've forgotten. Something like this, I guess."
> She patted my hair back in place. "Soon you will need bleach."
> [*Three*, 110]

In this case, something more resembling an exact pentimento has transpired; the "original lines" have accidentally shown through, allowing the viewer to see what has deliberately been covered over.

For Hellman, who says she is frightened by old women's bones—the body's "original lines"—but is attracted to the "thin man," pentimento becomes a synonym for her memory's cross-sectioning itself:

> (It is, indeed, strange to write of your own past. "In those days" I have written, and will leave here, but I am not at all sure that those days have been changed by time. All my life I believed in the changes I could, and sometimes did, make in a nature I so often didn't like, but now it seems to me that time made alterations and mutations rather than true reforms; and so I am left

with so much of the past that I have no right to think it very different from the present.) [*Three*, 330–31]

Because her books are nonchronological, crossing and recrossing the same time period, sometimes the same events, Hellman—like the Nabokov of *Speak, Memory*, who writes, "I like to fold my magic carpet, after use, in such a way as to superimpose one part of the pattern on another"[48]—relies on documents such as her cousin Bethe's partially legible letter, its pages torn in the folds, to compose the multiple redactions. In book after book, including the author's comments and comments on comments, Hellman eventually demonstrates the pentimento of her memory. *An Unfinished Woman* acts as a pentimento for *Pentimento*, the "original lines" having been covered up in the second memoir, just as *Scoundrel Time*'s version of the HCUA's effects on Hellman's life partially covers up the earlier versions given in the first two memoirs.

Hellman's pentimento technique reaches its conclusion in *Maybe* where she repents, not that she has revealed too much in her memoirs, but that she has covered up the "original lines" too much, pretended that her memory was more precise, more trustworthy, than she now realizes:

> *The piles and bundles and ribbons and rags turn into years, and then the years are gone. There is a light behind you certainly, but it is not bright enough to illuminate all of what you had hoped for. The light seems shadowed or masked with an unknown fabric.* [*Maybe*, 42]

In this description of a veiled light, which resembles the effect of backlighting through a theater scrim, Hellman echoes Nabokov's description of the artistic duplicity of memory:

> The individual mystery remains to tantalize the memoirist. Neither in environment nor in heredity can I find the exact instrument that fashioned me, the anonymous roller that pressed upon my life a certain intrinsic watermark whose unique design becomes visible when the lamp of art is made to shine through life's foolscap.[49]

In transferring the pentimento concept from painting to writing, Nabokov emphasizes another aspect of the autobiographer's use of the painter's metaphor. For an autobiographer, the false starts and rough drafts, which sometimes become available to researchers in special collections in libraries, are something like pentimenti. But for a writer like Hellman, whose personal papers have been closed to all except her official biographer, William Abrahams, pentimento can

also be thought of in literary terms as a palimpsest, which C. Hugh Holman defines as "a writing surface . . . which has been used twice or more for manuscript purposes. . . . With material so used a second time, it frequently happened that the earlier script either was not completely erased or that, with age, it showed through the new."[50]

Compared to Martha Gellhorn's article in which she claims that Hellman is an apocryphiar, Samuel McCracken's "'Julia' and Other Fictions by Lillian Hellman," published in *Commentary*, presents a far more serious, less biased argument, which raises numerous doubts about Hellman's veracity. In McCracken's essay, he never calls her a liar. Instead, he argues that the courts will have to determine whether Mary McCarthy's famous charge is a libel. But McCracken does say that extensive research into the Hellman memoirs raises grave doubts about her credibility because "she manipulated millions of readers and moviegoers into admiring her as an ethical exemplar, and as a ruthlessly honest writer."[51]

That McCracken uses "fictions" in his title and includes moviegoers among those misled suggests an initial problem with his argument—he apparently equates fiction with lie. It is one thing to claim that "Julia" is a fiction, another to claim, as he eventually does, that Hellman has plagiarized an actual person's life. Although Hellman admits that she uses "a lot of principles of fiction" in her personal narratives, she is insistent that she did not alter essential facts and that "Julia" is a true story. The truth-value of an autobiography should be treated in one category, the purported veracity of a movie in another. Hellman argues repeatedly that she did not write the script for the motion picture, did not even realize that she would be portrayed on the screen: "I don't want to be represented on the screen as me."[52] Although this protest might at first seem falsely naive, it becomes persuasive when we realize that Paramount Studios once projected a production of the "Willy" chapter of *Pentimento* and that Diane Johnson, the novelist and biographer of Hammett, is reportedly working on a screenplay of the first three memoirs to be produced by Sydney Pollack.[53] To further complicate the separation of life and art, the play *Lillian*, based on Hellman's autobiographies, was presented on Broadway as a monologue starring Zoe Caldwell; Nick and Nora Charles, based on both Hammett and Hellman, were portrayed in a popular motion picture and a later television series; and Hellman's house in Martha's Vineyard was decorated with furniture from the sets of her plays.

Because Hellman initially transformed her personal experiences into drama—a literary form that is not susceptible to the usual fiction-nonfiction dichotomy—her dramatic story of Julia in a nonfictional memoir results in a particularly problematic situation, especially since Hellman admits that the character Kurt Müller in *Watch on the Rhine* "was, of course, a form of Julia" (*Three*, 489). Part of McCracken's confusion comes from false expectations concerning autobiography, the nature of which Paul John Eakin describes so well by using a theatrical metaphor:

> When we settle into the theater of autobiography, what we are ready to believe—and what most autobiographers encourage us to expect—is that the play we witness is a historical one, a largely faithful and unmediated reconstruction of events that took place long ago, whereas in reality the play is that of the autobiographical act itself, in which the materials of the past are shaped by memory and imagination to serve the needs of present consciousness.[54]

Basically, McCracken and others who have attacked the "Julia" section of *Pentimento* make two arguments: first, "Julia" does not ring true; and second, although Hellman may have had Julia as a childhood friend, the story in which Hellman carries money to Berlin for antifascist purposes is a fabrication because the adult Julia is actually based on an American psychoanalyst named Muriel Gardiner, whose own autobiography, *Code Name "Mary,"* recounts *her* life as an underground anti-Nazi fighter in Vienna.

The argument that the "Julia" chapter does not seem plausible is based, in McCracken's words, on the feeling that "her account of this trip rings false wherever it is struck. Almost every detail is either improbable to a degree that would disgrace a third-rate thriller, or plainly contradicted by the historical record."[55] Given the improbability of the rest of Lillian Hellman's life, including her strikingly strict moral stances throughout four autobiographies filled with gangsters, prostitutes, murderers, and the Mafia, this charge is much like the usual complaint that Hellman's plays are melodramatic.

McCracken's specific examples of unbelievable events are no more unlikely than the probability that the name Julia is that of both Hellman's mother and the murder victim in *The Thin Man* or the chance that two of Hellman's antagonists would be named McCarthy. Many of McCracken's probing questions, designed to cast doubt on Hellman's credibility, appear to be motivated by political antagonism rather than by genuine curiosity. McCracken wonders, for instance, why the mission in Berlin is overstaffed and why Julia would allow her friend Lillian to risk her life. A simple answer to these questions might

be Hellman's own description of herself while on board the train to
Berlin: "I have known since childhood that faced with a certain kind
of simple problem, I sometimes make it so complex that there is no
way out. I simply do not see what another mind grasps immediately. I
was there now" (*Three*, 411).

More typical of McCracken's questions are the following:

> If the heavier of the two women is on her way to Cologne, why
> does she stay on the train to Berlin, 250 miles beyond her stop?
> What is the significance of the box of candy, which makes re-
> peated appearances but for no apparent reason? When Miss Hell-
> man is met in Berlin, why should her welcomers loudly announce
> that she will spend a few hours with them and then leave imme-
> diately after telling her to go straight to Julia? Why is the money
> transferred in public? Why does Julia tell Miss Hellman to take
> the train for Moscow at Bahnoff Zoo, requiring her to double
> back several miles to the west and use a small station, where she
> would be more conspicuous than at a large one? When Julia tells
> Miss Hellman that her escort will be in a car to the left, how can
> she know not only the order in which various carriages would be
> cut into the long train but also whether Miss Hellman's own car-
> riage would be positioned with the corridor on the left or
> right?[56]

McCracken's questions could be answered, in addition to his own
response—"To all these questions, one might answer that truth is
stranger than fiction"—by arguing that the whole point of the "Julia"
episode is not, as her critics seem to believe, to make Lillian Hellman
into a brave, heroic, radical, risking her life for the antifascist cause.
Nearly everything in *Pentimento*, as in the other Hellman autobiographies, presents the author—whose father said she "lived within a
question mark" (*Three*, 133)—as an awkward, passionate woman,
compensating for her lack of radical commitment by romanticizing
and revering those who are able to dedicate their lives to a cause. Part
of Hellman's point is to mock her own actions by presenting them
with comic overtones. She is not a character in a spy novel; she is a
character in an autobiography who remembers the entire incident,
like so many of her stories of evil, in an ironic, half-comic way, which
is not to suggest that she is less than serious.

Hellman does not tell us why the events of Julia's story happened as
they did because she does not know why. Essential to the whole story
is her lack of understanding of what was happening. She wants to
contrast her own inept bungling—her failure to recognize how safe

she really was and her lack of a sense of direction (politically as well as geographically)—with Julia's genuine commitments and sacrifices. Julia allowed her friend to experience a safely controlled version of political espionage—a grown-up version of the *World of Henry Orient* playacting they had indulged in as girls—in an effort to spur Hellman into giving up play writing for radical action and to allow herself to say farewell to her friend and to provide a safeguard for her child.

Much of McCracken's argument is centered on inconsistencies of travel accounts and street names, both in *Pentimento* and in the earlier sections of *An Unfinished Woman* that present roughly parallel versions. His argument is based on having checked such sources as phone books, directories, archives, and Thomas Cook's *Continental Railway Timetables*. To those who knew Hellman's total lack of geographic awareness—as related in John Hersey's remark that "her chromosomes took a nap when they should have been given a sense of direction"[57] or in Dashiell Hammett's story of her repeatedly getting lost on her own Pleasantville farm—the picture of her clumsy attempt at working underground is plausible.

Why would McCracken and others work so hard to pin down specific dates and names in a book of portraits, especially given Hellman's clear warning? "I have changed most of the names," she reveals; "Whenever in the past I wrote about that journey, I omitted the story of my trip through Berlin because I did not feel able to write about Julia" (*Three*, 401). In the additions included in *Three*, she explains further that she changed street names and addresses at the suggestion of her lawyers. That she chose to present Julia in *An Unfinished Woman* as the character Alice and that Anne-Marie and Sammy of *Pentimento* are called Marie-Louise and Hal in the first book are clear indications that the authenticity of the story, what it tells us about Lillian Hellman, should not be determined by the literal accuracy of its nouns. Hellman herself admits to having accidentally confused the issue because she could no longer remember which names she changed, which are original.

Judgments of Hellman's veracity based on such details as characters's names fail to see the larger significance of the story, taken in context. McCracken is being captious when he writes, "But Miss Hellman never mentions Julia's last name, so presumably what she means is not that she has changed it but that she has suppressed it. . . . We may in any event presume that Julia is a real name since we are told that Julia described Donne's poem 'To Julia' to her."[58] Not only does the claim that Julia is Muriel Gardiner make nonsense out of the counterclaim that Julia must be a real name, but also the comment on Donne's poem and the distinction between "changed" and "suppressed" are not persuasive. For instance, Maurice Brown writes of Hellman, "At twelve she and Julia . . . formed a secret espionage society of two and took to following strange characters about the streets of New York," a report based on a story in Margaret Case Harriman's *New Yorker* profile of Hellman. Brown's inaccurate interpretation reveals how complex Hellman's use of names becomes, for the actual name of the friend in New York—who is not directly identified with Julia—is Helen Schiff.[59] And if Helen *were* Julia, then Hellman could easily have substituted Donne's "To Julia" as a disguise for Poe's "To Helen." Questioning an autobiographer's veracity because of nominal inconsistencies makes little sense when the author labels her work a portrait and warns that names have been changed, not only for protection of the innocent, but also because one of Hellman's most consistent moral positions is her repeated refusal to name names.

The second major argument, that "Julia" is based on Muriel Gardiner's autobiography, is considerably more complex. When *Pentimento* was published, Gardiner began receiving inquiries from people who assumed that she was Julia because her story is so similar. She had been an American medical student in Vienna, was both a student and a patient with Dr. Ruth Mack Brunswick, a pupil and colleague of Freud, worked underground for the Social Democrats, and eventually married Joseph Buttinger, a socialist leader and later author of *In the Twilight of Socialism*, a history of Austrian socialism in the 1930s.[60]

Gardiner wrote to Hellman, asking about the coincidences, but received no reply, which is not surprising given that her letter, however polite, implies plagiarism and includes the words, "I hope you don't find this letter an intrusion. There is no need to answer it."[61] Hellman later remarks, "Miss Gardiner may have been the model for someone else's Julia, but she was certainly not the model for my Julia."[62]

In his *Journals*, Stephen Spender makes a curiously contradictory claim about the Gardiner controversy. He first says, "Lillian Hellman's long story 'Julia' is fiction written in autobiographical form with a narrator who purports to be Hellman"; but once he has actually read *Pentimento*, he writes, "Some of the events described and the general idea . . . are presumably taken from Muriel's life, but the character bears little resemblance to Muriel."[63] Spender, who was also accused by Martha Gellhorn of being an apocryphiar, is of course a biased witness. His *Journals* are dedicated to Gardiner who was his lover in Vienna, as recorded both in Gardiner's autobiography and in his *World within World: The Autobiography of Stephen Spender*. The whole issue of names is further confused because Muriel Gardiner, known by the underground name Mary and later Elizabeth and Gerda, is called Elizabeth in Spender's autobiography. There are other discrepancies between Spender's account of his life with Gardiner and her account, including the claim in Spender's work that she had been married twice when they met, a claim that contradicts her mention of only one marriage in *Code Name "Mary."*

Though Spender only claims that Hellman fictionalizes Gardiner's life—not in itself a dishonest action, especially for a playwright whose first production, *The Children's Hour*, was based on a historic case—most damaging of all is Gardiner's research, which includes a statement from Dr. Herbert Steiner, director of the Documentation Archives of the Austrian Resistance, stressing that no records show any other American women "deeply involved in the Austrian anti-Fascist or anti-Nazi underground."[64] To this charge Hellman has answered, "Underground socialist workers don't keep archives."[65]

Because the Hellman Collection at the University of Texas has been closed to all researchers, resolving this controversy is not possible, but speculating on answers is. One immediate answer may be that Julia lied to Hellman. Another possibility is that Gardiner, Spender, and Hellman have different conceptions of what the words "deeply involved" mean. To Hellman, Julia may have seemed deeply involved, but compared to Gardiner, she may not have been, in the same way that people who thought of themselves as actively involved in the Vietnam antiwar movement would have been totally unknown by name to leaders of various factions of what is collectively called the Movement. Spender writes of his time in Vienna, "Throughout those years I had always the sense of living on the circumference of a circle at whose centre I would never be," and he mentions that those in the underground that he met called themselves by "Christian names not their own" and "had in common the kind of anonymity which casts a certain drabness over the most eccentric, when they are bound together by exile, persecution and anxiety."[66]

Gardiner, like all autobiographers, admits to memory lapses. She is not certain in which year she met Freud nor whether she actually met his mother or saw her "only in my mind's eye," although meeting Freud, not to mention his mother, would seem fairly memorable for a psychoanalyst. Gardiner remarks that she "was never really part of the psychoanalytic community until my last years in Vienna."[67] Throughout her book, she mentions that few people were aware of her involvement in underground activities and that she was constantly surprised to discover the involvement of acquaintances.

was English, she traveled under both English and American passports,
a considerable aid in moving across borders. Since Julia's mother also
married an Englishman, it is plausible that Julia was thought to be
English, thereby offering another answer as to why her name, whatever it was, was not located in a search for American women who were
underground workers.

Another explanation lies in the nature of Gardiner's politics. She
was deeply involved in *Socialist* anti-Nazi activity but highly suspi-
cious of *Communist* anti-Nazi activity, a fact that makes sense of Hellman's claim that she was reluctant to reveal Julia's name because she
was "not sure that even now the Germans like their premature anti-
Nazis" (*Three*, 401). The term *premature anti-Fascist*, or PAF, is connected, as McCracken observes, with those "associated with the *Daily
Worker* and other Communist and Pro-Communist publications."[68]
Hellman's remark also seems less facetious in light of present-day Vienna's election of Kurt Waldheim as president of Austria, despite his
having lied about his direct connection to the Holocaust. Hellman's
wariness does not seem so paranoid when we realize that, in Mary
McCarthy's short story "The Perfect Host," a semifictional McCarthy
accuses a semifictional Hellman of being a spy for the Soviet Union.[69]
Another way of explaining the whole controversy over Julia's identity,
then, might be to argue that, in a situation where names and nation-
alities are constantly being altered for reasons of politics and survival,
Gardiner either did not know that she knew Julia or was not aware of
her because Julia was working for the Communist underground to
which Gardiner was antithetic.

Yet another way, less historical and more psychological, to approach
the problem has been suggested or assumed by a number of commentators. Spender, among others, sees Hellman as writing fiction, but
apparently he overlooks the possibility that she adopted the device he
admits to using in his autobiography: "Characters like the Communist lady novelist are portrayals of types and not of real personalities."[70] Gardiner first thought Julia a composite portrait, and Hellman's portrayal of Julia as Kurt Müller in *Watch on the Rhine* opens
the possibility that the childhood friend—called Alice in *An Unfinished Woman*—and the adult Julia were two different people, one female, the other male, combined by Hellman, not just as a means of
protecting her memory and assuaging her guilt over having told Julia's story (which she believed would not have pleased her friend),

but also as a psychological projection of her lifelong need for a heroic other against which to compare her own lack of political commitment.

Indeed, Philip French, reviewing the film version of *Julia*, writes, "In the morality play that is her autobiographical trilogy, [Dashiell Hammett] exists in the same imaginative dimension as Julia, who could quite easily be a projection of Miss Hellman's fantasies. In this reading Julia would be the beautiful playmate that every lonely child creates."[71] The screenwriter for *Julia*, Alvin Sargent, refers to the title character as "a memory, even an idea," and film critic Marc Green calls her "the nearly mythic Julia," echoing Vanessa Redgrave's remark that Julia is "an obscured character whom you can just catch through the varnish and smoke, but you only perceive outlines and contours."[72]

McCracken observes that "readers of a Freudian bent" will have much to make of the fact that "having inserted Alice/Julia into the narrative of her own life, Miss Hellman kills her off—in *An Unfinished Woman* in 1934, in *Pentimento* four years later (after first mutilating her by the loss of a leg)."[73] One of those who have seen "Julia" in Freudian terms is Alexander Cockburn who notes that the Julia controversy reminded him of yet another wealthy American woman connected to Freud and involved with rescuing political refugees from the Nazi *Anschluss* in Vienna—the poet H. D. As Janice Robinson notes in her biography of Hilda Doolittle, "H. D.'s whole orientation during the thirties had been antifascist, antitotalitarian, and anti-Hitler."[74] Robinson notes of H. D. and her lover, Bryher (Winifred Ellerman):

> Since the beginning of the 1920s both she and Bryher had been seriously concerned with the international political climate. . . . As the heiress of [Sir John Ellerman's] fortune in 1933, Bryher inherited the responsibility of directing funds to appropriate channels. H. D.'s 1933 and 1934 letters to Bryher reveal that a significant portion of her analytical hours with Freud were devoted to discussing the financing of the Jewish emigration, which Freud helped to coordinate and Bryher helped to pay for. As the political situation deteriorated, Bryher was actively involved in helping Jews cross the border from Germany to Switzerland.[75]

Although Bryher was British, H. D. was an American, and together they constitute another indication that Gardiner was not aware of everyone working underground against the Nazis. Neither Bryher nor H. D. appear in *Code Name "Mary,"* even though Bryher's autobiography, *A Heart to Artemis*, published in 1962, reports her presence in

Vienna. Cockburn's argument is not that Julia was Bryher or H. D. or some combination of the two, though he might be interested to know that H. D.'s name in her self-described roman à clef, *Bid Me to Live*, is Julia.[76] Instead, Cockburn remarks, "It seems to me that much of *Pentimento* is fantasy, in the respectable creative sense of an imaginative working of biographical material. 'Julia' is an amalgam of both sexual and heroic fantasies in which Hellman assumes the role of H. D. (her beautiful polar opposite) and renders Gardiner/Bryher as Julia but appropriates some of Julia's heroism for herself."[77] Cockburn's theory is a validation of Mary Mason's argument that women autobiographers develop self-identity primarily through their relationships with others, a theory applied specifically to Hellman by Marcus Bilson and Sidonie Smith.[78]

Cockburn's linking of Julia-Hellman with Bryher-H. D. also brings up the question of homosexuality that acts as a subtext to the whole controversy. Hellman writes that she was angered when Anne-Marie's brother Sammy drunkenly remarked that "everybody knew about Julia and Me" (*Three*, 420), apparently a reference to lesbianism. Such a relationship is hinted at later when Hellman notes, "In those years, and the years after Julia's death, I have had plenty of time to think about the love I had for her, too strong and too complicated to be defined as only the sexual yearnings of one girl for another. And yet certainly that was there" (*Three*, 414).

However deep the homosexual connection might have been, it provides another reason for Hellman's deliberately obfuscating the story. Although she asserts that her relationship with Julia did not include a physical aspect, Spender writes that "the heroism of Julia is partly a device for flattering herself since she portrays herself as Julia's dearest friend, in fact lover."[79] Pauline Kael, reviewing the movie version, also hints at homosexuality: "Who can believe in the Julia she describes— the ideal friend of her early youth? . . . If ever there was a character preserved in the ardor of a girlhood crush, she's it." Kael also implies lesbianism when she writes, "The friendship between Hellman and Julia was obviously the emotional basis—the original material—for *The Children's Hour*."[80] This last is an interesting observation for several reasons. *The Children's Hour* at first looks like the story of a "big lie": a child maliciously labels the main characters lesbians, but at the end we discover that, unknown to one of the women, the other apparently *is* a lesbian, and the lie turns out to be true. This story is especially complicated since many have seen the play as an allegory, not for homosexuality, but for the whole Joseph McCarthy era. Unlike Gertrude Stein, who was partially covering for homosexuality, or

Sherwood Anderson, whose androgyny was, if anything, played up in his autobiographies, Lillian Hellman's sexual preferences are considerably more ambiguous, adding another layer of obfuscation to her whole autobiographical performance.

Because both Cockburn and Spender, among others, see "Julia" as an attempt on Hellman's part to glorify her own heroism, I cannot accept their interpretations, since I read the whole episode as yet another example in which Hellman deliberately mocks her lack of political or physical heroism. The story of Julia is the usual story of Hellman's inability to understand what has happened, even as it is happening, the story of her difficulty in understanding what she means because nurses, hotel clerks, telephone operators, doctors, and others all speak in foreign languages and in cryptic ways. Hellman's story is not so much a record of Julia's bravery as it is a record of her own characteristic inability to resolve the mysteries of the lives to which she is attracted or to reconcile the shifting political movements that made Stalin and Hitler allies at one moment, Russia and America allies at another, followed by a period of bitter renunciation of one another. All of these mysteries and political movements are embodied in the shifting grounds of Julia's identity and in such unreconcilable facts as John Von Zimmer's alliance with Julia at one moment in Vienna, his marriage to Anne-Marie at another.

The inability to "finish" the "Julia" story is reflective of dozens of stories in her four autobiographies in which Lillian Hellman realizes that she has no way to trace someone from her past because she has lost the address, she has forgotten the name, or the person has unexpectedly died—for example, Horace Liveright; Sergei Eisenstein, the Russian captain who reads American novels; Pascal, the young Frenchman with whom she comes out of Spain; and Julia's daughter, Lillian. That this pattern is important to Hellman is reinforced by the stories of Arthur Cowan and Sarah Cameron, both of whom have contradictory, illusory lives that end ambiguously. From early childhood, Hellman has been attracted most profoundly by those unfinished and incomplete lives whose mysteries resonate most deeply with her own, the lives of people like Sophronia, Bethe, Willy, Cowan, Julia, Jimsie, and her own mother, lives that have in common large unanswered questions and ambiguous endings. True to the unfinished pattern of her books, Lillian Hellman died before the Mary McCarthy suit came to trial, just days after McCracken's article appeared.

She wrote, at the beginning of the "Julia" section of *Pentimento*, "I think I have always known about my memory: I know when it is to be trusted and when some dream or fantasy entered on the life, and the

dream, the need of dream, led to distortion of what happened. And so
I knew early that the rampage angers of an only child were distorted
nightmares of reality. But I trust absolutely what I remember about
Julia" (*Three*, 412). This statement, when examined closely, does not
preclude the possibility that "Julia" is a composite portrait of some
kind, for as Hellman argued in an interview, "Memory, of course, is
not the same thing as what really happened in the real minute of pleasure or pain."[81] Although I am not oblivious to the fact that Hellman
sometimes lied in real life, it is more important, finally, from the autobiographical standpoint that Hellman needed to present the "Julia"
episode as she did; for all its confusion, inaccuracy, incompleteness,
and possible fictive components, the most telling aspect of the story
resides in the fact that at age sixty-seven Lillian Hellman was com-
pelled to write the story so as to deliberately point up its shadowy,
unfinished nature.

Scoundrel Time: Not Naming Names

I'd rather lie to him than have him think I'm lying.
—Dashiell Hammett, *The Thin Man*

"Are you now or have you ever been a member of the Communist
party?"—the classic question of the House Committee on Un-American Activities—parallels in grammatical structure the classic question
asked by all autobiographers: how much of what I am as I write depends on what I once was? The HCUA question also parallels, stylis-
tically, Lillian Hellman's natural autobiographical rhythm—her simul-
taneous layering of past and present—the "I didn't understand it then
and I don't now" (*Three*, 700) style that in her second autobiography begins with the dedication: "For Barbara and John / Ruth and
Marshall / with gratitude for then and now" (*Three*, 602).

Hellman begins *Scoundrel Time* by admitting that she did not like
her previous attempts at writing about the Joseph McCarthy period,
mainly because, in those writings, she had seen McCarthy and Nixon
as clownlike bumblers rather than villains. Her genuine anger, she
explains, has always been reserved for those liberal intellectuals who
failed to speak out about the HCUA's tactics. Interestingly, the figure
who was at the time of the Watergate trial called "the new Nixon"
seems to have been the stimulus for her finally writing her third memoir. Hellman now refers to Nixon as "a villainous liar" (*Three*, 649).

At first glance, *Scoundrel Time* would seem to be memoir because its focus is on the author's place within an historical event; however, as Hellman makes clear throughout the work, her concentration is still inward. "But I don't want to write about my historical conclusions— it isn't my game. I tell myself that this third time out, if I stick to what I know, what happened to me, and a few others, I have a chance to write my own history of the time" (*Three*, 607). Although this book, like her others, is informed by notebooks, diaries, memos, and the official record of the HCUA, Hellman insists that she is after a personal, rather than historical, version of what happened. "IT IS IM-POSSIBLE to write about any part of the McCarthy period in a clear-dated, annotated form; much crossed with much else, nothing obeyed a neat plan" (*Three*, 642).

This autobiographical, rather than memoiristic, focus is just what Thom Andersen objects to in his excellent essay "Red Hollywood": "If Hellman had tried to write about her political commitments and her political activities instead of about the persecution they brought on her, she might have created an important work."[82] But for Lillian Hellman, what is important about her experiences with McCarthyism is, not her past's emphasis on political activity, but her present's belief that she is after all less political than the record might indicate.

The controversy that followed *Scoundrel Time*'s publication, reminiscent of the manifesto against Gertrude Stein, takes its shrillest form in William F. Buckley's "*Scoundrel Time*: and Who Is the Ugliest of Them All?," a title that suggests both Buckley's idea that Hellman lacks self-reflection and an ad hominem argument about Hellman's facial features, an echo of the various claims that her face resembled the figurehead of a ship, a primitive statue on Easter Island, or George Washington, although her detractors hardly claim that she cannot tell a lie.[83] The more moderate attacks against *Scoundrel Time* generally claim that Hellman has falsely presented herself as a model of integrity by simplifying the complex nature of the period and underplaying her commitment to Stalinism in a book characterized by a tone of obfuscation, self-righteousness, and a lack of forgiveness.

Hellman answers most of her detractors within *Scoundrel Time*, agreeing with their objections before they have been voiced. "I am, of course, making my political history too simple" (*Three*, 613), she admits, after having confessed that "the traceries from what you were to what you became are always too raw and too simple" (*Three*, 612). Claiming that a history of herself in terms of political beliefs is impossible, she nevertheless admits that she was wrong about Stalin. To her antagonists, her apologies seem inadequate—too little, too late. But to Hellman, and other victims of the blacklisting period, the demand for a public statement of remorse smacks of what Victor Navasky, in his *Naming Names*, calls "degradation ceremonies," one of the main purposes of the HCUA purge.[84]

When Pauline Kael asks about the word *pentimento* in a review of the film *Julia*—"Of what is Hellman repenting?"[85]—she echoes those antagonists who have failed to see that throughout her autobiographies Hellman is repenting virtually everything, confessing, in the traditional autobiographical sense, that she really was never the brave and decisive figure she appeared to be. Her nature was given to rages and rash acts, motivated by a stern sense of social injustice, powered by angry passion rather than logic; yet brusqueness and anger were often simply the covering mask for a constant inner feeling of vagueness and indecision. "Simply, then and now, I feel betrayed by the nonsense I had believed" (*Three*, 606), she writes, placing the blame on herself. In earlier portions of *Three*, Hellman has admitted that she is "slow at leaving anything" (*Three*, 505), an echo of her only defense for not speaking out against Stalinism's horrors. Unlike her critics, who have never publicly admitted their political errors in not standing more firmly against the HCUA, Hellman says repeatedly, though in a deliberately low-key voice, that she was wrong because she was slow to recognize her errors. Throughout her account, she shows herself to be slow in understanding, late at letting go, a sort of person on whom, politically, everything is lost. "It took me months to understand what I was listening to" (*Three*, 607), she says of overt anti-Semitism in pre–World War II Germany. "It is comically late to admit that I did not even consider the fierce, sweeping, violent nonsense-tragedies that break out in America from time to time" (*Three*, 615), she says in distinguishing her romantic notions of radicalism from Hammett's pragmatic approach. Speaking of the anti-Communist writers who oppose her, she writes, "Such people would have a right to say that I, and many like me, took too long to see what was going on in the Soviet Union" (*Three*, 720). In always linking her admissions to a sense of bad timing, Hellman is consistent, both with her statements in *An Unfinished Woman* and *Pentimento* about these charges of pro-Stalinism and with her recurring theme of being awkward and out of step.

Hellman begins her defense of her actions toward Communism in the first autobiography where she argues that what we now know about the 1937–38 purges in Russia seemed then far less certain, part of a propagandistic smoke screen made out of equal parts of anti-

Communist press releases and a Soviet determination to cover up what happened by never admitting it. She writes of the confusion that typified the Russian intellectual of the day:

> The accusations against his friends or his heroes were only half understood and were, therefore, more frightening. Such men and women tell you that one day they knew a criminal charge of treason or disloyalty could not be true, the next day felt uncertain, and within a short time were half convinced that perhaps their country, their revolution might have been betrayed. Great honor must and will be paid those who did protest the criminal purges. It is hard to judge those who tossed about in silent doubt and despair, but it is even harder to believe that they did not understand what was happening. [*Three*, 150]

Chapter 12 of *An Unfinished Woman* consists of a flashback to all that occurred during the Joseph McCarthy era and the consequences, given in the form of the recollection of a conversation with Raya, Hellman's Russian translator and friend. "I was also shy and stumbling when I tried to talk about the McCarthy period" (*Three*, 182). Similar to the ankle turns produced by her physical clumsiness, a difficulty with turns, Hellman reveals, is also characteristic of her political stumbling. *"All through my childhood and youth I had an interest in all sharp turns of history"* (*Three*, 204); however, she admits, "I cannot make quick turns . . . cannot ever adjust fast to a new pattern, have not the mind or the nature to do one thing, maybe wiser, when I am prepared for another" (*Three*, 668). For a person not capable of quick turns, the period after the Spanish civil war was particularly problematic. Having been attracted in varying degrees to Communism, liberals of all persuasions, suddenly made aware of Stalin's purges and the Nazi-Soviet Pact of 1939, were faced with a sudden political turn, made more confusing when Russia later became an American ally during World War II. Frank Warren asserts boldly in *Liberals and Communism*, "If Trotsky were not guilty and the trials were a monstrous frame-up, one could not distinguish morally between Communism and Fascism."[86]

The majority of Hellman's politically oriented critics attack her attitudes toward Stalin and the Moscow trials with the same argument that Larry Ceplair and Steven Englund apply to Hollywood Communists in *The Inquisition in Hollywood*:

> Communist screenwriters defended the Stalinest regime, accepted the Comintern's policies and about-faces, and criticized

enemies and allies alike with an infuriating self-righteousness, superiority, and selective memory which eventually alienated all but the staunchest fellow travelers. As defenders of the Soviet regime the screen artist Reds became apologists for crimes of monstrous dimensions, though they claimed to have known nothing about such crimes, and indeed shouted down, or ignored, those who did.[87]

This summary, which echoes virtually every anti-*Scoundrel Time* essay, fails to make an important distinction. As Thom Andersen astutely notices, a difference exists between supporting and apologizing for the horrors of Stalin's actions and denying that they took place at all. "They did not claim to know nothing of such crimes," writes Andersen of the Hollywood Communists, which would certainly include such supporters as Lillian Hellman; "they claimed, rather, that the reports of them were untrustworthy products of anti-Soviet propaganda." "How could they not have known?" asks Andersen, adding, "This is a difficult question because we have always already known; we have known as we know our own names."[88]

For Hellman—whose deepest sentiment has always been against naming names, and whose childhood includes a romantic admiration for the passionate and emotional actions of gangsters, and whose financial difficulties as a result of the blacklisting required her to work as a salesclerk at Macy's department store under an assumed name—this is an impossibly difficult question. Just as we now wonder how the people of Poland could claim to be unaware of the Nazi concentration camps within their midst, or how intellectuals and otherwise reasonable southerners could have failed to see the evil of slavery that surrounded them, Hellman—like the majority of those who supported Communism in this period—can offer few answers for her own blindness.

That she shares the generic liberal failure to imagine the most monstrous of political machinations is one answer. Another lies in the realm of psychoanalysis: "the impulse to obscure dark facts" that Daniel Goleman refers to as those "vital lies" that "come from the need to preserve the integrity of the self."[89] Hellman repeatedly describes herself as exhausted, dizzy, on the verge of vomiting, disoriented, accident prone, following clues that lead nowhere. Often unable to communicate at crucial moments because of comical ineptness at understanding, she admits, "Increasingly I find myself most comfortable with conversations I don't understand" (*Three*, 94). These psychological, sometimes physical, traits grow stronger until in *Maybe* they become physical manifestations directly linked to despair over loss of memory and the difficulty of maintaining integrity. First, her vision literally fails her: "A strange thing is happening to me. I can't see the other side of the room" (*Maybe*, 94). Later, while swimming, she is inexplicably unable to locate the shore: "I am not frightened in water. Something else was happening to me: I was collapsing in a way that had never happened before" (*Maybe*, 100).

Actually, something similar had happened before. Throughout *Three*, there are examples of Hellman's loss of bodily control, physical parallels to her lifelong rages. One example occurs when she is on a streetcar returning from police headquarters after having discovered Bethe's connection to the Mafia: "I think of it now as the closest I have ever come to a conscious semiconsciousness, as if I were coming through an anesthetic, not back into a world of reality, but into a new body and time, moving toward something, running back at the moment I could have reached it" (*Three*, 345). Another example occurs when she describes herself testifying before the HCUA as moving her "right hand as if I had a tic, unexpected, and couldn't stop it. . . . I felt the sweat on my face and arms and knew that something was going to happen to me, something out of control, and I turned to Joe, remembering the suggested toilet intermission" (*Three*, 674).

What many of her antagonists most dislike about *Scoundrel Time* is her tone. Although many of their objections are really to Garry Wills's introduction, those who publicly dislike this book often mention a querulous, quibbling tone characterized by mean spiritedness. Although Andersen, in the following passage, is describing Hellman's tone in *Scoundrel Time*, his description is also suggestive of *An Unfinished Woman*: "There is in her memoir an almost solipsistic remoteness, a lack of solidarity."[90] Actually, these are the very qualities she is deliberately stressing, not as instances of withholding or covering up, but as examples of how she remembers the past. Even if we accept her angriest critics' views that her tone is less self-doubt and more disingenuousness and false modesty, this tone, according to Andersen, is true to the spirit of the age: "Her tone of disappointment and petulant disillusionment is unexpectedly prevalent in political memoirs of the fifties, no matter what the politics of the author. It is, it seems, the authentic voice of the times."[91]

It is true that Hellman has simplified her mistakes, but she has also simplified her apologies. Repeatedly she confesses her errors; of "Stalin Communism," she states clearly, "There were plenty of sins and plenty that for a long time I mistakenly denied" (*Three*, 606). Her most straightforward apology, however, is the following: "I thought

that in the end Russia, having achieved a state socialism, would stop
its infringements on personal liberty. I was wrong" (*Three*, 612).

For a number of Hellman's critics, little difference seems to exist
between autobiographical truth and legal testimony, between simpli-
fication of a complex political time and perjury. Despite her repeated
warnings that she is not after historical accuracy and that she does not
"like to talk about convictions" because, as she clearly admits, "I'm
never sure I'm telling the truth" (*Three*, 631), *Scoundrel Time* has been
judged as if it were legal testimony. For Hellman, the point is not to
compete with the contemporary record but to discover how she sees
the whole period twenty-four years later. As Glen Cavaliero writes in
"Autobiography and Fiction," "In autobiographical form the freely
associative portrait of the self-with-others relies on a perceptiveness
that offsets its unreliability as court-room evidence."[92]

In addition to exhibiting a lack of sophistication about autobiographical theory, many of Hellman's critics are guilty of the same
charge they level against her—oversimplification. William Phillips,
for instance, notes that "Lillian Hellman's questions as to why we did
not come to the defense of those who had been attacked by McCarthy
is not as simple as it appears. First of all some were communists and
what one was asked to defend was their right to lie about it."[93] With
the phrase "their right to lie," Phillips is alluding to the taking of the
Fifth Amendment, the legitimate refusal to answer a question that
might be considered incriminating. The Fifth Amendment is a perfectly legal strategy, stemming from an ethical tradition established
long before the HCUA. In 1907, for instance, in his "Classification of
Duties—Veracity," Henry Sidgwick stated that "it is obviously a most
effective protection for legitimate secrets that it should be universally
understood and expected that those who ask questions which they
have no right to ask will have lies told to them,"[94] as we have seen
with Mary McCarthy's mental reservations.

This philosophical version of "Ask me no questions, I'll tell you no
lies" is amplified by Sissela Bok's contention, in her "Lying to Liars"
chapter, that not only is there "an undoubted psychological easing of
standards of truthfulness toward those believed to be liars" but also
"if, finally, the liar to whom one wishes to lie is also in a position to do
one harm, then the balance may shift; not because he is a liar, but
because of the threat he poses."[95]

During the HCUA inquests of the 1950s, the actual words of the
Fifth Amendment shifted their surface meanings depending on the
audience. Joseph McCarthy himself explained to Dashiell Hammett
on 23 March 1953:

Well, now, you have told us that you will not tell us whether you are a member of the Communist Party today or not, on the ground that if you told us the answer might incriminate you. That is normally taken by this committee and the country as a whole to mean that you are a member of the party, because if you were not you would simply say, "No," and it would not incriminate you. You see, the only reason that you have the right to refuse to answer is if you feel a truthful answer would incriminate you. An answer that you were not a Communist, if you were not a Communist, could not incriminate you. Therefore, you should know considerable about the Communist movement, I assume.[96]

Liberal anti-Communists often explained that McCarthy's tactics did not speak for them; however, Sidney Hook, writing with the perspective of time, still insists that taking the Fifth Amendment is tantamount to lying: "In Miss Hellman's case, since she explicitly claims that she was *not* a member of the Communist Party—and that her refusal to say so was motivated only by reluctance to incriminate others—her invocation of the Fifth Amendment was really illegitimate because her truthful testimony could never have incriminated others."[97] To HCUA members and supporters, then, invoking the Fifth Amendment meant, "I refuse to answer because I'm really a Communist, since no one who was not would hide behind such an obvious legal out." Even to Hellman, this tactic was also suspect:

The Fifth Amendment has catches: if I were asked if I knew Harriman or President Roosevelt, I would have to say yes because I could not claim that knowing them could harm me; but if I were asked if I knew Chaplin or Hammett, for example, I would have to refuse to answer because they could, in the eyes of the Committee, incriminate me. Thus, of course, one puts a finger on certain people and possibly on people about whom you know little and whose history you can only guess at. Maybe it is all legally necessary, well thought out, but it can be ugly stuff in practice. [*Three*, 666]

Her testimony is filled with a personalized version of the Fifth Amendment, a Hellmanesque attempt to accomplish what Richard Mayne calls "a case of double-indemnity—the Fifth Amendment and defiance too."[98] Instead of replying with the standard "I refuse to answer . . . ," Hellman often said, "I *must* refuse to answer . . . ," thereby expressing her contempt for a legalistic trick forced on her by the inverted rules of the game.

Hellman notes, "Once in a while I slipped on the Fifth Amendment, and made Rauh [her lawyer] very nervous."[99] Because she made some mistakes in her testimony—she says, "At times I couldn't follow the reasoning" (*Three*, 674)—her antagonists have seen her as a liar rather than as a person who repeatedly tells us that she is not adept at being heroic, though forced by her nature to appear heroic in public. As she said in an interview, "There was no question of heroics. There was a question of legalities."[100] In addition, Hellman claims that she still distrusts the printed documents of her testimony, both because the words do not reveal the spoken tone and because "the court stenographer missed some of what was said . . . or the documents were, in part, edited" (*Three*, 673).

The now-famous Hellman letter to the HCUA in which she pledges to waive her Fifth Amendment rights if not required to testify about others, a strategy she attributes to Abe Fortas, is not an example of what Eric Bentley calls "legal gymnastics."[101] Instead, it was a straightforward attempt on Hellman's part to maintain one of the most consistent patterns of her life—the refusal to name names, especially when someone is in trouble. "Don't go through life making trouble for people" (*Three*, 25), says Sophronia Mason, on the occasion of young Lillian's having discovered her father is having an affair. "Oh, Sophronia, it's you I want back always," confesses Hellman; "it's by you I still so often measure, guess, transmute, translate and act" (*Three*, 255). Using this black woman as her only inviolable standard, her life's lodestone, Lillian Hellman—who as a child once tried to pass for black by claiming she was related to Sophronia—is consistent in not naming names. She will not give Julia's name now, as she refused earlier, at the time of her abortion, to reveal the name of her lover, though they eventually married.

Hellman constantly asserts that she is not happy with her HCUA stand and the excessive admiration it eventually attained. Of an earlier version of her letter, with its famous line "I cannot and will not cut my conscience to fit this year's fashions," Hellman notes, "I didn't like it much because it didn't sound like me" (*Three*, 658). Like Henry Adams, who saw his autobiographical protagonist as a manikin whose clothing is tailored by his narrator, Hellman frequently uses clothes metaphors throughout *Scoundrel Time* to describe both the events of the blacklisting era and her subsequent attempts at understanding what it meant. "If facts are facts," she writes, "and should not be altered, then which of us, as individuals or in groups, did the alterations and why?" (*Three*, 650). For Hellman, who is most inaccurate when she deals in facts—and who later appeared in an advertisement for a full-length Blackgama mink coat under the heading "What Becomes a Legend the Most?"—clothes are a suitable metaphor, both for concealment and for the difference between the way things were and the way they appear in retrospect. As with the mink coat advertisement, which Hellman is too embarrassed about to explain, although twice asked about it by Dan Rather, she sees herself as having become an ironic legend, years after the events being described in *Scoundrel Time*.[102] According to William Wright, "Hellman herself misunderstood the slogan, giving it the subjective reading of 'What human raw material is most likely to develop into a legend?' "[103]

To those who see the accuracy of *Scoundrel Time* as suspect, she agrees, adding in her later commentary in *Three*, "*I wrote the book and I misrepresented myself in the book*" (*Three*, 725). She means both that she made herself too heroic and that her tone appears too restrained. But most of her errors are the result of the complex, conflicting motives behind her writing of *Scoundrel Time*, her searching for "a truth I couldn't name" (*Three*, 344), yet another example of her difficulty in naming names. Finally writing *Scoundrel Time*, after not being able to write about the period for years, represents her attempt at recovering through art a time in her life she earlier described as a sort of amnesia:

> I had taken a whole period of my life and thrown it somewhere, always intending to call for it again, but now that it came time to call, I couldn't remember where I had left it. Did other people do this, drop the past in a used car lot and leave it for so long that one couldn't even remember the name of the road? [*Three*, 184]

If psychologist Ernest Schachtel is right in claiming that "adult memory reflects life as a road with occasional signposts and milestones rather than as the landscape through which this road has led,"[104] then Lillian Hellman, in writing *Scoundrel Time* and being faced with a road whose name she has suppressed, has recovered, if not the literal landscape, then certainly an authentic reproduction. When the obstacles are taken into consideration, *Scoundrel Time* is, as Murray Kempton notes, a triumph of honesty:

> When we consider the general practice of using memory so earnestly as an instrument for mendacity, it is a sufficient miracle for Miss Hellman to be so honest a witness; and our admiration for her integrity cannot grow smaller for a final impression that *Scoundrel Time* is not quite true. Honesty and truth are not just the same thing, since the first has to do with character and the second with self-understanding of a cruder kind than hers.[105]

Nobody can shake me on what I believe I can remember.—Lillian Hellman

In *Maybe*, Hellman returns to biography, absent from *Scoundrel Time*, in the curious combination of autobiography-biography that Linda Wagner-Martin describes as "near biography set in an autobiographical frame."[106] Although *Maybe*'s subtitle, "A Story by Lillian Hellman," would seem to put this fourth personal narrative into a different category from its three predecessors, the title applies equally to itself as to everything else in the book. "Maybe a story, maybe not," writes Eakin, who sees the book as "an inquiry into authorial motivation and narrative epistemology," presented as Hellman's "sense of her life, as 'a life.'"[107] Henri Peyre argues that "there is scant question of total sincerity in memoirs" because the memoirist's "gift is to be that of a picturesque storyteller"; Desmond McCarthy, however, sees a biographer as "an artist upon oath."[108] But in *Maybe*, we have the typical Hellman mixture of drama, autobiography, memoir, biography, and storytelling, and though she is neither "upon oath" nor insincere, she is, in *Maybe*, most doubtful of capturing the whole truth of any life, including her own.

Following her usual practice of writing biography about uncelebrated, though certainly not ordinary, lives, she focuses on those parts of the story of Sarah Cameron that connect with the life of Lillian Hellman. She asks: *"Why am I writing about Sarah? I really only began to think about her a few years ago, and then not often. Although I always rather liked her, she is of no importance to my life and never was. I do not know the truth about her or much of what I write here"* (*Maybe*, 50).

The truth about Sarah Cameron is less important than the way she is remembered and the fact that Hellman finds herself, toward the end of her life, writing about someone she claims is not important. "Autobiography is a necessary stratagem to gain something more important than itself," Alfred Kazin explains;[109] and for Hellman, her confused, collapsing memories about Sarah act somewhat as an answer to those who attacked *Pentimento* and *Scoundrel Time* for dubious veracity. The strategy of *Maybe*, according to Eakin, is partially "motivated by apology" and partially inspired by a need to explain—"the need to make clear to her detractors . . . that in this, as in her three earlier 'memoir books,'" the whole truth is "an inherently unstable category."[110]

In the early pages of *An Unfinished Woman*, Hellman isolates a central component of her psychological makeup: "I was first puzzled by the conflict which would haunt me, harm me, and benefit me the rest of my life: simply, the stubborn, relentless, driving desire to be alone as it came into conflict with the desire not to be alone when I wanted not to be" (*Three*, 22). This essential conflict produced a lifelong attraction for people whose own lives would allow, to varying degrees, off-and-on relationships with Hellman that are characterized by not asking too many personal questions on either side. She lived, for instance, with Dashiell Hammett off and on for thirty years, yet she never asked him if he was actually a member of the Communist party nor why he stopped writing novels after *The Thin Man*. The majority of the portraits in all four personal narratives are of people who, from Hellman's perspective, have mysterious, evasive, unfinished lives, which occasionally cross and recross her own. Although Sarah Cameron is not in herself important to the author, the elusive, fugitive quality of her life resonates with Hellman's need for puzzling lives.

Sarah Cameron is also important because Hellman's memory of her, which is repeatedly undercut by new revelations—now confirming, now disconfirming some story—is characteristic of Hellman's memory in general. Because Sarah is deliberately unreliable, her contradictory versions of her life are particularly taxing to the author, who was undoubtedly distressed at her memory's factual distortions and lapses that the Gellhorn-McCracken-McCarthy investigations had revealed to her. As Hellman writes in *Maybe*, "As time and much of life has passed, my memory—which for the purpose of this tale has kept me awake sorting out what I am certain of, what maybe I added to what, because I didn't see or know the people—won't supply what I need to know" (*Maybe*, 63). Psychologists have stressed that even the memory in our unconscious is not necessarily the literal truth, although Adrienne Rich argues that "the unconscious wants truth. It ceases to speak to those who want something else more than truth."[111] But as Daniel Goleman observes, "Memory is attention in the past tense: what you remember now is what you noticed before."[112]

Trying as she composes *Maybe* to remember Sarah's telling of her own life story, Hellman remarks, "But it was not a question of memory: I was only half listening. There was no other way because there was no coherence. I had wanted to have my dinner alone" (*Maybe*, 56). Hellman is apparently unaware how memory works and that she is describing her most characteristic need—to be alone when she wants. Throughout *Maybe*, she struggles with what she imagines are her memory's lies, trying to reconcile her own "messy and tipsy life" (*Maybe*, 59), including the disconnected story of Sarah's life that "had been deposited" with her (*Maybe*, 12) and that puzzles and la-

ter frightens her because she instinctively suspects that none of her
memories is entirely trustworthy, that "memory for us all is so nuts"
(*Maybe*, 63), and that "*near an edge is nothing*" (*Maybe*, 42).

Increasingly aware of the duplicity of memory, Hellman fears that
her own identity—which is partially composed of what F. C. Bartlett
named "memory schemata," which are "socially and culturally determined patterns of reconstruction of the past"[113]—is collapsing in-
wardly, paralleling the accelerating physical collapses she has begun to
experience and the collapse of the narrative of Sarah Cameron she is
trying to write. Caught in a complex network of lies told by Sarah and
Carter Cameron and by Sarah's college roommate, Ferry Dixon, that
part of Hellman's self identified as a woman is confused about what
Pamela Bromberg calls "her own gynophobia," her "crippling obsession with her own body odor";[114] the portion tied to her role as an
author is frustrated by an inability to make a story out of Sarah's narrative. Together, these double needs produce the one Hellman autobiography whose veracity has not been challenged and, therefore, the
only one that appears true to both supporters and detractors alike.

Part of the reason for *Maybe*'s truthful feel resides in Hellman's ap-
plication of Goethe's principle—"Was früchtbar ist, allein ist wahr"
(that is, "Only what is fruitful is true").[115] According to Donald
Spence, the only fruitful truth, "truth in the service of self-coherence,"
is constructed in two stages: "first, finding a verbal expression for the
anomalous event, and, second, finding a narrative home for the verbal expression."[116] What Pamela Bromberg calls *Maybe*'s central metaphor, "finding how things 'fit,'"[117] is another way of expressing
Spence's conception of narrative as opposed to historical truth.

Spence's stages are the very steps Hellman is struggling with in
Maybe: first, finding a way to narrate Sarah's story and, second, giving
the story a narrative home within *Maybe* and by extension within all
four personal narratives and within her own memory, with "MISSING
PIECES EVERYPLACE" (*Maybe*, 101).

Conclusion: "What Is Remembered"

Memory, then, is not only a backward retrieval of a vanished event, but also a post-
ing forward, at the remembered instant to all other future moments of corresponding circumstance.—Richard Powers, *Three Farmers on Their Way to a Dance*

Alice B. Toklas's actual autobiography, *What Is Remembered*, deliberately written without a question mark, would make an apt title for the

four volumes of Lillian Hellman's autobiography. In moving from the first sentence, "I was born," to the last, "I hung up"—from "the sweetest smelling baby in New Orleans" to an adult forever unsure about the spuriousness of a misogynist's charge that she had a particularly strong personal odor—Hellman has, in one sense, deconstructed herself. But in another sense, she has reconstructed herself, ratifying A. O. J. Cockshut's claim that "it is the privilege of a great autobiography to give us data for disagreeing with its conclusions."[118] Throughout these four books, she has repeated the self-made charge that she must pay a price for having once believed in absolute truth. The price, she explains, is having "gone through my life blaming myself for almost anything that harmed me: what anybody did to me, what work failed, what meanness or malice was given . . . it was I who was the fool for not guessing it in time, for accepting lies I should have known to be lies" (*Maybe*, 19).

In writing her four autobiographies, however, Lillian Hellman has finally triumphed over the lies she told herself; she has, in the end, gained "the final courage to say that I refuse to preside over violations against myself" (*Three*, 213). She has gained, through the writing of her autobiographies, the personal courage so long falsely ascribed to her by the legend of Lillian Hellman.

Her lifelong struggle between being alone and acting on political feelings is illustrated in the shape and direction of these four books and in her final breakthrough in *Maybe*—allowing herself to feel comfortable with an autobiography that is satisfied with its own inconclusive rhetorical stance. For Lillian Hellman, who once thought of her own life as unfinished, the act of repenting through mastery of the art of palimpsestic autobiography has ultimately produced a completed woman, at home with an ordering of memory, not into an idealistic yes, nor into a Hawthornian "no in thunder," but into a resolute, self-satisfying, self-defining *maybe*.

"You Must Remember This"

[Twentieth-century autobiographers] no longer believe that autobiography can offer a faithful and unmediated reconstruction of a historically verifiable past; instead, it expresses the play of the autobiographical act itself, in which the materials of the past are shaped by memory and imagination to serve the needs of present consciousness.—Paul John Eakin

Most of us love ourselves too dearly to be autobiographers.—Roy Pascal

Throughout *Telling Lies in Modern American Autobiography*, I have attempted to show that even those autobiographers who have been publicly labeled liars should not be considered culpable, though each author makes statements that research has shown to be contrary to fact. Although each of these five writers has been accused of lying, what is more remarkable, considering the inherent complications of the autobiographical act, is the relative degree of authenticity in each autobiography. Writers who have an overwhelming wish to conceal their personal lives do not turn to autobiography. Any autobiography subjected to the intense scrutiny of a lawyer or an angry antagonist could be expected to reveal discrepancies. But what is more important is how each writer's individual approach to the problems of lying in autobiography, as I have detailed in the preceding pages, reveals far more than inaccuracies conceal.

Also important is the nature of what each writer is said to lie about, what those making the accusations of lying have thought was to be gained by each autobiographer. Gertrude Stein's antagonists charge her with making herself look more important as an artist, and Sherwood Anderson's opponents think that his major flaw is romanticizing his escape from Elyria. But time, and the continuing interest in *The Autobiography of Alice B. Toklas*, has made Stein's position as an artist important to generations of readers, whereas many of her antagonists have been virtually forgotten. Anderson's legend has always been more important to others than to the author, who uses the legend, particularly the escape from Elyria, as a personal myth rather than as a historical account. Those who find Richard Wright's autobiography untruthful, including Mary McCarthy, fail to see that his exaggerations and patently obvious lies are meant not to fool the reader but to be taken in the spirit of Flannery O'Connor's statement, "To the hard of hearing you shout, and for the almost-blind you draw large and startling figures."[1] Mary McCarthy, about whom Eakin writes, "Telling of lies is inextricably implicated in the writing of her memories,"[2] has been treated less harshly, in terms of lying, than the other figures I have discussed, even though her first autobiography contains more admissions of lying than either of the autobiographers she attacks. The most likely explanation for McCarthy not being branded a liar—and an explanation for Lillian Hellman's failure to have her lawyers examine *Memories of a Catholic Girlhood* for lies—is that McCarthy's autobiographies focus primarily on her childhood.

McCarthy sees that her life stories contain fiction, but for her, fiction must be as accurate as nonfiction: "I have this fanatical obsession with accuracy. The events in my books may be improbable or lightly fantastic, but the characters have to take real airplanes that can be found on a schedule."[3] Lillian Hellman's autobiographies, because they have been seen as self-aggrandizing, have received the harshest criticism of any of the five figures I have treated. As a result, Hellman is frequently characterized as completely mendacious, even though she is certainly as trustworthy as any of the others. McCarthy's obsession with such factual details as plane schedules, even in a work of fiction, explains why she finds Lillian Hellman's autobiographies so unacceptable, even though McCarthy writes, "I have a belief that the only documentation that is any good is that which remains in the memory."[4]

Despite her reverence for factual accuracy, McCarthy, like Hellman, must have been disconcerted to discover how manipulative memory is. Speaking of the scene in which she claims to have seen Hellman talking to students of Sarah Lawrence College about John Dos Passos, McCarthy says:

> The Spenders' memory of my Sarah Lawrence meeting with Hellman is different from mine. They say that it was at their home, not Harold Taylor's, that I arrived punctually and she arrived late and that two separate, hostile groups at once formed. Whatever was said between her and me they think they did not hear; this jibes with my memory in that my version there was nobody present but her and me and the Sarah Lawrence girls. But the variance nevertheless worries me. They're so sure, and so had I been.[5]

No matter how hard she tries to remember, or how important getting at the truth is for her, McCarthy's memory, like everyone's, is overwhelmed by memory's mendacity. As a result, "the only documentation that is any good," to use McCarthy's phrase, is bound to be unreliable. That an autobiography is a story created out of the author's memory in terms of his or her private mythologies suggests that autobiography is, in some ways, similar to mythology in the larger sense. Like the mythology of a community, or of a nation, autobiography seeks to refine the self's folk stories, those successive versions of events we tell ourselves, consciously and unconsciously. Because the human memory, unlike a computer's circuits, is not a written text, it operates in a manner remarkably similar to those primitive cultures without reading and writing, cultures that must learn their collective stories by heart and constantly maintain their stock of stories through repetition. What constitutes a self or an identity is a set of memories-turned-into-stories, memories shared by the successive series of personae occupying an individual mind. And like the most ancient mythologist, we tend to remember according to the needs of memory.

In the chapter of *The Creation of Mythology* called "By Mouth and by Ear," Marcel Detienne writes of "the most fundamental fact of shared memory: that what is memorable, that which this kind of memory remembers, far from being a recorded past or a collection of archives, consists in present knowledge, proceeding through reinterpretations but whose unceasing variations within tradition relayed by speech are imperceptible."[6] Because autobiographical memory is like the oral memory of traditional storytellers, we must be careful not to confuse the use of memory by the autobiographer—even when aided by such written documents as diaries, letters, or newspaper accounts—with the other kind of memory, what Detienne calls "mnemonic activity." "Mnemonic activity," or mechanical memory, "consists in stockpiling and reproducing *faithfully* series of statements or pieces of information."[7] This second sort of memory, what we mean when we say that we have learned material by heart, depends on a written document for comparison, a record against which to check for literal accuracy. The autobiographer's memory, in contrast, consists of material learned, not by heart, but by soul, by a complicated pattern of psychological self-deceptions and constructions that are explained in detail in Daniel Goleman's *Vital Lies, Simple Truths: The Psychology of Self-Defense.*

According to Goleman, "memory is autobiography, its author is the 'self,' an especially potent organization of schemas."[8] By schemas, Goleman means patterns of perception built up over the years, something similar to what we ordinarily call self-concept: "Memory is in double jeopardy, for apart from an initial skew in what is noticed, there can be later biases in what is recalled."[9] If memory is the self's autobiography, an unwritten narrative with an unreliable narrator, then the actual autobiographer trying to record the story of the self faces a virtually impossible task. As Goleman explains: "The self-system sculpts the way a person filters and interprets experience. . . . In doing so, the self has in its power all the tools—and temptations—of a totalitarian state. The self acts as a censor, selecting and deleting the flow of imagination."[10]

What makes autobiography valuable then is not its fidelity to fact but its revelations—to the writer as much as to the reader—of self. Rather than blaming our autobiographers for discrepancies between their stories and supposedly verifiable facts, we should realize, on the one hand, that memory's deceptions are not always conscious and, on the other, that the duplicity of memory affords us one of the most powerful avenues of entry into the self-identity of the writer. "Such self-serving reinterpretation of reality goes on for most of us some of the time," concludes Goleman, "but we are rarely found out. After all, the dissembling goes on discreetly, behind the screen of our unconscious; we are only its recipients, innocent self-deceivers. A convenient arrangement."[11]

Although we make distinctions between short-term and long-term memory, we usually speak of the self who is writing as the culmination of a lifetime of selves. Sissela Bok reminds us that, among the many attempts at defining truth, a pre-Socratic Greek version of truth was *aletheia*—literally a-lethe, that is, "all that we remember singled out through memory from everything that is destined for Lethe, 'the river of forgetfulness.'" Bok continues by describing *aletheia* in terms of mythology: "The oral tradition required that information be memorized and repeated, often in song, so as not to be forgotten. Everything thus memorized . . . all partook of truth, even if in another sense completely fabricated or erroneous."[12]

Using *aletheia* as a definition—which is not so farfetched if we realize that in our minds we are still relying on oral tradition—suggests that what we remember, despite its obvious fallibility, can even be thought of as what is true for us. This idea is directly supported by the Hebrew concept of truth, which Dafna Allon explains in an essay called "Reflections on the Art of Lying." "The Hebrew conception of truth is less removed: truth is what remains and endures through time, what can be trusted to stay true. . . . In the last analysis, then, the truth is what you believe."[13] Allon continues her discussion by asking: "In what way are some stories felt to be 'true' and others not? 'True to life' is the phrase often used, but we think we recognize this quality in stories about lives we know nothing of."[14]

When Alice B. Toklas titled her real autobiography, *What Is Re-*

membered, she was actually expressing this paradoxical truth: what we remember—which is a mysterious amalgam of what we choose, what we really want, what actually happened, and what we are forced to remember—once turned into language and written down, becomes our personal truth without much consideration for its literal accuracy.

That the actual act of writing an autobiography is fraught with complexities because of memory is clearly illustrated in Patricia Hampl's combination essay-autobiography "Memory and Imagination," which begins as autobiography, then breaks off sharply into a meditation on what happened as she wrote. In the course of her discussion, Hampl reveals—to herself as much as to her readers—that she has told stories that are not accurate: "I wasn't writing fiction. I was writing memoir—or was trying to. My desire was to be accurate. I wished to embody the myth of memoir: to write as an act of dutiful transcription." Facing the fact that she has not merely transcribed, she goes on to say, "I am forced to admit that memoir is not a matter of transcription, that memory itself is not a warehouse of finished stories, not a static gallery of framed pictures." Having come that far, she must ask herself, "Two whys: why did I invent, and then, if a memoirist must inevitably invent rather than transcribe, why do I—why should anybody—write memoir at all?"[15]

Her answer is a particularly clear expression of the way an autobiographer looks at autobiographical truth:

> Memoir seeks a permanent home for feeling and image, a habitation where they can live together in harmony. . . . It was only in reviewing the piece after writing it that I saw my inaccuracy. In pondering this "lie," I came to see what I was up to: I was getting what I wanted. At last. . . . For meaning is not "attached" to the detail by the memoirist, meaning is revealed. Here memory impulsively reaches out its arms and embraces imagination. That is the resort to invention. It isn't a lie but an act of necessity, as the innate urge to locate personal truth always is.
>
> Memoirs must be written because each of us must have a created version of the past. Created: that is, real, tangible, made of the stuff of a life lived in place and in history. . . . We must acquiesce to our experience and our gift to transform experience into meaning and value. . . . If we refuse to do the work of creating this personal version of the past, someone else will do it for us. . . . What is remembered is what becomes reality.[16]

Of course a difference exists between remembering events from childhood, between Hampl's changing a school friend's name and historical situation to satisfy a psychological truth about herself, and deliberately altering someone else's historical truth, as Janet Cooke did in inventing "Jimmy." But little difference exists between deliberately playing with reader's expectations in a genre such as the eighteenth-century novel, which gained its power by pretending to be nonfiction, or in modern American autobiography, which uses its indeterminate generic position as a rhetorical strategy. According to Alfred Kazin, this strategy, which he calls "autobiography as narrative," consists of "fiction that uses facts, that deliberately retains the facts behind the story in order to show the imaginative possibilities inherent in fact, and yet which is designed, even when the author does not say so, to make a fable of his life."[17]

Because lying in autobiography is such a public act, the autobiographer must be aware of the possibility of being found out, a possibility that leads to the question, why would anyone think they could get away with massive lying in a personal narrative? Part of the answer comes from Anthony Brandt's claim that we deliberately lie as a way to test our sense of truth:

> I am suggesting that "true" honesty, innocence, simplicity, directness of manner are not traits to be *practiced* by always being good, honest, and simple, by always, in situations of moral choice, choosing "rightly"; rather they are a residue, what remains after a life has been purified by anxiety and suffering. Such traits are not real except to the extent that they have been tested, and the only real tests are those terrifying, transforming experiences which pit us against our own most powerful impulses, experiences where simple moral choices are impossible and tragedy is inevitable.[18]

According to Sissela Bok, "The whole truth *is* out of reach. But this fact has very little to do with our choices about whether to lie or to speak honestly, about what to say and what to hold back."[19] Although I want to agree with the simple wisdom of this statement, I must argue, finally, that her claim is not applicable to autobiography. For the autobiographer, autobiography is one of these "transforming experiences" that Brandt describes, and though tragedy is not inevitable for the autobiographer, it is for the person who never looks at his or her life autobiographically.

Whatever they were in actual life, Gertrude Stein, Sherwood Anderson, Richard Wright, Mary McCarthy, and Lillian Hellman, in their autobiographies, are autobiographers, not liars. This declaration is true because general readers, literary theorists, and autobiographers have different ideas of what an autobiography is and consequently

different notions of the truth standards required; because sociological, sexual, and political circumstances surrounding these authors affected their capacity for openness; because each's sense of identity as a self was partly created anew through the mixture of memory and imagination that responded to their needs as they wrote; and finally because, especially for autobiographers who are also novelists, personal narrative always includes a fictive aspect that is created by the tension between the "I" who writes and the "I" being written about. For these problem cases that I have covered in detail, as for all autobiography, autobiographers are not telling lies but telling their lives.

NOTES

Preface

1. Pascal, *Design and Truth in Autobiography*, 189.
2. Stephen, *Hours in a Library*, 3:237.
3. Eck, *Lies and Truth*, 160.

Chapter 1: Introduction

1. Spengemann and Lundquist, "Autobiography and the American Myth," 518.
2. De Man, "Autobiography as De-facement," 919.
3. See Blasing, *The Art of Life*, and Mandel, "Full of Life Now."
4. De Man, "Autobiography as De-facement," 921.
5. Fleishman, *Figures of Autobiography*, 39.
6. Loesberg, "Autobiography as Genre, Act of Consciousness, Text," 171.
7. Olney, "Autobiography and the Cultural Moment," 4.
8. Fishkin, *From Fact to Fiction*, 215.
9. See Adams, "'A Momentary Stay against Confusion.'"
10. Lawrence, *Studies in Classic American Literature*, viii.
11. See Adams, "The Contemporary American Mock-Autobiography."
12. Barth, *Lost in the Funhouse*, 186.
13. Mandel, "Full of Life Now," 54.
14. Fowles, *The French Lieutenant's Woman*, 82.
15. Bok, *Lying*, 6.
16. Translation of Lejeune, *Le Pact Autobiographique*.
17. Eakin, *Fictions in Autobiography*, 5.
18. Neuman, "The Observer Observed," 319.
19. Ibid., 321.
20. Loesberg, "Autobiography as Genre, Act of Consciousness, Text," 173.
21. Eakin, *Fictions in Autobiography*, 3–4.
22. Koelb, *The Incredulous Reader*, 31.
23. Hayden White, "Fictions of Factual Representation," 24.
24. Scholes, Klaus, and Silverman, *Elements of Literature*, 101.
25. Stevick, "Lies, Fictions, and Mock-Facts"; Doctorow, "False Documents."
26. Merle Brown, "The Idea of Fiction as Fictive or Fictitious," 62.
27. Eakin, *Fictions in Autobiography*, 276.
28. Shapiro, "The Dark Continent of Literature," 426.
29. Neuman, "The Observer Observed," 328.
30. Spender, "Confessions and Autobiography," 116.

31. Quoted in Neuman, "The Observer Observed," 319.
32. Spence, *Narrative Truth and Historical Truth*, 28.
33. Ibid., 31.
34. Gunn, *Autobiography*, 143.
35. Coles and Vopat, *What Makes Writing Good?*, xi.
36. Cebik, *Fictional Narrative and Truth*, 39.
37. Roberts, "Fiction outside of Literature," 5.
38. Ibid., 6.
39. Quoted in Bok, *Lying*, 3.
40. Cebik, *Fictional Narrative and Truth*, 9.
41. Quoted in Bok, *Lying*, 35. See Bok for a discussion of general misunderstandings of Augustine's definition (314).
42. Orwell, *1984*, 176–77.
43. Maxwell, *So Long, See You Tomorrow*, 27.
44. Abrams, *A Glossary of Literary Terms*, 80.
45. Brandt, "Lies, Lies, Lies," 63.
46. Gusdorf, "Conditions and Limits of Autobiography," 43.

Chapter 2: Gertrude Stein

1. Matisse et al., "Testimony against Gertrude Stein," 6.
2. Gertrude Stein, *Everybody's Autobiography*, 194.
3. Leo Stein, *Journey into the Self*, 134.
4. Quoted in Brinnin, *The Third Rose*, 311.
5. Leo Stein, *Journey into the Self*, 189.
6. Matisse et al., "Testimony against Gertrude Stein," 11, 13.
7. Hoffman, *Gertrude Stein*, 117.
8. Wasserstrom, "The Sursymamericubealism of Gertrude Stein," 104.
9. Simon, *The Biography of Alice B. Toklas*, 74.
10. Flanner, *Paris Was Yesterday, 1925–1930*, 90.
11. Wasserstrom, "The Sursymamericubealism of Gertrude Stein," 94.
12. Mellow, *Charmed Circle*, 195.
13. Toklas, *What Is Remembered*, vi.
14. Quoted in Simon, *The Biography of Alice B. Toklas*, 247.
15. Quoted in ibid., 60.
16. Ibid., 62.
17. Gertrude Stein, *Everybody's Autobiography*, 44.
18. Pascal, *Design and Truth in Autobiography*, 71.
19. Starobinski, "The Style of Autobiography," 77.
20. Lejeune, "Autobiography in the Third Person," 34.
21. Ibid., 33.
22. Gertrude Stein, *The Autobiography of Alice B. Toklas*, 60; subsequent citations appear as page numbers within the text. For citation of pet names, see Bridgman, *Gertrude Stein in Pieces*, 209.
23. Bloom, "Gertrude Is Alice Is Everybody," 83.
24. Lejeune, "Autobiography in the Third Person," 27.

25. Ibid., 44.

26. Quoted in ibid., 43.

27. Quoted in Mellow, *Charmed Circle*, 445.

28. Cited in Simon, *The Biography of Alice B. Toklas*, 152.

29. Bridgman, *Gertrude Stein in Pieces*, 205.

30. Simon, *The Biography of Alice B. Toklas*, 150.

31. Sutherland, *Gertrude Stein*, 148–49.

32. Mellow, *Charmed Circle*, 524.

33. Ibid., 268.

34. W. G. Rogers, *When This You See Remember Me*, 179–80.

35. Hemingway, *A Moveable Feast*, 118.

36. Gertrude Stein, *The Geographical History of America*, 155.

37. Rich, *On Lies, Secrets, and Silence*, 190, 191.

38. Simon, *The Biography of Alice B. Toklas*, 25.

39. Quoted in ibid., 187.

40. Wilson, *Gertrude Stein*, 183.

41. Minter, *The Interpretive Design as a Structural Principle in American Prose*, 5.

42. Ibid., 20–21.

43. Neuman, "The Observer Observed," 320.

44. Author's introduction to *Biography and Truth*, by Stanley Weintraub, 5.

45. Hoffman, *Gertrude Stein*, 117.

46. Author's introduction to *Biography and Truth*, by Stanley Weintraub, 5.

47. Bridgman, *Gertrude Stein in Pieces*, 212.

48. Matisse et al., "Testimony against Gertrude Stein," 6.

49. Copeland, *Language and Time and Gertrude Stein*, 127.

50. Ibid., 139.

51. Bilson, "The Memoir," 271.

52. Quoted in ibid., 278.

53. Misch, *A History of Autobiography in Antiquity*, 1:240.

54. Hoffman, *Gertrude Stein*, 117.

55. Munz, *The Shapes of Time*, 338.

56. Gertrude Stein, *Everybody's Autobiography*, 163.

57. Gertrude Stein, *Tender Buttons*, 64.

58. Gertrude Stein, *Stanzas in Meditations and Other Poems*, 77.

59. Bridgman, *Gertrude Stein in Pieces*, 219.

60. Roberts, *When Is Something Fiction?*, 9, 10.

61. Ibid., 23.

62. Bridgman, *Gertrude Stein in Pieces*, 21.

63. Gertrude Stein, *Everybody's Autobiography*, 69.

64. Wellek and Warren, *Theory of Literature*, 212–13.

65. Quoted in Ross, introduction to *The Life and Adventures of Robinson Crusoe*, by Daniel Defoe, 11.

66. Author's preface to *The Life and Adventures of Robinson Crusoe*, by Daniel Defoe, 25.

67. Ross, introduction to *The Life and Adventures of Robinson Crusoe*, by Daniel Defoe, 11.

68. Davis, *Factual Fictions*, 156.

69. Quoted in Novak, "Defoe's Theory of Fiction," 654.

70. Gertrude Stein, *Narration*, 45, 30–31.

71. Gertrude Stein, *Everybody's Autobiography*, 302.

72. Novak, "Defoe's Theory of Fiction," 651.

73. Ross, introduction to *The Life and Adventures of Robinson Crusoe*, by Daniel Defoe, 8.

74. Quoted in McAlmon, *McAlmon and the Lost Generation*, 204.

75. Holman, *A Handbook to Literature*, 524.

76. Hauck, *A Cheerful Nihilism*, 51–52.

77. Gertrude Stein, *What Are Masterpieces?*, 84.

78. Gertrude Stein, *Everybody's Autobiography*, 121.

79. Evans, "Gertrude Stein as Humorist," 97.

80. Ibid.

81. Hauck, *A Cheerful Nihilism*, 42.

Chapter 3: Sherwood Anderson

1. See Ray Lewis White, *Sherwood Anderson/Gertrude Stein*, for the most complete account of the Anderson-Stein relationship. Stein's valentine appeared originally in *Little Review* 9 (1923): 5–9; "Sherwood's Sweetness" is part of the Anderson memorial issue of *Story* 19 (1941): 63. Both works are reprinted in *Sherwood Anderson/Gertrude Stein*, as is Sherwood Anderson's introduction to Gertrude Stein's *Geography and Plays* (Boston: Four Seas, 1922), 5–8.

2. Sherwood Anderson, *Sherwood Anderson's Memoirs*, 11; subsequent citations appear as *Memoirs* plus page numbers within the text.

3. Feibleman, "Memories of Sherwood Anderson," 32.

4. Sherwood Anderson, "Sherwood Anderson's Earliest Autobiography," 345.

5. Fleishman, *Figures of Autobiography*, 478.

6. Rosengarten, *All God's Dangers*, xviii.

7. Sherwood Anderson, *A Story Teller's Story*, 190; subsequent citations appear as *Story* plus page numbers within the text.

8. Howe, *Sherwood Anderson*, 143.

9. Gertrude Stein, review of *A Story Teller's Story*, by Sherwood Anderson, 45.

10. These terms, in the order given in the text, come from Klein, "Sherwood Anderson," 40; Douglas G. Rogers, *Sherwood Anderson*, 9; David D. Anderson, "A Photographic Gallery," 18; David D. Anderson, introduction to *Critical Essays on Sherwood Anderson*, 2; Eden, "A Critical Approach to Autobiography," 105; Crowley, "The Education of Sherwood Anderson," 186; and Burbank, *Sherwood Anderson*, 21, 118.

11. Cooley, *Educated Lives*, 145–49.

12. Sherwood Anderson, *Tar*, 10; subsequent citations appear as *Tar* plus page numbers within the text.

13. Coe, *When the Grass Was Taller*, xi.

14. Grossman, "The Strange Case of a Man Who Offers No Apologies," 12.

15. Burbank, *Sherwood Anderson*, 137.

16. Cockshut, *The Art of Autobiography in 19th and 20th Century England*, 6.

17. Couser, *American Autobiography*, 7.

18. Cooley, *Educated Lives*, xi.

19. Gohdes, "Three Books for the Student of America," 335.

20. Bok, *Lying*, 104.

21. Young, "A Marginal Note," 195.

22. Boynton, *More Contemporary Americans*, 184; Geismar, "Babbitt on Pegasus," 184.

23. Lionel Trilling, *Sincerity and Authenticity*, 10–11.

24. Howe, *Sherwood Anderson*, 18.

25. Miller, "Anderson the Storyteller," 71; Thomas, *Literary Admirers of Alfred Stieglitz*, 73–74.

26. Karl James Anderson, "My Brother, Sherwood Anderson," 26.

27. Matthews, *Tales of the Ohio Land*, viii.

28. Sherwood Anderson, *Sherwood Anderson's Notebook*, 184.

29. Jones, *Letters of Sherwood Anderson*, 129.

30. Curry, The *"Writer's Book,"* 275–76.

31. Ibid., 276.

32. Quoted in Sutton, *The Road to Winesburg*, 479.

33. Ibid., 477.

34. Hecht, "Go, Scholar-Gypsy!," 92.

35. Feibleman, "Memories of Sherwood Anderson," 35.

36. Sherwood Anderson, *Sherwood Anderson's Notebook*, 33, 34–35.

37. Tintner, "Autobiography as Fiction," 258.

38. Ibid.

39. Lionel Trilling, "Sherwood Anderson," 213.

40. Hecht, *A Child of the Century*, 211.

41. Neuman, "The Observer Observed," 320.

42. Gregory, *The Portable Sherwood Anderson*, 15.

43. Marriner, "Sherwood Anderson," 109, 115.

44. Ibid., 109.

45. Sutton, *The Road to Winesburg*, 20.

46. Ibid., 97.

47. Marriner, "Sherwood Anderson," 112.

48. William L. Phillips, "How Sherwood Anderson Wrote *Winesburg, Ohio*," 74–75.

49. Quoted in Sutton, *The Road to Winesburg*, 172.

50. Ibid., 196.

51. Ibid., 185, 191.

52. Townsend, *Sherwood Anderson*, 81.

53. Howe, *Sherwood Anderson*, 48.

54. Quoted in Sutton, *The Road to Winesburg*, 561.

55. Quoted in ibid., 191.

56. Jones, *Letters of Sherwood Anderson*, viii.

57. David D. Anderson, "Anderson and Myth," 125.

58. Steinbeck, *East of Eden*, 84.

59. Howe, *Sherwood Anderson*, 18–19.

60. Sutton, *The Road to Winesburg*, 482.

61. Townsend, *Sherwood Anderson*, 13.

62. Sherwood Anderson, *Windy McPherson's Son*, 22.

63. Wolff, "Minor Lives," 69.

64. Pascal, *Design and Truth in Autobiography*, 4.

65. Henley, "Transformations of Experience," 7.

66. Ibid., 1.

67. For permission to quote this unpublished passage from Memoirs Box 2 of the Sherwood Anderson Collection, Newberry Library, Chicago, Ill., I thank Diana Haskell, modern manuscripts curator.

68. Geismar, *The Last of the Provincials*, 262.

69. Quoted in Sutton, *The Road to Winesburg*, 473.

70. In an earlier, unpublished version of this story, "A Father and Son and the Hand," the father is not so silent; see Memoirs Box 2 of the Sherwood Anderson Collection, Newberry Library, Chicago, Ill.

71. Rideout, preface to *A Story Teller's Story*, by Sherwood Anderson, n.p.

72. Howe, *Sherwood Anderson*, 19.

73. Ibid., 143.

74. Rideout, "Sherwood Anderson," 5.

75. Abbott, *Diary Fiction*.

76. Scholes and Kellogg, *The Nature of Narrative*, 151.

77. Kazin, "Autobiography as Narrative," 212.

Chapter 4: Richard Wright

1. Ralph K. White, *"Black Boy,"* 442–43.

2. Du Bois, "Richard Wright Looks Back," 133.

3. For these terms, see the following in Reilly, *Richard Wright*, 122–76: Gottlieb, Creighton, Du Bois, Garlington, Bentley, Richter, and Hamilton.

4. Quoted in Fabre, *The Unfinished Quest of Richard Wright*, 578.

5. Ibid.

6. Ibid., 250.

7. Quoted in Fabre, "Afterword," 138.

8. Alternate titles cited in Webb, *Richard Wright*, 706–7, and in Davis and Fabre, *Richard Wright*, 56.

9. Fabre, *The Unfinished Quest of Richard Wright*, 259, 578.

10. Webb, *Richard Wright*, 198, 207–8.

11. For a discussion of *Black Boy* and slave narratives, see Stepto, *From behind the Veil*; Smith, *Where I'm Bound*; and Butterfield, *Black Autobiography in America*.

12. Richard Wright, *Black Boy*, 83; subsequent citations appear as page numbers within the text.

13. See Webb, *Richard Wright*, 402, and Richard Wright, "How 'Bigger' Was Born."

14. Pascal, *Design and Truth in Autobiography*, 63, 82.

15. Fabre, *The Unfinished Quest of Richard Wright*, 47.

16. Ibid., 6.

17. Ibid., 56.

18. Cited in Webb, *Richard Wright*, 419.

19. Margolies, *The Art of Richard Wright*, 16.

20. Olney, "Some Versions of Memory / Some Versions of Bios," 244–45.

21. Ellison, "Richard Wright's Blues," 89.

22. Stone, *Autobiographical Occasions and Original Acts*, 124.

23. Lionel Trilling, *Sincerity and Authenticity*, 139.

24. Ibid., 135.

25. Mandel, "Full of Life Now," 65.

26. Ibid.

27. Ibid., 66.

28. Stepto, *From behind the Veil*, 143.

29. Stone, *Autobiographical Occasions and Original Acts*, 126.

30. Richard Wright, "The Ethics of Living Jim Crow," 4–5.

31. High, *Past Titan Rock*, 65.

32. Richard Wright, *Uncle Tom's Children*, 2.

33. Rosenblatt, "Black Autobiography," 173.

34. Angelou, *I Know Why the Caged Bird Sings*, 164.

35. Ellison, *Invisible Man*, 8.

36. Margolies, *The Art of Richard Wright*, 19.

37. Felgar, *Richard Wright*, 46.

38. Graves, "Opportunity," 173.

39. Spence, *Narrative Truth and Historical Truth*, 31.

40. Kazin, "The Self as History," 89.

Chapter 5: Mary McCarthy

1. Mary McCarthy, "Portrait of a Typical Negro," 10.

2. Ibid.

3. Niebuhr, "Mary McCarthy," 310–11.

4. Grumbach, *The Company She Kept*, 29.

5. Cook, "Mary McCarthy," 40.

6. Quoted in Gelderman, *Mary McCarthy*, 204.

7. Antonia White, "Withered on the Stalk," 740.

8. Spacks, *The Female Imagination*, 182.

9. Mary McCarthy, *Memories of a Catholic Girlhood*, 5; subsequent citations appear as *Memories* plus page numbers within the text; passages appearing in italics are italicized in *Memories*.

10. Goleman, *Vital Lies, Simple Truths*, 173.

11. Quoted in Niebuhr, "Mary McCarthy," 314.

12. Eakin, *Fictions in Autobiography*, 39.

13. Howarth, "Some Principles of Autobiography," 100.

14. Goldman, *Mary McCarthy*, viii.

15. McKenzie, *Mary McCarthy*, 26.

16. Lange, "The Woman and the Orphan Child," 18.

17. Grumbach, *The Company She Kept*, 15.

18. Ibid., 20.

19. Quoted in Niebuhr, "Mary McCarthy," 291.

20. Moore, *Collected Poems*, 41.

21. Mary McCarthy, "Settling the Colonel's Hash," 88.

22. Ibid., 89.

23. Mansell, "Unsettling the Colonel's Hash," 126.

24. Mary McCarthy, "Artists in Uniform," 81.

25. Mary McCarthy, *The Company She Keeps*, 262–63.

26. Mary McCarthy, "Settling the Colonel's Hash," 89.

27. Quoted in Grumbach, *The Company She Kept*, 86.

28. Eakin, *Fictions in Autobiography*, 16, 7.

29. Roth, "Don't Try to Get to the Bottom of Things," 24.

30. Eakin, *Fictions in Autobiography*, 17.

31. Mary McCarthy, *Memories of a Catholic Girlhood*, 4, 10, 11, 48, 52, 101, 193, 193, 194, 210, 237, 240.

32. Mary McCarthy, *How I Grew*, 5, 44, 44, 47, 48, 73, 80, 102; subsequent citations appear as *How I Grew* plus page numbers within the text.

33. Niebuhr, "Mary McCarthy," 286.

34. Latko, "Confession," 131.

35. McKeever, "Penance," 78.

36. Ibid., 81.

37. Quoted in Brower, "Mary McCarthyism," 63.

38. Kazin, "The Self as History," 87.

39. McKeever, "Penance," 81.

40. Rudge, "Confession," 214.

41. De Man, "Autobiography as De-facement."

42. Stelzig, "Poetry and/or Truth," 29.

43. Misch, *A History of Autobiography in Antiquity*, 2:582.

44. Shaw, "*In Memoriam* and the Rhetoric of Confession," 83.

45. Eakin, *Fictions in Autobiography*, 34.

46. Widner, "Finally a Lady," 95.

47. Spacks, *The Female Imagination*, 185.

48. Minnich, "Why Not Lie?," 505.

49. Lange, "The Woman and the Orphan Child," 18.

50. Mary McCarthy, "Settling the Colonel's Hash," 89.

51. Eakin, *Fictions in Autobiography*, 42.

52. Trow, "Truth but without Respect for Truth," 24.

53. Eakin, *Fictions in Autobiography*; Taylor, *Chapters of Experience*.

54. Eakin, *Fictions in Autobiography*, 54.

55. Ignatieff, "Family Photo Albums," 28.
56. Quoted in Brower, "Mary McCarthyism," 64.
57. Mary McCarthy, "The Fact in Fiction," 186.
58. Berthoff, *Fictions and Events*, 39–40.
59. Mary McCarthy, "Portrait of a Typical Negro," 10.
60. Erikson, *Young Man Luther*, 111–12.
61. Mailer, "An Appeal to Lillian Hellman and Mary McCarthy," 3.
62. Rich, *On Lies, Secrets, and Silence*, 187.
63. Arendt, *Thinking*, 27.
64. Quoted in and translated by Schachtel, *Metamorphosis*, 281–82.
65. Lifson, "Allegory of the Secret," 259.
66. Hughes, "Mental Reservation," 662–63.
67. Ibid., 663.
68. Hardwick, "Mary McCarthy," 38.
69. Sheed, "Her Youth Observed," 5.
70. Brower, "Mary McCarthyism," 63.

Chapter 6: Lillian Hellman

1. Quoted in Mailer, "An Appeal to Lillian Hellman and Mary McCarthy," 3.
2. Quoted in Gelderman, *Mary McCarthy*, 338.
3. Doudna, "A Still Unfinished Woman," 198.
4. See Rollyson, *Lillian Hellman*, 482.
5. Mary McCarthy, "Mary McCarthy Goes to the Movies," 33.
6. Mary McCarthy, "Theater Chronicles," 577; Kevin McCarthy, "In Her Own Words," 99.
7. Mailer, " An Appeal to Lillian Hellman and Mary McCarthy," 3.
8. See *Pentimento* in Hellman, *Three*, 365; subsequent citations of Hellman's first three autobiographies (*An Unfinished Woman*, *Pentimento*, and *Scoundrel Time*) appear as *Three* plus page numbers within the text.
9. Eakin, *Fictions in Autobiography*, 36.
10. Pynchon, *V*, 286.
11. Wagner-Martin, "Lillian Hellman," 275.
12. Scott-Maxwell, *The Measure of My Days*, 96.
13. Wagner-Martin, "Lillian Hellman," 278.
14. Janeway, "Women's Literature," 345; Spacks, *The Female Imagination*, 409.
15. Gardner, "An Interview with Lillian Hellman," 123; Albert, "Sweetest Smelling Baby in New Orleans," 176.
16. Pascal, *Design and Truth in Autobiography*, 4.
17. Ibid., 6.
18. Bilson, "The Memoir," 265.
19. Ibid.
20. See, for example, Hellman's "Day in Spain," 297–98, and "I Meet the Front-Line Russians," 11, 68, 71.
21. Originally called "Dashiell Hammett: A Memoir" when published in

the *New York Review of Books* 5 (24 November 1965): 16–18, 20–23, this piece served as an introduction to the Hellman-edited *The Big Knockover*.

22. Eakin, *Fictions in Autobiography*, 5.

23. Gellhorn, "On Apocryphism," 280–81.

24. Spender, *Journals, 1939–1983*, 482–83.

25. McCracken, "'Julia' and Other Fictions by Lillian Hellman," 43.

26. Hook, "The Scoundrel in the Looking Glass," 226, 237.

27. Kramer, "The Life and Death of Lillian Hellman," 2, 4.

28. Ibid., 5.

29. Diana Trilling, *We Must March My Darlings*, 42.

30. Ibid., 46.

31. Hellman, *Maybe*, 50; subsequent citations appear as *Maybe* plus page numbers within the text.

32. Bilson, "The Memoir," 264.

33. Norman, "Lillian Hellman's Gift to a Young Playwright," 7.

34. Gellhorn, "On Apocryphism," 286, 297.

35. William Wright, *Lillian Hellman*, 412.

36. Gellhorn, "On Apocryphism," 301.

37. Spender, "Stephen Spender Replies," 304.

38. Lederer, *Lillian Hellman*, 114; Doudna, "A Still Unfinished Woman," 195.

39. Gellhorn, "On Apocryphism," 286, 297.

40. Brandt, "Lies, Lies, Lies," 63.

41. Quoted in Johnson, *The Life of Dashiell Hammett*, 317.

42. Pascal, *Design and Truth in Autobiography*, 79.

43. Spacks, *The Female Imagination*, 383.

44. Ibid., 381.

45. Ibid., 383.

46. Quoted in Rather, "A Profile of Lillian Hellman," 215.

47. Harriman, "Miss Lily of New Orleans," 22.

48. Nabokov, *Speak, Memory*, 139.

49. Ibid., 25.

50. Holman, *A Handbook to Literature*, 315.

51. McCracken, "'Julia' and Other Fictions by Lillian Hellman," 35, 43.

52. Quoted in Doudna, "A Still Unfinished Woman," 194, 198.

53. Quoted in Rollyson, *Lillian Hellman*, 470; Drake, "Lillian Hellman as Herself," 292.

54. Eakin, *Fictions in Autobiography*, 56.

55. McCracken, "'Julia' and Other Fictions by Lillian Hellman," 38.

56. Ibid.

57. Hersey, "Lillian Hellman," 26.

58. McCracken, "'Julia' and Other Fictions by Lillian Hellman," 38.

59. Maurice H. Brown, "Autobiography and Memory," 5; Harriman, "Miss Lily of New Orleans," 23.

60. Gardiner, *Code Name "Mary,"* 69.

61. Quoted in Witt, "Nazi Era Saga," 1.

62. Quoted in William Wright, *Lillian Hellman*, 404.

63. Spender, *Journals, 1939–1983*, 482.

64. Quoted in Gardiner, *Code Name "Mary,"* xv.

65. Quoted in Spender, *Journals, 1939–1983*, 483.

66. Ibid., 165, 170.

67. Gardiner, *Code Name "Mary,"* 37, 43.

68. McCracken, "'Julia' and Other Fictions by Lillian Hellman," 40.

69. Quoted in William Wright, *Lillian Hellman*, 388.

70. Spender, *World within World*, 81.

71. French, review of *Julia*, 53–54.

72. Quoted in Knight, "Writing the Screenplay for *Julia*," 6; Marc Green, "Lillian Hellman, Embellished for the Screen," 19; and Judith Weintraub, "Two Feisty Feminists Filming Hellman's *Pentimento*," 17.

73. McCracken, "'Julia' and Other Fictions by Lillian Hellman," 41.

74. Robinson, *H. D.*, 304.

75. Ibid., 303–4.

76. Ibid., 133.

77. Cockburn, "Who Was Julia?," 201.

78. Mason, "The Other Voice," 210; Bilson and Smith, "Lillian Hellman and the Strategy of the 'Other.'"

79. Spender, *Journals, 1939–1983*, 483.

80. Kael, "The Current Cinema," 94.

81. Doudna, "A Still Unfinished Woman," 200.

82. Andersen, "Red Hollywood," 153.

83. A number of people, including Tallulah Bankhead, Louis Kronenberger, and Margaret Case Harriman, are responsible for the George Washington remark; Geoffrey Wolff for the Easter Island comparison; and John Hersey for the ship's figurehead comparison.

84. Navasky, *Naming Names*, 314–29.

85. Kael, "The Current Cinema," 94.

86. Warren, *Liberals and Communism*, 163.

87. Ceplair and Englund, *The Inquisition in Hollywood*, 279.

88. Andersen, "Red Hollywood," 157.

89. Goleman, *Vital Lies, Simple Truths*, 239–40.

90. Andersen, "Red Hollywood," 151.

91. Ibid.

92. Cavaliero, "Autobiography and Fiction," 160.

93. William Phillips, "What Happened in the Fifties," 338.

94. Quoted in Bok, *Lying*, 154.

95. Ibid., 134, 140.

96. Quoted in Layman, *Shadow Man*, 227.

97. Hook, "The Scoundrel in the Looking Glass," 227.

98. Mayne, "Ishmael and the Inquisitors," 1413.

99. Quoted in Berger, "Profile," 253.

100. Ibid., 254.

101. Bentley, "The Greatest Show on Earth," 284.

102. Rather, "A Profile of Lillian Hellman," 216.

103. William Wright, *Lillian Hellman*, 370.

104. Schachtel, *Metamorphosis*, 287.

105. Kempton, "Witnesses," 22–25.

106. Wagner-Martin, "Lillian Hellman," 278.

107. Eakin, "Reference and the Representative in American Autobiography," 20, 23.

108. Peyre, *Literature and Sincerity*, 205; Desmond McCarthy quoted in Kendall, "Walking the Boundaries," 40.

109. Kazin, "The Self as History," 88.

110. Eakin, "Reference and the Representative in American Autobiography," 23.

111. Rich, *On Lies, Secrets, and Silence*, 187.

112. Goleman, *Vital Lies, Simple Truths*, 95.

113. Bartlett, *Remembering*, 53.

114. Bromberg, "The Duplicity of Memory in Lillian Hellman's Memoirs," 1, 7.

115. Quoted in Spence, *Narrative Truth and Historical Truth*, 164.

116. Ibid., 165.

117. Bromberg, "The Duplicity of Memory in Lillian Hellman's Memoirs."

118. Cockshut, *The Art of Autobiography in 19th and 20th Century England*, 101.

Chapter 7: Conclusion

1. O'Connor, *Mystery and Manners*, 34.

2. Eakin, *Fictions in Autobiography*, 55.

3. Quoted in Gelderman, *Mary McCarthy*, 329.

4. Ibid., 254–55.

5. Ibid., 408.

6. Detienne, *The Creation of Mythology*, 36–37.

7. Ibid., 38.

8. Goleman, *Vital Lies, Simple Truths*, 96.

9. Ibid., 95.

10. Ibid.

11. Ibid., 96.

12. Bok, *Lying*, 5.

13. Allon, "Reflections on the Art of Lying," 47.

14. Ibid., 53.

15. Hampl, "Memory and Imagination," 1006–7.

16. Ibid., 1011.

17. Kazin, "Autobiography as Narrative," 211.

18. Brandt, "Lies, Lies, Lies," 59.

19. Bok, *Lying*, 4.

WORKS CITED

Abbott, H. Porter. *Diary Fiction: Writing as Action*. Ithaca, N.Y.: Cornell University Press, 1984.

Abrams, M. H. *A Glossary of Literary Terms*. 3d ed. New York: Holt, Rinehart and Winston, 1971.

Adams, Timothy Dow. "The Contemporary American Mock-Autobiography." *Clio* 8 (1979): 417–28.

_____. "'A Momentary Stay against Confusion': Frank Conroy's *Stop-Time*." *Critique* 27 (1986): 153–66.

Albert, Jan. "Sweetest Smelling Baby in New Orleans." In *Conversations with Lillian Hellman*, pp. 165–78. See Bryer.

Allon, Dafna. "Reflections on the Art of Lying." *Commentary* 61 (1986): 47–54.

Andersen, Thom. "Red Hollywood." In *Literature and the Visual Arts in Contemporary Society*, edited by Suzanne Ferguson and Barbara Groseclose, pp. 141–96. Columbus: Ohio State University Press, 1985.

Anderson, David D. "Anderson and Myth." In *Sherwood Anderson: Dimensions of His Work*, edited by David D. Anderson, pp. 118–41. East Lansing: Michigan State University Press, 1976.

_____. "A Photographic Gallery." *Twentieth-Century Literature* 23 (1977): 17–39.

_____, ed. *Critical Essays on Sherwood Anderson*. Boston: G. K. Hall and Co., 1981.

Anderson, Karl James. "My Brother, Sherwood Anderson." *Saturday Review of Literature* 31 (1948): 6–7, 26–27.

Anderson, Sherwood. "Sherwood Anderson's Earliest Autobiography." Appendix to *A Story Teller's Story: A Critical Edition*. Edited by Ray Lewis White. Cleveland: Press of Case Western Reserve University, 1968.

_____. *Sherwood Anderson's Memoirs: A Critical Edition*. Edited by Ray Lewis White. Chapel Hill: University of North Carolina Press, 1969.

_____. *Sherwood Anderson's Notebook*. New York: Boni and Liveright, 1926.

_____. *A Story Teller's Story: A Critical Edition*. Edited by Ray Lewis White. Cleveland: Press of Case Western Reserve University, 1968.

_____. *Tar: A Midwest Childhood. A Critical Text*. Edited by Ray Lewis White. Cleveland: Press of Case Western Reserve University, 1969.

_____. *Windy McPherson's Son*. New York: B. W. Huebsch, 1916.

_____. *Winesburg, Ohio*. New York: B. W. Huebsch, 1919.

Angelou, Maya. *I Know Why the Caged Bird Sings*. New York: Bantam Books, 1971.

Arendt, Hannah. *Thinking: Life of the Mind*. New York: Harcourt Brace Jovanovich, 1977.

188

Barth, John. *Lost in the Funhouse*. New York: Bantam Books, 1969.

Bartlett, F. C. *Remembering: A Study in Experimental and Social Psychology*. Cambridge: Harvard University Press, 1932.

Bentley, Eric. "The Greatest Show on Earth." In *Theatre of War*, pp. 283–305. New York: Viking Press, 1972.

Berger, Marilyn. "Profile: Lillian Hellman." In *Conversations with Lillian Hellman*, pp. 232–73. See Bryer.

Berthoff, Warner. *Fictions and Events: Essays in Criticism and Literary History*. New York: E. P. Dutton and Co., 1971.

Bilson, Marcus K. "The Memoir: New Perspectives on a Forgotten Genre." *Genre* 10 (1977): 259–83.

Bilson, Marcus K., and Sidonie Smith. "Lillian Hellman and the Strategy of the 'Other.'" In *Woman's Autobiography: Essays in Criticism*, edited by Estelle Jelinek, pp. 163–79. Bloomington: Indiana University Press, 1980.

Blasing, Mutlu Konuk. *The Art of Life: Studies in American Autobiographical Literature*. Austin: University of Texas Press, 1977.

Bloom, Lynn Z. "Gertrude Is Alice Is Everybody: Innovation and Point of View in Gertrude Stein's Autobiographies." *Twentieth-Century Literature* 24 (1978): 81–93.

Bok, Sissela. *Lying: Moral Choice in Public and Private Life*. New York: Random House, Vintage Books, 1979.

Boynton, Percy. *More Contemporary Americans*. Chicago: University of Chicago Press, 1940.

Brandt, Anthony. "Lies, Lies, Lies." *Atlantic* 240 (November 1977): 58–63.

Bridgman, Richard. *Gertrude Stein in Pieces*. New York: Oxford University Press, 1970.

Brinnin, John Michael. *The Third Rose: Gertrude Stein and Her World*. Boston: Little, Brown and Co., 1959.

Bromberg, Pamela. "The Duplicity of Memory in Lillian Hellman's Memoirs." Paper presented at the annual meeting of the Modern Language Association, Washington, D.C., December 1984.

Brower, Brock. "Mary McCarthyism." *Esquire* (July 1962): 62–67, 113.

Brown, Maurice H. "Autobiography and Memory: The Case of Lillian Hellman." *Biography* 8 (1985): 1–11.

Brown, Merle. "The Idea of Fiction as Fictive or Fictitious." *Bulletin of the Midwest Modern Language Association* 6 (1973): 62–73.

Bryer, Jackson R., ed. *Conversations with Lillian Hellman*. Jackson: University Press of Mississippi, 1986.

Buckley, William F. "*Scoundrel Time* and Who Is the Ugliest of Them All?" *National Review* 29 (21 January 1977): 101–6.

Burbank, Rex. *Sherwood Anderson*. New York: Twayne Publishers, 1964.

Butterfield, Steven. *Black Autobiography in America*. Amherst: University of Massachusetts Press, 1974.

Cavaliero, Glen. "Autobiography and Fiction." In *Modern Selves: Essays on British and American Autobiography*, edited by Philip Dodd, pp. 157–71. London: Frank Cass, 1986.

Cebik, L. B. *Fictional Narrative and Truth: An Epistemic Analysis.* Washington, D.C.: University Press of America, 1984.

Ceplair, Larry, and Steven Englund. *The Inquisition in Hollywood: Politics in the Film Community, 1930–1960.* Garden City, N.Y.: Doubleday and Co., 1980.

Cockburn, Alexander. "Who Was Julia?" *Nation* 240 (23 February 1985): 200–201.

Cockshut, A. O. J. *The Art of Autobiography in 19th and 20th Century England.* New Haven, Conn.: Yale University Press, 1984.

Coe, Richard. *When the Grass Was Taller: Autobiography and the Experience of Childhood.* New Haven, Conn.: Yale University Press, 1984.

Coles, William E., and James Vopat. *What Makes Writing Good?* Lexington, Mass.: D. C. Heath and Co., 1985.

Cook, Rev. Bruce. "Mary McCarthy: One of Ours?" *Catholic World* 199 (1964): 34–42.

Cooley, Thomas. *Educated Lives: The Rise of Modern Autobiography in America.* Columbus: Ohio State University Press, 1976.

Copeland, Carolyn Faunce. *Language and Time and Gertrude Stein.* Iowa City: University of Iowa Press, 1975.

Couser, Thomas G. *American Autobiography: The Prophetic Mode.* Amherst: University of Massachusetts Press, 1979.

Crowley, John W. "The Education of Sherwood Anderson." In *Sherwood Anderson: Centennial Essays,* edited by Hilbert H. Campbell and Charles E. Modlin, pp. 185–201. Troy, N.Y.: Whitston Publishing Co., 1976.

Curry, Martha Mulroy, ed. *The "Writer's Book".* Metuchen, N.J.: Scarecrow Press, 1975.

Davis, Charles T., and Michel Fabre. *Richard Wright: A Primary Bibliography.* Boston: G. K. Hall and Co., 1982.

Davis, Lennard J. *Factual Fictions: The Origins of the English Novel.* New York: Columbia University Press, 1983.

Defoe, Daniel. Preface to *The Life and Adventures of Robinson Crusoe.* Baltimore: Penguin Books, 1965.

De Man, Paul. "Autobiography as De-facement." *Modern Language Notes* 94 (1979): 919–30.

Detienne, Marcel. *The Creation of Mythology.* Translated by Margaret Cook. Chicago: University of Chicago Press, 1986.

Doctorow, E. L. "False Documents." *American Review* 26 (1977): 215–32.

Dodd, Philip, ed. *Modern Selves: Essays on British and American Autobiography.* London: Frank Cass, 1986.

Doudna, Christine. "A Still Unfinished Woman: A Conversation." In *Conversations with Lillian Hellman,* pp. 192–209. See Bryer.

Drake, Sylvie. "Lillian Hellman as Herself." In *Conversations with Lillian Hellman,* pp. 287–92. See Bryer.

Du Bois, W. E. B. "Richard Wright Looks Back." In *Richard Wright: The Critical Reception,* edited by John M. Reilly, pp. 132–33. New York: Burt Franklin, 1978.

Eakin, Paul John. *Fictions in Autobiography: Studies in the Art of Self-Invention*. Princeton, N.J.: Princeton University Press, 1985.

———. "Reference and the Representative in American Autobiography: Mary McCarthy and Lillian Hellman." Paper presented at the Symposium on American Autobiography, Rome, May 1985.

Eck, Marcel. *Lies and Truth*. Translated by Bernard Murchland. New York: Macmillan Co., 1970.

Eden, Walter Anthony. *A Critical Approach to Autobiography: Technique and Theme in Sherwood Anderson, Benedetto Croce, Jean-Paul Sartre, and Richard Wright*. Ph.D. dissertation, New York University, 1975.

Ellison, Ralph. *Invisible Man*. New York: Random House, Vintage Books, 1972.

———. "Richard Wright's Blues." In *Shadow and Act*, pp. 89–104. New York: New American Library, 1966.

Erikson, Erik. *Young Man Luther: A Study in Psychoanalysis and History*. New York: W. W. Norton and Co., 1962.

Evans, Oliver. "Gertrude Stein as Humorist." *Prairie Schooner* 21 (1947): 97–101.

Fabre, Michel. "Afterword." In *American Hunger*, by Richard Wright, pp. 136–46. New York: Harper and Row, 1977.

———. *The Unfinished Quest of Richard Wright*. Translated by Isabel Barzun. New York: W. W. Norton and Co., 1973.

Feibleman, James K. "Memories of Sherwood Anderson." *Shenandoah* 3 (1962): 32–45.

Felgar, Robert. *Richard Wright*. Boston: Twayne Publishers, 1980.

Fishkin, Shelley. *From Fact to Fiction: Journalism and Imaginative Writing in America*. Baltimore: Johns Hopkins University Press, 1985.

Flanner, Janet. *Paris Was Yesterday, 1925–1930*. Edited by Irving Drutman. New York: Viking Press, 1972.

Fleishman, Avrom. *Figures of Autobiography: The Language of Self-Writing*. Berkeley: University of California Press, 1983.

Fowles, John. *The French Lieutenant's Woman*. New York: Signet, 1969.

French, Philip. Review of *Julia*. *Sight and Sound* 47 (1977–78): 53–54.

Gardiner, Muriel. *Code Name "Mary": Memoirs of an American Woman in the Austrian Underground*. New Haven, Conn.: Yale University Press, 1983.

Gardner, Fred. "An Interview with Lillian Hellman." In *Conversations with Lillian Hellman*, pp. 107–23. See Bryer.

Geismar, Maxwell. "Babbitt on Pegasus." *Yale Review* 32 (1942–43): 183–85.

———. *The Last of the Provincials*. London: Seeker and Warburg, 1947.

Gelderman, Carol. *Mary McCarthy: A Life*. New York: St. Martin's Press, 1988.

Gellhorn, Martha. "On Apocryphism." *Paris Review* 79 (1981): 280–301.

Gohdes, Clarence. "Three Books for the Student of America." *South Atlantic Quarterly* 41 (1942): 335.

Goldman, Sherli Evens. *Mary McCarthy: A Bibliography*. New York: Harcourt, Brace and World, 1968.

Goleman, Daniel. *Vital Lies, Simple Truths: The Psychology of Self-Deception.* New York: Simon and Schuster, 1985.

Graves, Patsy. "Opportunity." In *Richard Wright: The Critical Reception,* edited by John M. Reilly, pp. 173–74. New York: Burt Franklin, 1978.

Green, Marc. "Lillian Hellman, Embellished for the Screen." *Chronicle of Higher Education* 15 (7 November 1977): 19.

Gregory, Horace, ed. *The Portable Sherwood Anderson.* New York: Viking Press, 1949.

Grossman, Max. "The Strange Case of a Man Who Offers No Apologies." *Boston Post,* 12 April 1942, 12.

Grumbach, Doris. *The Company She Kept.* New York: Coward-McCann, 1967.

Gunn, Janet Varner. *Autobiography: Towards a Poetics of Experience.* Philadelphia: University of Pennsylvania Press, 1982.

Gusdorf, Georges. "Conditions and Limits of Autobiography." Translated by James Olney. In *Autobiography: Essays Theoretical and Critical,* pp. 28–48. See Olney, ed.

Hampl, Patricia. "Memory and Imagination." In *The Dolphin Reader,* edited by Douglas Hunt, pp. 1003–14. Boston: Houghton Mifflin Co., 1986.

Hardwick, Elizabeth. "Mary McCarthy." In *A View of My Own: Essays in Literature and Society,* pp. 33–40. New York: Farrar, Straus and Cudahy, 1962.

Harriman, Margaret Case. "Miss Lily of New Orleans." *New Yorker* 17 (8 November 1941): 22–33.

Hauck, Richard. *A Cheerful Nihilism: Confidence and the "Absurd" in American Humorous Fiction.* Bloomington: Indiana University Press, 1971.

Hecht, Ben. *A Child of the Century.* New York: Playbill/Ballantine, 1954.

———. "Go, Scholar-Gypsy!" *Story* 19 (1941): 92–93.

Hellman, Lillian. "Day in Spain." *New Republic* 94 (13 April 1938): 297–98.

———. "I Meet the Front-Line Russians." *Collier's* 115 (31 March 1945): 11, 68, 71.

———. *Maybe: A Story by Lillian Hellman.* Boston: Little, Brown and Co., 1980.

———. *Three: "An Unfinished Woman," "Pentimento," "Scoundrel Time."* Boston: Little, Brown and Co., 1979.

———, ed. *The Big Knockover: Selected Stories and Short Novels of Dashiell Hammett.* New York: Random House, 1966.

Hemingway, Ernest. *A Moveable Feast.* New York: Charles Scribner's Sons, 1964.

Henley, Joan. "Transformations of Experience: The Autobiographical Writings of Sherwood Anderson." Paper presented at the annual meeting of the Modern Language Association, New York 1978.

Hersey, John. "Lillian Hellman." *New Republic* 175 (18 September 1976): 25–27.

High, Ellesa Clay. *Past Titan Rock: Journeys into an Appalachian Valley.* Lexington: University Press of Kentucky, 1984.

Hoffman, Michael J. *Gertrude Stein.* Boston: Twayne Publishers, 1976.

192

Holman, C. Hugh. *A Handbook to Literature*. 4th ed. Indianapolis: Bobbs-Merrill Co., 1980.

Hook, Sidney. "The Scoundrel in the Looking Glass." In *Philosophy and Public Policy*, pp. 218–37. Carbondale: Southern Illinois University Press, 1980.

Howarth, William L. "Some Principles of Autobiography." In *Autobiography: Essays Theoretical and Critical*, pp. 84–114. See Olney, ed.

Howe, Irving. *Sherwood Anderson: A Biographical and Critical Study*. Stanford, Calif.: Stanford University Press, 1961.

Hughes, D. "Lying." In *New Catholic Encyclopedia*, 8:1107–10. New York: McGraw-Hill, 1967.

————. "Mental Reservation." In *New Catholic Encyclopedia*, 9:662–63. New York: McGraw-Hill, 1967.

Ignatieff, Michael. "Family Photo Albums." *Harper's* 274 (1987): 27–28.

Janeway, Elizabeth. "Women's Literature." In *Harvard Guide to Contemporary Writing*, edited by Daniel Hoffman, pp. 342–95. Cambridge: Harvard University Press, Belknap Press, 1979.

Johnson, Diane. *The Life of Dashiell Hammett*. London: Chatto and Windus, 1984.

Jones, Howard Mumford, ed. *Letters of Sherwood Anderson*. Boston: Little, Brown and Co., 1953.

Kael, Pauline. "The Current Cinema: A Woman for All Seasons?" *New Yorker* 53 (10 October 1977): 94, 99–102.

Kazin, Alfred. "Autobiography as Narrative." *Michigan Quarterly Review* 3 (1964): 210–16.

————. "The Self as History: Reflections on Autobiography." In *Telling Lives: The Biographer's Art*, edited by Marc Pachter, pp. 74–89. Washington, D.C.: New Republic Books/National Portrait Gallery, 1979.

Kempton, Murray. "Witnesses." *New York Review of Books* 23 (10 June 1976): 22–25.

Kendall, Paul Murray. "Walking the Boundaries." In *Biography as High Adventure: Life-Writers Speak on Their Art*, edited by Stephen B. Oates, pp. 32–49. Amherst: University of Massachusetts Press, 1986.

Klein, Mia. "Sherwood Anderson: The Artist's Struggle for Self-Respect." *Twentieth-Century Literature* 23 (1977): 40–52.

Knight, Arthur. "Writing the Screenplay for *Julia*: An Interview with Screenwriter Alvin Sargent." *Films Incorporated's Chairman's Choice* 2 (1977): 6.

Koelb, Clayton. *The Incredulous Reader: Literature and the Function of Disbelief*. Ithaca, N.Y.: Cornell University Press, 1984.

Kramer, Hilton. "The Life and Death of Lillian Hellman." *New Criterion* (October 1984): 1–6.

Lange, Victor. "The Woman and the Orphan Child." Review of *Memories of a Catholic Girlhood*, by Mary McCarthy. *New Republic* 136 (1957): 18.

Lanham, Jon. "The Genre of *A Portrait of the Artist as a Young Man* and 'The Rhythm of Its Structure.'" *Genre* 10 (1977): 77–82.

Latko, E. F. "Confession." In *New Catholic Encyclopedia*, 4:131–34. New York: McGraw-Hill, 1967.

Lawrence, D. H. *Studies in Classic American Literature*. New York: Viking Press, 1964.

Layman, Richard. *Shadow Man: The Life of Dashiell Hammett*. New York: Harcourt Brace Jovanovich, 1983.

Lederer, Katherine. *Lillian Hellman*. Boston: Twayne Publishers, 1979.

Lejeune, Philippe. "Autobiography in the Third Person." *New Literary History* 9 (1977): 27–50.

————. *Le Pact Autobiographique*. Paris: Editions du Seuil, 1975.

Lifson, Martha F. "Allegory of the Secret: Mary McCarthy." *Biography* 4 (1981): 249–67.

Loesberg, Jonathan. "Autobiography as Genre, Act of Consciousness, Text." *Prose Studies* 4 (1981): 169–85.

McAlmon, Robert. *McAlmon and the Lost Generation: A Self-Portrait*. Edited by Rogert E. Knoll. Lincoln: University of Nebraska Press, 1962.

McCarthy, Kevin. "In Her Own Words." *People Weekly* 12 (12 November 1979): 92, 95–96, 99.

McCarthy, Mary. "Artists in Uniform." In *The Humanist in the Bathtub*, pp. 68–86. New York: New American Library, 1964.

————. *The Company She Keeps*. New York: Harcourt, Brace and World, 1942.

————. "The Fact in Fiction." In *The Humanist in the Bathtub*, pp. 173–94. New York: New American Library, 1964.

————. *How I Grew*. New York: Harcourt Brace Jovanovich, 1987.

————. "Mary McCarthy Goes to the Movies." *Film Comment* 12 (1976): 32–34.

————. *Memories of a Catholic Girlhood*. New York: Harcourt, Brace and Co., 1957.

————. "Portrait of a Typical Negro." Review of *Black Boy*, by Richard Wright. *New Leader* 28 (23 June 1945): 10.

————. "Settling the Colonel's Hash." In *The Humanist in the Bathtub*, pp. 87–103. New York: New American Library, 1964.

————. "Theater Chronicles: Dry Ice." *Partisan Review* 13 (1946): 577–79.

McCracken, Samuel. "'Julia' and Other Fictions by Lillian Hellman." *Commentary* 77 (1984): 35–43.

McKeever, P. E. "Penance." In *New Catholic Encyclopedia*, 11:78–84. New York: McGraw-Hill, 1967.

McKenzie, Barbara. *Mary McCarthy*. New York: Twayne Publishers, 1966.

Mailer, Norman. "An Appeal to Lillian Hellman and Mary McCarthy." *New York Times Book Review*, 11 May 1980, 3, 33.

Mandel, Barrett John "Full of Life Now." In *Autobiography: Essays Theoretical and Critical*, pp. 49–72. See Olney, ed.

Mansell, Darrel. "Unsettling the Colonel's Hash: 'Fact' in Autobiography." *Modern Language Quarterly* 37 (1976): 115–32.

Margolies, Edward. *The Art of Richard Wright*. Carbondale: Southern Illinois University Press, 1969.

Marriner, Gerald L. "Sherwood Anderson: The Myth of the Artist." *Texas Quarterly* 14 (1971): 105–16.

194

Works Cited

Mason, Mary G. "The Other Voice: Autobiography of Women Writers." In *Autobiography: Essays Theoretical and Critical*, pp. 207–35. See Olney, ed.

Matisse, Henri, Georges Braque, André Salmon, Tristan Tzara, Eugene Jolas, and Maria Jolas. "Testimony against Gertrude Stein." Supplement to *transition* 23 (1935): 1–16.

Matthews, Jack. *Tales of the Ohio Land*. Columbus: Ohio Historical Society, 1978.

Maxwell, William. *So Long, See You Tomorrow*. New York: Alfred A. Knopf, 1980.

Mayne, Richard. "Ishmael and the Inquisitors." Review of *Scoundrel Time*, by Lillian Hellman. *Times Literary Supplement*, 12 November 1976, 1413.

Mellow, James R. *Charmed Circle: Gertrude Stein and Company*. New York: Avon Books, 1974.

Miller, Henry. "Anderson the Story-Teller." *Story* 19 (1941): 70–74.

Minnich, Elizabeth Kamarck. "Why Not Lie?" *Soundings* 67 (1985): 493–509.

Minter, David V. *The Interpretive Design as a Structural Principle in American Prose*. New Haven, Conn.: Yale University Press, 1969.

Misch, Georg. *A History of Autobiography in Antiquity*. Translated by E. W. Dickes. 2 vols. Cambridge: Harvard University Press, 1951.

Moore, Marianne. *Collected Poems*. New York: Macmillan Co., 1951.

Munz, Peter. *The Shapes of Time: A New Look at the Philosophy of History*. Middletown, Conn.: Wesleyan University Press, 1977.

Nabokov, Vladimir. *Speak, Memory: An Autobiography Revisited*. New York: G. P. Putnam's Sons, 1966.

Navasky, Victor. *Naming Names*. New York: Viking Press, 1980.

Neuman, Shirley. "The Observer Observed: Distancing the Self in Autobiography." *Prose Studies* 4 (1981): 317–36.

Niebuhr, Elisabeth. "Mary McCarthy." In *Writers at Work: The Paris Review Interviews*, 2d ser., pp. 285–315. New York: Viking Press, 1963.

Norman, Marsha. "Lillian Hellman's Gift to a Young Playwright." *New York Times*, sec. 7, 27 August 1984, 7.

Novak, Maximillian E. "Defoe's Theory of Fiction." *Studies in Philology* 61 (1964): 650–68.

Oates, Stephen B., ed. *Biography as High Adventure: Life-Writers Speak on Their Art*. Amherst: University of Massachusetts Press, 1986.

O'Connor, Flannery. *Mystery and Manners: Occasional Prose, Selected and Edited by Sally and Robert Fitzgerald*. New York: Farrar, Straus and Giroux, 1969.

Olney, James. "Autobiography and the Cultural Moment: A Thematic, Historical, and Bibliographical Introduction." In *Autobiography: Essays Theoretical and Critical*, pp. 3–27. See Olney, ed.

————. "Some Versions of Memory / Some Versions of Bios: The Ontology of Autobiography." In *Autobiography: Essays Theoretical and Critical*, pp. 236–67. See Olney, ed.

————, ed. *Autobiography: Essays Theoretical and Critical*. Princeton, N.J.: Princeton University Press, 1980.

Orwell, George. *1984*. New York: New American Library, 1961.

Pachter, Marc, ed. *Telling Lives: The Biographer's Art*. Washington, D.C.: New Republic Books/National Portrait Gallery, 1979.

Pascal, Roy. "The Autobiographical Novel and the Autobiography." *Essays in Criticism* 9 (1959): 134–50.

————. *Design and Truth in Autobiography*. Cambridge: Harvard University Press, 1960.

Peyre, Henri. *Literature and Sincerity*. New Haven, Conn.: Yale University Press, 1963.

Phillips, William. "What Happened in the Fifties." *Partisan Review* 43 (1976): 337–40.

Phillips, William L. "How Sherwood Anderson Wrote *Winesburg, Ohio*." In *The Achievement of Sherwood Anderson*, edited by Ray Lewis White, pp. 62–85. Chapel Hill: University of North Carolina Press, 1966.

Poirier, Richard. Introduction to *Three: "An Unfinished Woman," "Pentimento," "Scoundrel Time,"* by Lillian Hellman. Boston: Little, Brown and Co., 1979.

Pynchon, Thomas. *V*. New York: Bantam Classics, 1964.

Rather, Dan. "A Profile of Lillian Hellman." In *Conversations with Lillian Hellman*, pp. 210–17. See Bryer.

Reilly, John M., ed. *Richard Wright: The Critical Reception*. New York: Burt Franklin, 1978.

Rich, Adrienne. *On Lies, Secrets, and Silence: Selected Prose, 1966–1978*. New York: W. W. Norton and Co., 1979.

Rideout, Walter B. Preface to *A Story Teller's Story*, by Sherwood Anderson. New York: Viking Press, 1969.

————. "Sherwood Anderson." In *Sixteen Modern American Authors: A Survey of Research and Criticism*, edited by Jackson R. Bryer, pp. 3–28. New York: W. W. Norton and Co., 1973.

Roberts, Thomas J. "Fiction outside of Literature." *Literary Review* 22 (1978): 5–21.

————. *When Is Something Fiction?* Carbondale: Southern Illinois University Press, 1972.

Robinson, Janice S. *H. D.: The Life and Work of an American Poet*. Boston: Houghton Mifflin Co., 1982.

Rogers, Douglas G. *Sherwood Anderson: A Selected, Annotated Bibliography*. Metuchen, N.J.: Scarecrow Press, 1976.

Rogers, W. G. *When This You See Remember Me: Gertrude Stein in Person*. New York: Holt, Rinehart and Winston, 1948.

Rollyson, Carl. *Lillian Hellman: Her Legend and Her Legacy*. New York: St. Martin's Press, 1988.

Rosenblatt, Roger. "Black Autobiography: Life as the Death Weapon." In *Autobiography: Essays Theoretical and Critical*, pp. 169–80. See Olney, ed.

Rosengarten, Theodore. *All God's Dangers: The Life of Nate Shaw*. New York: Alfred A. Knopf, 1975.

Ross, Angus. Introduction to *The Life and Adventures of Robinson Crusoe*, by Daniel Defoe. Baltimore: Penguin, 1965.

Roth, Philip. "Don't Try to Get to the Bottom of Things." *New York Times Book Review*, 4 January 1987, 24.

Rudge, Florence M. "Confession." In *The Catholic Encyclopedia*, 4:214. New York: The Encyclopedia Press, 1913.

Schachtel, Ernest G. *Metamorphosis: On the Development of Affect, Perception, Attention, and Memory*. New York: Basic Books, 1959.

Scholes, Robert, Carl H. Klaus, and Michael Silverman, eds. *Elements of Literature*. New York: Oxford University Press, 1978.

Scholes, Robert, and Robert Kellogg. *The Nature of Narrative*. New York: Oxford University Press, 1966.

Scott-Maxwell, Florida. *The Measure of My Days*. New York: Alfred A. Knopf, 1968.

Shapiro, Stephen A. "The Dark Continent of Literature: Autobiography." *Comparative Literature Studies* 5 (1968): 421–54.

Shaw, W. David. "*In Memoriam* and the Rhetoric of Confession." *ELH* 38 (1971): 80–103.

Sheed, Wilfrid. "Her Youth Observed." Review of *How I Grew*, by Mary McCarthy. *New York Times Book Review*, 9 April 1987, 5–6.

Simon, Linda. *The Biography of Alice B. Toklas*. Garden City, N.Y.: Doubleday and Co., 1977.

Smith, Sidonie. *Where I'm Bound: Patterns of Slavery and Freedom in Black Autobiography*. Westport, Conn.: Greenwood Press, 1974.

Spacks, Patricia Meyer. *The Female Imagination*. New York: Avon Books, 1972.

Spence, Donald. *Narrative Truth and Historical Truth: Meaning and Interpretation in Psychoanalysis*. New York: W. W. Norton and Co., 1982.

Spender, Stephen. "Confessions and Autobiography." In *Autobiography: Essays Theoretical and Critical*, pp. 115–22. See Olney, ed.

———. *Journals, 1939–1983*. Edited by John Goldsmith. New York: Random House, 1986.

———. "Stephen Spender Replies." *Paris Review* 79 (1981): 304–7.

———. *World within World: The Autobiography of Stephen Spender*. London: Reader's Union, 1953.

Spengemann, William C., and L. R. Lundquist. "Autobiography and the American Myth." *American Quarterly* 17 (1965): 501–19.

Starobinski, Jean. "The Style of Autobiography." Translated by Seymour Chatman. In *Autobiography: Essays Theoretical and Critical*, pp. 73–83. See Olney, ed.

Stein, Gertrude. *The Autobiography of Alice B. Toklas*. New York: Random House, Vintage Books, 1960.

———. *Everybody's Autobiography*. New York: Random House, 1937.

———. *The Geographical History of America*. New York: Random House, 1936.

———. *Narration: Four Lectures by Gertrude Stein*. Chicago: University of Chicago Press, 1935.

———. Review of *A Story Teller's Story*, by Sherwood Anderson. In *Sherwood Anderson/Gertrude Stein: Correspondence and Personal Essays*, edited by Ray

Lewis White, p. 45. Chapel Hill: University of North Carolina Press, 1972.

———. *Stanzas in Meditation and Other Poems*. Edited by Donald Sutherland. Yale edition of the Unpublished Works of Gertrude Stein. New Haven, Conn.: Yale University Press, 1956.

———. *Tender Buttons*. New York: Claire Marie Press, 1914.

———. *What Are Masterpieces?* New York: Pitman Publishing Co., 1970.

Stein, Leo. *Journey into the Self*. Edited by Edmund Fuller. New York: Crown, 1950.

Steinbeck, John. *East of Eden*. New York: Bantam Books, 1952.

Stelzig, Eugene. "Poetry and/or Truth: An Essay on the Confessional Imagination." *University of Toronto Quarterly* 54 (1984): 17–37.

Stephen, Leslie. *Hours in a Library*. 3 vols. London: Smith, Elder and Co., 1892.

Stepto, Robert B. *From behind the Veil: A Study of Afro-American Narrative*. Urbana: University of Illinois Press, 1979.

Stevick, Philip. "Lies, Fictions, and Mock-Facts." *Western Humanities Review* 30 (1976): 1–12.

Stone, Albert E., Jr. *Autobiographical Occasions and Original Acts: Versions of American Identity from Henry Adams to Nate Shaw*. Philadelphia: University of Pennsylvania Press, 1982.

Sutherland, Donald. *Gertrude Stein: A Biography of Her Work*. New Haven, Conn.: Yale University Press, 1951.

Sutton, William A. "The Diaries of Sherwood Anderson's Parents." Appendix to *Tar: A Midwest Childhood. A Critical Edition*. Edited by Ray Lewis White. Cleveland: Press of Case Western Reserve University, 1969.

———. *The Road to Winesburg: A Mosaic of the Imaginative Life of Sherwood Anderson*. Metuchen, N.J.: Scarecrow Press, 1972.

Taylor, Gordon O. *Chapters of Experience: Studies in Modern American Autobiography*. New York: St. Martin's Press, 1983.

Thomas, F. Richard. *Literary Admirers of Alfred Stieglitz*. Carbondale: Southern Illinois University Press, 1983.

Tintner, Adeline R. "Autobiography as Fiction: 'The Usurping Consciousness' as Hero of James's *Memoirs*." *Twentieth-Century Literature* 23 (1977): 239–60.

Toklas, Alice B. *What Is Remembered*. New York: Holt, Rinehart and Winston, 1963.

Townsend, Kim. *Sherwood Anderson: A Biography*. Boston: Houghton Mifflin Co., 1987.

Trilling, Diana. *We Must March My Darlings: A Critical Decade*. New York: Harcourt Brace Jovanovich, 1977.

Trilling, Lionel. "Sherwood Anderson." In *The Achievement of Sherwood Anderson*, edited by Ray Lewis White, pp. 212–23. Chapel Hill: University of North Carolina Press, 1966.

———. *Sincerity and Authenticity*. Cambridge: Harvard University Press, 1972.

Trow, George W. S. "Truth but without Respect for Truth." *Harper's* 274 (April 1986): 23–25.

Wagner-Martin, Linda. "Lillian Hellman: Autobiography and Truth." *Southern Review* 19 (1983): 275–88.

Warren, Frank A. *Liberals and Communism: The "Red" Decade Revisited.* Bloomington: Indiana University Press, 1966.

Wasserstrom, William. "The Sursymamericubealism of Gertrude Stein." *Twentieth-Century Literature* 21 (1975): 90–107.

Webb, Constance. *Richard Wright: A Biography*. New York: G. P. Putnam's Sons, 1968.

Weintraub, Judith. "Two Feisty Feminists Filming Hellman's *Pentimento*." *New York Times*, sec. 2, 31 October 1976, 17.

Weintraub, Stanley. *Biography and Truth*. Indianapolis: Bobbs-Merrill Co., 1967.

Wellek, René, and Austin Warren. *Theory of Literature*. New York: Harcourt, Brace and World, 1956.

White, Antonia. "Withered on the Stalk." Review of *Memories of a Catholic Girlhood*, by Mary McCarthy. *New Statesman* 54 (1957): 740.

White, Hayden. "Fictions of Factual Representation." In *The Literature of Fact*, edited by Angus Fletcher, pp. 21–44. New York: Columbia University Press, 1976.

White, Ralph K. "*Black Boy*: A Value Analysis." *Journal of Abnormal and Social Psychology* 42 (1947): 440–61.

White, Ray Lewis, ed. *Sherwood Anderson/Gertrude Stein: Correspondence and Personal Essays*. Chapel Hill: University of North Carolina Press, 1972.

Widner, Eleanor. "Finally a Lady: Mary McCarthy." In *The Fifties: Fiction, Poetry, Drama*, edited by Warren French, pp. 93–102. Deland, Fla.: Everett/Edwards, 1970.

Wilson, Robert A. *Gertrude Stein: A Bibliography*. New York: Phoenix Bookshop, 1974.

Witt, Linda. "Nazi Era Saga: A Real 'Julia' Disputes History." *Chicago Tribune*, sec. 2, 25 November 1984, 1–2.

Wolff, Geoffrey. "Minor Lives." In *Telling Lives: The Biographer's Art*, edited by Marc Pachter, pp. 56–72. Washington, D.C.: New Republic Books/National Portrait Gallery, 1979.

Wright, Richard. *Black Boy: A Record of Childhood and Youth*. New York: Harper and Row, 1945.

———. "The Ethics of Living Jim Crow." In *Uncle Tom's Children*, pp. 9–22. New York: Harper and Brothers, 1940.

———. "How 'Bigger' Was Born." Introduction to *Native Son*. New York: Harper and Row, 1940.

———. *Uncle Tom's Children*. New York: Harper and Brothers, 1938.

Wright, William. *Lillian Hellman: The Image, the Woman*. New York: Simon and Schuster, 1986.

Young, Stark. "A Marginal Note." In *Voyager in the Arts*, by Paul Rosenfeld, edited by Jerome Mellquist and Lucie Wiese, pp. 195–97. New York: Creative Arts Press, 1948.

INDEX

Abrahams, William, 143
Accuracy, 11
Adams, Henry: *The Education of Henry Adams*, 22, 41, 135, 161
Aiken, Conrad: *Ushant*, 41
Albert, Jan, 124
Allon, Dafna, 170
Anania, Michael, 6
Andersen, Thom, 154, 157, 158
Anderson, Cornelia, 55
Anderson, David D., 56, 66
Anderson, Eleanor Copenhaver, 42
Anderson, Karl, 47, 49, 56
Anderson, Margaret, 56
Anderson, Sherwood, ix, x, 4, 69, 135, 167, 172; androgyny of, 39, 47, 152; legend, 51–66; mother of, 48–49, 58–60, 66–68; father of, 53–54, 58, 60–65, 67–68; and Mary McCarthy, 102, 110. *See also* Persona; Tall tale
—Works: *Notebook*, 50; *Sherwood Anderson's Memoirs*, x, 3, 40–44, 46, 49, 50, 54, 58, 59, 62–66, 68; *A Story Teller's Story*, x, 3, 40, 41, 43, 44, 46, 48, 49, 52–68; *Tar*, x, 3, 40, 44–45, 54, 59, 60, 62, 67; *Windy McPherson's Son*, 46, 60
Anderson, Stella, 49
Angelou, Maya, 80
Anti-Semitism: of Mary McCarthy, 114, 116–20; of Hellman, 155
Apollinaire, Guillaume, 18, 21, 29
Arendt, Hannah, 119
Augustine, Saint, 3, 11, 15, 176 (n. 41)
Autobiographical novel, ix, 7
Autobiography: and memory, ix, x, 1, 3, 12, 15, 17, 25, 29, 50, 67, 73, 86, 87, 89, 91, 95, 105–8, 110, 111, 114–16, 118, 121–23, 129, 137, 140–42, 148, 152, 153, 158, 164, 165, 168–72; and fiction, ix, 11, 41, 91–92, 114, 129, 143; and myth, x, 1, 7, 14, 18, 37, 52, 169–70; and fraud, x, 1, 13, 14, 16, 130; and hoax, x, 5, 17–18, 31, 92; and authenticity, x, 6, 17, 47, 52, 69, 73–75, 94, 146, 158, 167; and mask, x, 14, 30, 88, 98, 112; and figure, 1, 2, 11, 21, 74; and design, 1, 3, 4, 8, 27; and self, 1, 11, 87, 112, 123, 169; and identity, 1, 24, 25, 56, 85, 87, 94, 105, 106, 108, 111, 122, 123, 124, 149, 169, 170, 172; and imagination, 3, 12, 50, 89, 105, 172; and metaphor of self, 3, 26, 35, 69, 88, 104; and fabrication, 5, 7, 132; and historicity, 8, 12, 30, 34, 45, 67, 80, 82, 107, 130, 131, 154; and fact, 10, 45, 91, 92; and irony, 15, 16, 38, 40, 135. *See also* Autobiographical novel; Biography; Diary; Indian captivity narrative; Memoir; Nonfiction; Roman à clef; Slave narrative; Tall tale

Babel, Isaak, 129
Baker, Carlos, 132
Baldwin, James, 73
Bankhead, Tallulah, 185 (n. 83)
Barth, John, 3, 7
Barthes, Roland, 22
Bartlett, F. C., 165
Baumbach, Jonathan, 7